The Causes of War

THE CAUSES OF WAR

DAVID SOBEK

polity

First published in 2009 by Polity Press

Polity Press
65 Bridge Street
Cambridge CB2 1UR, UK.

Polity Press
350 Main Street
Malden, MA 02148, USA

ISBN-13: 978-0-7456-4198-0
ISBN-13: 978-0-7456-4199-7(pb)

A catalogue record for this book is available from the British Library.

Typeset in 10.5 on 12 pt Times
by SNP Best-set Typesetter Ltd., Hong Kong
Printed and bound in Great Britain by MPG Books Ltd, Bodmin, Cornwall.

The publisher has used its best endeavours to ensure that the URLs for external websites referred to in this book are correct and active at the time of going to press. However, the publisher has no responsibility for the websites and can make no guarantee that a site will remain live or that the content is or will remain appropriate.

For further information on Polity, visit our website: www.polity.co.uk

CONTENTS

ACKNOWLEDGMENTS

I would like to thank both Rode Abouharb and Cameron Thies for reading various parts of this book. In addition, I would like to thank Sam Robison and Caroline Payne for their research assistance. Finally, thanks go to Challen, for listening to me talk about the book and giving me the needed encouragement, and Emily, who cheered me up every day when I came home.

INTRODUCTION

The 1964 classic movie from Stanley Kubrick (*Dr Strangelove or: How I Learned to Stop Worrying and Love the Bomb*) portrays the United States and Soviet Union on the verge of nuclear Armageddon. As the crisis evolves, Kubrick depicts both American and Soviet leaders scrambling to avert the impending conflict. To limit misunderstanding, the leaders stay in contact over the phone and the American president even allows the Soviet ambassador into the war room. As rational as they appear in their attempts to resolve the crisis, the two sides are constantly vexed by the irrational. Whether it is the insanity of an American general, the paranoia of both sides, or the drunkenness of the Soviet premier, war appears almost inevitable. As the movie ends, the viewers find that the doomsday devices, which were believed to be the most rational of weapons, ultimately lead to the most irrational of outcomes (nuclear war). How accurately, however, does this movie depict the onset of interstate war?

Wars often appear the epitome of both rationality and irrationality. On the one hand, it makes perfect sense that a state would occasionally use its military to further its national self-interest. On the other hand, wars often exact exorbitant costs on both the defeated and the victor. As such, why would either side of the conflict simply not negotiate a solution and avoid all of the costs associated with war? In many ways, understanding why states choose conflict over diplomacy is the crux of the problem. The onset of war implies an end to diplomacy just as the end of war signals the start of diplomacy. So why do states choose war over diplomacy, given that the vast majority of time they rely on diplomacy to resolve their differences?

Unfortunately no single answer to that question exists. Just as all illnesses of the human body do not derive from a single cause, conflicts of the body politic do not have a single source. This does not mean that one can never understand the onset of war, or discover methods that limit its occurrence or severity. In fact, scholars have developed a number of generalizations about the onset of war. The problem is that none of these individual theories can explain all wars, but they all represent risk factors that are important to any analysis of international conflict.

From this perspective, context matters. A factor that was critical in generating a war in one case may have little effect in another. For instance, researchers have found a significant amount of evidence showing that democracies are less likely to have militarized conflicts with one another. Does this general finding apply equally to all types of democracies? Are poor democracies just as peaceful as rich democracies? Are newly democratized states just as peaceful as consolidated democracies? The answers to these questions touch on the crux of the matter. If the effect on the democratic peace is conditioned on the context, then it becomes vitally important to understand these limits. This book bridges the gaps between risk factors, conditionality, and war.

Understanding war

It is not new to investigate the causes of war but often the theoretical explanations concentrate on a single "cause." For instance, Waltz (1979) focused on the systemic distribution of resources, Blainey (1988) examined disagreements over the distribution of capabilities, and Organski and Kugler (1980) looked at power transitions. While the single-cause explanations have an intuitive appeal, reality is often not cooperative. If one wants to truly understand war, then the first step is to move away from the "magic bullet" theories that purport to fully explain the onset of international war with a single theory.

The risk of war is influenced by a number of factors, each of which individually alters the probability of conflict. The magic bullet theories of conflict tend to concentrate on one cause as the primary source of war but in reality multiple factors push and pull states closer to, or farther from, armed conflict. In addition, the conditionality of war implies that the importance of the individual causes of war differs from case to case. So the balance of power may have mattered to the Germans in their decision to attack France in 1940 but played a lesser role in the American decision to invade Iraq in 2003. Why would the cause of war change so dramatically from case to case?

Part of the problem is that international politics can be viewed from a variety of perspectives (or levels of analysis). For instance, one could look at the decision of individual states to initiate wars or how pairs of states (dyads) enter into conflict or even how the structure of the international system affects the amount of conflict. All of these areas of research address the causes of war but they do so at drastically different levels of analysis. So while the characteristics of an individual state may affect its decision to initiate war, they may have little to no effect on the overall level of conflict in the international system. As such, the choice to examine a certain level of analysis may emphasize one cause of war over others. This does not necessarily mean that the other factors do not matter. In fact, this is one place where context enters into the equation.

The democratic peace argues that pairs of democracies are less likely to experience conflict. This theory is clearly cast at the dyadic level of analysis which generates a degree of parsimony. Sacrificing that parsimony, however, allows for a more nuanced picture. So while pairs of democratic states are more peaceful, researchers have found that this may not apply to newly democratized states. In this instance, a factor for the state level of analysis (democratization) affects a dyadic theory (democratic peace). The effect of context, however, is more than simply the interaction of the levels of analysis; rather, certain contexts may alter the way states perceive the international system.

While states often find themselves confronted by situations that could lead to war, the precise costs and benefits associated with war differ from case to case. For instance, domestic politics can play a critical role in determining the perception of national interests of the state. In addition, the domestic institutions can constrain leaders in varying ways. As such, we would not expect an elected democratic leader to calculate the costs and benefits of a war in the same way as a military dictator. This means that two states facing the same situation may make vastly different choices. So for Hitler in 1940 the balance of power mattered more than domestic support but for Bush in 2003 domestic support played an important role.

In many ways, context provides a structure for the interaction of states that emphasizes some causes of war over others. Theories that ignore the role of context may mistakenly believe that an individual factor is more (or less) important than it is in reality. As such, the effects of context do not make understanding war impossible but provide a way to deepen our knowledge both of the dynamics of individual cases and of the explanatory power of different theories of war. From this perspective, context generates an interactive, as opposed to additive, effect.

The difference between additive and interactive effects is critical. For instance, assume that two factors affect the likelihood that a state will initiate an international war. Factor A generates a 10 percent probability that a state will initiate a war, while factor B generates a 20 percent probability. We can imagine four possible situations: neither factor A nor B is present, factor A is present but not B, factor B is present but not A, and both factors A and B are present. This means that when neither factor is present, the probability of war is 0 percent. The presence of factor A but not B leads to a 10 percent chance and the presence of factor B but not A creates a 20 percent probability. So what happens when both A and B are present?

Perhaps the best way to answer that question is to look not at the odds of war but at the probability of peace. Since only one of the factors is needed to trigger a war, in order to maintain peace both factors need to generate peace (or not war). So the question becomes what are the odds that both factors A and B will generate peace? The answer is simply the multiplication of the two individual probabilities of peace, i.e., 90 percent (factor A) times 80 percent (factor B). So when both factors A and B are present, we would expect peace 72 percent of the time and war 28 percent of the time. While we determined the probability by multiplying the two probabilities, the effects are assumed to be "additive" in the sense that the result was a simple combination of the two individual effects.

The joint presence of A and B, however, could also produce an interactive effect. Imagine that, when we empirically examine the international system, we find that our predictions about the effects of A and B are accurate except for one case. In particular, what if the probability of conflict when they are both present is 40 percent instead of 28 percent? What does this imply? It could be the case that the theory is incorrect but it could also be the case that the presence of both A and B generates an interactive effect. When an interactive effect is present, it leads to an outcome that is more than the sum of its parts. This interactive effect is similar to the concept of emergence, i.e., the component units interact and generate an outcome not explainable by their "simple laws," or general patterns of behavior. Systems that contain emergence are "driven by the behavior of individual actors who are moved by their own incentives, goals, and calculations" (Jervis 1997: 16).

The interactive effects can be seen in the rush to the First World War. In the years leading up to the war, the political and military leaders felt that the offense had become dominant. As a result, the leaders felt that the first state to successfully mobilize their forces would gain a tremendous advantage in any conflict. In addition, the major powers of Europe had entangled themselves in a set of tight alliances that essentially split them into two main groups: the Triple Alliance (Germany, Italy, and Austria-Hungary) and the Triple Entente (Britain, France, and Russia). While the belief in the offense and the tight alliances would each individually increase the risk of war, these two factors interacted to create an exceptionally unstable environment. So when Austria-Hungary began to mobilize against Serbia and the Russians mobilized to defend Serbia, it started a chain reaction which led to German mobilization, followed by French and British mobilization, and then ultimately to Germany's attack against France.

Emergence, or the interactive effects, occurs in systems that are composed of copies of a limited number of components, such as states. The individual components obey simple laws and are connected to one another, forming an array that may change (Holland 1999: 6–10). In general, emergence is used to explain a system where the whole is greater than the sum of its parts (Mainzer 1997: 3–5; Holland 1999: 121–2). As Holland notes (1999: 225), "there are regularities in system behavior that are not revealed by direct inspection of the laws satisfied by the components." In fact, Jervis (1999: 61) argues that actions in an emergent system "have unintended effects on the actor, others, and the system as a whole, which means that one cannot infer results from desires and expectations and vice versa."

Emergent phenomena are embedded in a context that determines their function (Holland 1999: 226). So wind-generated waves could strike rocks in one instance, leading to erosion and the formation of a beach, but on other occasions the waves could hit a sandy beach and spur erosion that ultimately weakens the size of the waves. In terms of international politics, it is often argued that the democratic peace is generated by some conflict-dampening effect of either norms or institutions. Harrison (2002: 150), however, found that "many sections of Kant's writings appear not to rely on the benign tendencies of liberal states, but stress conflict as the source of the emergence of pacific relations." This does not mean that the democratic peace is incorrect.

What it implies is that the democratic peace may be an emergent phenomenon.

This discussion of emergence and context does not mean that understanding international politics is impossible. In fact, the presence of emergence offers an opportunity to better understand the outcomes that we see in the international system. To reach this promise, however, theories require a mechanism that allows for the generation of the emergent behavior, i.e., they cannot simply be aggregations of component unit interactions. In addition, the theories need to take into account the possibility that the effect is not constant, i.e., context matters.

Building truly emergent theories of international relations requires researchers to think in term of interactions, i.e., how do the various conditions affect the probability of conflict when they occur simultaneously? Perhaps the easiest analogy for emergent theories is to think of them as recipes. A cake, for example, does not simply require the correct ingredients; it also matters how they are combined, heated, and so on. Simply placing flour, milk, eggs, and sugar into a bowl (without mixing or baking) would not make a cake. Would this outcome imply that flour, milk, eggs, and sugar are not ingredients found in cakes? Of course not. Cakes are more than simply the sum of their ingredients. A cake is an emergent outcome when the ingredients are combined in the proper manner.

Just as there are recipes for cakes, one can also think about recipes for war. The critical question is really how these ingredients combine to generate international conflict. Scholars implicitly build emergent theories of international conflict, although they do not often speak of it as such. For instance, Copeland (2000) builds his theory by integrating three strands of realist thought (classical realism, neo-realism, and hegemonic stability theory). Vasquez (1993) builds his "steps to war" theory by detailing how the actions of the states interact to greatly increase the risk of war.

Understanding war also requires one to move across the levels of analysis. In other words, the onset of conflict in a given dyad is certainly related to the characteristics of that dyad (joint democracies, balance of capabilities, amount of trade, and so on), but it is also related to the characteristics of both the individual states and the international system. For instance, it could be the case that democratic peace theory is accurate but the effect may be magnified when the international system is bipolar or when international trade is relatively open and free. It could also be the case that democratic peace is less effective when the states are major powers with global concerns.

Determinism versus probabilistic theory

Theories, regardless of their level of analysis, can fall into two broad categories: deterministic or probabilistic. Deterministic theories offer a set of cause-and-effect relationships that always hold; in other words, if condition X is present then outcome Y will always happen. Probabilistic theories offer a set of cause-and-effect relationships that hold more often than one would expect simply by chance alone. In other words, a probabilistic theory would argue that the presence of condition X increases the likelihood of outcome Y. While at first glance it appears that a theorist should strive for deterministic theories, the choice between developing probabilistic or deterministic theories is often contingent on the area of study.

Deterministic theories are mostly found in the natural sciences, such as physics and chemistry. For example, the law of gravity argues that two masses will attract one another along a straight line connecting the two center masses. Practically, this means that all objects on earth, unless acted upon by another force, will fall. Because this theory is deterministic, any instance where this does not occur automatically disproves the theory. For example, Einstein's theory of gravitational lensing, which argues that massive bodies would bend light waves, was tested during a solar eclipse in 1919. When astronomers found that the sun bent light exactly as Einstein predicted, it was seen as confirmation of the theory. If, however, the light did not bend, then the theory would have been discredited.

This method of testing theories is generally referred to as naive falsificationism and is most often associated with the work of Karl Popper. In general, most scholars believe that falsifiability differentiates scientific from unscientific fields of study, i.e., falsifiability makes astronomy a science and astrology not a science. Popper conceptualized science as the replacement of a falsified theory with another falsifiable theory, which may or may not be replaced in the future. Over the long run, this implies that scientific fields see a general increase in understanding across time. This process, however, works best in areas that have deterministic processes.

Unlike the natural sciences, probabilistic theories generally occur in the social sciences, such as political science, sociology, and economics. Theories in these fields do not make equivocal statements as to cause-and-effect relationships. For instance, the aforementioned democratic peace argues that democracies are less likely to go to war with one another but it does not state that they will never go to war (although such an outcome would still support the theory). For this theory, one example of two democracies engaging in a war will not disprove the democratic peace. Disconfirming evidence of the democratic peace would occur if democracies went to war with one another just as often as they entered into wars with non-democracies.

Probabilistic theories make naive falsificationism, as Popper describes it, an unrealistic standard. This does not mean, however, that theories of international relations should be unfalsifiable. Imre Lakatos argued that scientific fields progressed across time by increasing their understanding. This is done by the replacement of an old theory with one that accounts for everything explained by the old theory and offers some new insight (known as excess empirical content). In this case, scientific fields are differentiated from unscientific fields by the progression of knowledge. So for Lakatos a theory does not need to explain everything, just more than the alternatives.

Why probabilistic theories?

Why would social sciences, in general, and international relations, in particular, rely on probabilistic theories? Would it not be better to strive for laws of human behavior that detail unerring cause-and-effect relationships? The short answer to these questions is that it is simply not possible, or a lot less likely, for law-like relationships to develop in the social sciences. The choice of probabilistic theories in social sciences is driven by the nature of subjects of observation. In other words, when one wants to study human behaviors, probabilistic theories are the best set of explanations. Cioffi-Revilla (1998: 5) was correct when he argued that political outcomes are uncertain, where they are "neither predetermined (with probability 1) nor impossible (with probability 0)."

One of the main reasons that probabilistic theories are needed in the social sciences is the reflective nature of individuals. Unlike in physics or chemistry, the units of analysis in the social sciences are generally self-aware. Often these units examine past behaviors to determine the best course of action. This reflectivity means that any strong relationship that occurs will be observed and this will cause the units to change their behaviors. So imagine that one found a law of international war where the use of strategy X guarantees victory. How would states react to this information? Obviously, they would all adopt strategy X which would inevitably lead to a war where a state using strategy X loses. This creates an ironic situation where the stronger the relationship, the less likely it will maintain in the future.

Another major obstacle to the use of deterministic theory in the social sciences deals with the (ir)rationality of individuals. In order for international politics to develop truly deterministic theories, states (and individuals within states) would need to act consistently in a rational manner. While it may be the case that states and individuals often behave rationally, this may not be universally true. The implication for theory building is that irrational acts will create errors. For example, condition X may lead a state to choose policy Y but in some instances a leader will act irrationally and choose Z. If theories of international politics were deterministic, then this one case would be sufficient to refute the theory. Probabilistic theories, however, can incorporate these sorts of errors when analyzing the validity of a theory.

Finally, probabilistic theories may be most appropriate simply because portions of political outcomes are simply uncertain and unpredictable. In *The Prince*, Machiavelli noted this when he argued that "I think it may be true that fortune determines one half of our actions, but that, even so, she leaves us to control the other half." Whether Machiavelli was correct in his estimate of 50 percent is debatable but it is clear that some portion of political outcomes is simply uncertain. In some ways, predicting political outcomes is similar to predicting the outcome of a sporting event. While a large part of the outcome is determined by the skill of the players and coaches, the outcomes are not completely determined. As a result, we have the stylized quotes so often used by sports announcers: "any given Sunday," "that is why they play the game," and so on.

Testing the theories of international relations

The testing of theories in international relations has been dominated by the divide between qualitative (case study) and quantitative (statistical) research. Often the debate has been intense and divisive, although the division between the two methods may not be as stark as the intensity of the debate implies. Qualitative scholars often argue that the use of cases allows a researcher to better understand the hypothesized cause-and-effect relationship. The in-depth analysis of a case, or set of cases, can demonstrate a causal factor at work. Quantitative scholars, however, believe that the concentration on a single (or a few) case(s)

may obfuscate a more general pattern. In other words, can you estimate the approval rating of a president by asking one person?

In general, most of the empirical evidence cited in this book comes
from quantitative work. This reliance derives from the nature of theories discussed above. If the causes of war are driven by probabilistic
factors, can the examination of a single case offer a definitive test?
Quantitative scholars would obviously answer that question with a
negative. Gerring (2004: 348) makes a similar point about testing
probabilistic phenomena by arguing that the "researcher must examine
several instances of this phenomenon to gauge the average causal effect
of X on Y and the random element of that variation." The ultimate
argument for the use of quantitative analyses comes down to the
probabilistic nature of the phenomenon: if the onset of war is not a
deterministic process, then the examination of a single case cannot
prove (or disprove) a theoretical explanation. Obviously not everyone
agrees that quantitative methods are the best for testing theories. In
fact, Van Evera (1999: 12) explicitly dismisses the arguments of "ortho-
dox social science methodology."

Statistical analyses, however, are not a panacea for testing theories.
Quantitative analyses are exceptionally useful at finding generalizable
correlations between variables. Correlation is not causation. So where
a statistical analysis could discover if a pair of dice is fair or loaded,
it could not help us understand how or why. The same is true in the
study of international politics. For example, the literature is replete
with statistical analyses that confirm the democratic peace but these
models cannot easily differentiate between the various theories of the
democratic peace.

Qualitative analyses provide the opportunity to trace causal mechanisms within a set of cases. This sort of analysis serves two critical
purposes. First, it allows scholars to move closer to understanding
causation as opposed to the correlation. In order to truly confirm a
theory, one needs to demonstrate both a general, statistically significant correlation and a causal pattern within a set of cases. So we know
that a correlation exists between joint democracy and a lack of conflict,
but how do the democratic institutions and norms operate? Only by
looking at cases can one trace the causal mechanisms. Gerring
(2004: 348) argues this point when he notes that "case studies, if well
constructed, allow one to peer into the box of causality to the
intermediate cases lying between some cause and its purported
effect."

Aside from discovering causal patterns, case studies also aid in
theory development. As one delves into cases, patterns may emerge

that were not obvious from the more abstract statistical analyses. It may also be the case that causal mechanisms that we expected to find do not exist. In these situations, the case study allows one to generate new hypotheses that could be tested in a statistical model. In this way the difference between qualitative and quantitative is not an either/or choice; rather, they represent two different tools that have various benefits and costs. It is the researcher's job to use the method that best fits their purpose.

This book will rely on the use of case studies as opposed to statistical analyses. This does not mean that quantitative work will be downplayed. In fact, in the development of the theory, I will heavily rely on the previous statistical work. The case studies will build upon this work by both tracing causal mechanism and building the theory. Ultimately, however, the theory developed in this book needs to be confirmed with a general quantitative analysis but, in order to fully espouse the theory, that task will be relegated to future work.

Plan of the book

The rest of the book is organized around the levels of analysis and moves from the state to the dyadic and then finishes at the systemic level. At each level of analysis, some of the most important theories are examined in two main ways. First, the general quantitative evidence in support of (or against) a given theory is presented. Second, two to three important cases are then inspected to further elaborate the theory and understand how context matters.

The next chapter looks at how the power of a state affects the risk of war. In some ways it seems almost axiomatic that stronger states have a greater stake in the international system, which leads them into conflict more often than their weaker brethren. Yet the vast majority of wars involve states that are not major powers. How strong, then, is the relationship between the power of a state and its propensity to enter into wars? Do major powers enter into conflict because they have a greater stake in the international system, or are warlike, aggressive states more likely to become major powers? In general, the bulk of the evidence demonstrates that major powers are more prone to conflicts than minor powers but the evidence cannot conclusively show what drives their aggressive behaviors.

Chapter 2 continues the emphasis on the state but turns to the role of domestic politics. In particular, what happens when the powerful state is democratic? Would democratic institutions make the state less aggressive? The answers to these questions are actually quite mixed. At first, scholars believed that democracies were more peaceful because the citizens, who would bear the costs of a war, would not elect aggressive leaders. Continued research into the topic, however, found that democracies are just as war-prone as non-democratic states. In fact, one only needs to see the popular support that the Olmert government in Israel had for its initial attacks against Lebanon and Hezbollah. These results do not mean that democratic institutions have no effect on the behavior of a state; rather, they show that being a democracy does not necessarily make a state dovish.

Chapter 3 turns back to the role of power but, where chapter 2 examines the power of the state, this chapter turns to the balance of power in a dyad. Scholars have long argued that the distribution of capabilities (power) is critical in the onset of war but no consensus has developed as to what sorts of distributions lead to war. At first, theorists argued that a balance of capabilities would lead to peace because the sides would be risk-averse and avoid conflict. In contrast, an asymmetry would encourage conflict because the more powerful states would frequently start wars that they knew they would win. Blainey (1988), however, argues the opposite. For Blainey, wars occur because the two sides disagree as to the ultimate outcome of a war. In this case, in a dyad with asymmetry the outcome is quite obvious. So when the stronger state makes a demand, how will the weaker state react? By engaging in a war it knows it will lose? Of course not; it will seek a compromise short of war. When power is balanced, however, both sides will believe they can win which means that neither side has an incentive to seek a negotiated solution. Recent empirical testing has found fairly consistent evidence that balances of power are more war-prone.

Chapter 4 continues to look at dyadic theories but turns to the democratic peace. Where the evidence for democratic pacifism may be scant (chapter 3), ample research has found that democracies are much more peaceful with each other. In other words, democracies are just as conflict-prone as autocracies but they simply do not fight one another (Russett and Oneal 2001). Numerous theories have been developed to explain the democratic peace. First, the structural explanation argues that the institutions of democracies, such as the separation of powers, create time for diplomacy to find a peaceful solution. The second theory, however, relies on the norms (a bargaining culture and peaceful resolution of disputes) that develop in democratic societies. When two democracies encounter one another in the international system, the norms are triggered but, when a democracy interacts with an autocracy, the norms remain dormant.

Chapter 5 is the last of the dyadic analyses and addresses the role of international trade in lowering (or increasing) the risk of war. Trade has often been cited as a cure for international conflict. Whether it results from the economic interdependence described by Russett and Oneal (2001) or the rise of the "trading state" (Rosecrance 1986), scholars have consistently expected international trade to act as a source of peace. While it may be the case that trade and trading generates connections that enhance peace, some have argued that trade can actually produce conflict (Barbieri 2002). What, then, is the ultimate effect of trade? Could Hegre (2002) offer a solution in that the relationship between trade and war is conditioned by the level of development, where trade produces peace only when both states are wealthy?

The sixth chapter once again investigates the role of power but this time from the systemic level of analysis. Perhaps one of the most enduring debates in international relations is about the effect of the systemic distribution of power. Are multipolar systems (three or more poles/major powers) a source of peace or conflict? Is bipolarity, as argued by Waltz (1979), the most stable or is it hegemony (dominance by a single state)? Oftentimes, the debate surrounding these questions revolves around one's definition of stability. The bipolar Cold War was peaceful but only if one looks at major power wars. Shift the focus in the Cold War to minor powers and then it does not seem nearly as peaceful. In addition, does stability really mean peace or does it simply mean that states will survive?

The debate over the effect of the systemic distribution of power on international conflict has developed into a debate over the risk-taking propensities of states, where the propensity of states to take risks alters their behavior in the international system (Bueno de Mesquita 1980; Huth, Bennett, and Gelpi 1992). Waltz's (1979) argument about the dangers of external balancing, for example, is contingent on states being risk-acceptant. In systems with high levels of uncertainty (diffusion of capabilities), states are willing to take the risk of conflict to protect their positions. Deutsch and Singer (1964), however, assume states are risk-averse and thus argue that a diffusion of capabilities inhibits conflict.

Chapter 7 continues to examine the role of power but, rather than focus on its distribution, this chapter examines how changes in the distribution of power affect the international system (mainly in terms of the amount of international conflict). In particular, history has shown that a state's position as hegemon of the international system is never permanent. While a state can maintain its position for centuries, history has shown a consistent cycle of states rising and falling as the hegemon. Part of this process is the actual surpassing of the hegemon by the second most powerful state in the system. This transition has often been seen as a high-risk scenario in term of major power wars. As the challenger approaches the hegemon in power, the hegemon has a strong incentive to launch a pre-emptive war while it still has a military advantage. This implies that hegemonic wars will occur when a challenger is about to pass the hegemon. Recent work by Lemke (2002) has extended this theory to include regional powers and power transitions within these sub-sets of the international system.

The final two chapters of the book both bring together the previous chapters but also look into the role of other forms of violence. Chapter 8 loosens the state-centric view of war and examines violent engagements with non-state actors. The non-state actors can be broadly grouped into purely domestic or transnational in nature. When domestic groups fight the state, it is often characterized as a civil war. Recently, however, we have seen states have conflicts with transnational groups, i.e., Israel versus Hezbollah or United States versus al-Qaeda. These wars, while similar to the interstate conflicts described above, have many divergent characteristics. This chapter is meant to highlight these similarities and differences.

Civil wars (those versus purely domestic groups) differ from interstate conflicts in three main ways. First, the distribution of power between the two sides is often asymmetric, with the state having an overwhelming advantage. Second, the winner of a civil war is most often the side that wins the hearts and minds of the population, i.e., military victory is secondary to political victory. Finally, the belligerents often have to live together within a single state after the end of the conflict. Because of these differences, civil wars tend to have a longer duration, recur more often, and cluster on states with natural resources.

The "war on terror" and Israel's recent engagements with Hezbollah highlight the renewed importance of transnational groups. While the effect of transnational actors is not unique (see the *Condotierri* of Renaissance Italy), they seem to have taken on renewed importance in the twenty-first century. Conflicts with these organizations differ from interstate wars in two main ways. First, transnational organizations often require either the support of a state, or a region outside the control of a state, to establish a central base of operation. Second, transnational organizations have fairly diffused (cellular) organizational structures, especially as their geographic reach increases. As with civil wars, these differences make wars against transnational actors different from interstate conflicts. In particular, these conflicts tend to be drawn out, often involve the use of terrorism, and are targeted against regional (Israel) or global powers (United States).

Chapter 9 ends the book by tying together the separate levels of analysis. The ultimate conclusion from the book is not that a single recipe for war exists, just as there is no single recipe for making cookies. What scholars have found, however, is a set of risk factors which increase the probability that a war will occur. The biggest gap in our current understanding is what causes a pair of states to move from the at-risk category to war. In some ways it seems almost accidental, as in the case of the assassination of the Archduke Franz Ferdinand, which led to the First World War. In other cases, it seems as if the precipitating factor was almost redundant, such as the German invasion of Poland that led to the Second World War. This does not mean that we know nothing, or little, about conflict. Quite the contrary, our multitude of theoretical explanations of war allows both scholars and policy-makers to focus their attention on the states most at risk of war. In some ways our knowledge about conflict can be represented by islands of theories that now need to be connected with bridges.

PART I THE BEHAVIOR OF STATES

1 THE POWER OF STATES

Guns will make us powerful; butter will only make us fat.

Reichmarshal Hermann Goering, 1936

Peace is the most powerful weapon of mankind. It takes more courage to take a blow than give one. It takes more courage to try and talk things through than to start a war.

Mahatma Gandhi

Power certainly plays a role in the international system. Hermann Goering's quote represents a fairly common conception of power and alludes to why states strive to gain it. From this perspective, power represents an important means and end for a state. States need to acquire power both to protect their interests and expand their influence. When states fail to act on this imperative, they place themselves at risk. The implication of this view is that powerful states will be consistently wielding it in a belligerent manner which will ultimately lead to involvement in numerous wars.

Truly powerful states, however, may not need to actually use their power to gain their desired ends. Late in the Peloponnesian War, the ancient Athenians were facing a prospective revolt from one of their tributary city-states, Melos. Before attacking, the Athenians attempted to persuade the Melians into surrendering, just as the Melians attempted to dissuade the Athenians from attacking. Part of the Melian argument centered on the reputation of the Athenians, where attacking (and presumably defeating) the Melians would signal the weakness of Athens. A truly powerful Athens would not need to bother with a small city-state that wanted to exit from the Athenian alliance. In this way, peace between Athens and Melos would signal the strength of Athens.

Unfortunately for the Melians, Athens did not accept their argument. In fact, the Athenians uttered perhaps one of the most well-known quotes on the role of power in the international system: the strong do as they will and the weak suffer as they must. In other words, the Melian argument was moot simply because their power (relative) to the Athenians was insignificant. As such, Athens felt that the Melians merely needed to recognize reality and submit to the will of the Athenians. Ultimately, Melos decided to resist, which precipitated an attack. The Athenians eventually triumphed, after which they killed all the men, sold the women and children into slavery, and then salted their fields. So was the behavior of the Athenians representative of powerful states or does power mean not having to enter into wars?

A cursory perusal of the empirical record seems to support the claim that the most powerful states in the international system are also the most belligerent. Germany's climb to major power status in the nineteenth and twentieth centuries led to three wars with France, two with Britain, two with Russia, two with the United States, and a number of additional conflicts against both major and minor powers. Despite this history, however, the Cold War saw roughly 40 years of peace between the superpowers and not a single war between the other major powers. So are the most powerful states in the international system the most conflict-prone, or do they simply fight the most well-known wars, which makes them appear more belligerent?

The empirical evidence has found fairly consistent support for the argument that major powers are more war-prone than minor powers. Small and Singer (1970, 1982), using the correlates of war data, found that major powers are more likely than minor powers to engage in war. Bremer (1980) additionally showed that states with higher rank orders (most powerful state is ranked number 1, second most is ranked number 2, and so on) are involved in and initiate more conflicts. Eberwein (1982) additionally found that power status accounts for 60 percent of the variance in terms of states joining ongoing conflicts. Geller (1988) noted that major powers are more likely to fight the most severe wars (more than 15,000 battle deaths). Finally, and perhaps more compelling, Kohler (1975) looked at 15 "imperial leaders" and found that once a state loses its dominance, it becomes more peaceful. So what explains the belligerence of the major powers?

In general, states act to gain power both to maintain the security of their state and to effect change in the international system. The only way to secure a state's interest in the international system is to defend against other states. That being said, the cases of both Germany and Japan point to two additional factors. First, revisionist states (i.e., those that want to change the status quo) tend to have the willingness to use force before they gain the capacity. These states will seek to increase their power so that they can change the international system at some future point. Second, the domestic context matters in that even non-democratic states require a population willing to support aggressive behavior. It would be too costly for a state to fight both opponents at home and enemies abroad so states actively shape public opinion in ways that would support aggressive actions abroad. Before we can delve into these cases, however, we first must understand power.

What is power?

As important as power is as an explanation for the patterns of behavior seen in international politics, it is fairly difficult to define. At its most basic level, power is simply military capabilities. Yet to develop those capabilities a state is required to both finance the purchases of the equipment and recruit individuals to serve in the armed forces; as such, we would expect both economic and demographic characteristics to affect the power of a state. In addition, technological advantages, quality leadership, and morale can all change the balance of power. So what are the component parts of power and how have scholars traditionally measured the power of states?

At its broadest conception, power exists, and matters, outside of the international system. As such, it is useful to start with a broad conception of power and then contextualize it in terms of international politics. Poggi (1990: 1) prefers the term social power and notes that:

> in all societies, some people clearly and consistently appear more capable than others of pursuing their own objectives; and if these are incompatible with those envisaged by others, the former manage to somehow ignore or override the latter's preferences. Indeed, they are often able to mobilize, in the pursuit of their own ends, the others' energies, even against their will.

In many ways, a shorthand version of that definition is that power is able to get someone to do what they otherwise would not have done.

Social power, however, is not simply defined by coercion. In fact, Poggi (1990: 2–3) defines three separate forms of social power: economic, ideological, and political. Economic power derives from an actor possessing a good that is rare or held to be rare (Saudi Arabia and its oil reserves, for instance). Ideological power occurs when individuals endow, through a system of beliefs, an object or person with authority. For example, Roman Catholics, through their systems of beliefs, grant the Pope a degree of ideological power. The third form of social power, political, is what most individuals mean when they discuss power in relation to international politics and occurs when an actor has the ability to physically coerce another. In other words, political power comes from the use, or threat, of physical violence.

Political power occupies a relatively unique position among the forms of social power. Poggi argues that political power is both paramount and ultimate. Political power is paramount because it has the capacity to limit the ability of actors to exercise their economic and/or ideological powers. For instance, governments can use their political power to break monopolies (economic power) or bar certain religious sects (ideological power). Political power is ultimate because "violence – or the threat of it – appears as the facility of last resort in shaping and managing interpersonal relations" (Poggi 1990: 9). These aspects of political power become much more apt in the anarchy of the international system where no overarching authority exists.

Political power in the international system, however, is not simply the ability to coerce. Carr (1939a) divides the power of states into three components: military power, economic power, and power over opinion. In many ways, the divisions employed by Carr overlap those used by Poggi when describing social power (military power is political power, economic power is economic power, and power over opinion is ideological power). Of the three, Carr (1939a: 109) clearly places the most importance on military power because "potential war being thus a dominant factor in international politics, military strength becomes the recognized standard of political values."

Even if one narrows down the definition of power to simply the military capacity of a state, it still does not resolve all of the relevant issues. For instance, how does one weigh the latent versus manifest power of a state? According to Mearsheimer (2001: 55), latent power derives from "the socio-economic ingredients that go into building military power; it is largely based on a state's wealth and the overall size of its population." When a state utilizes its latent power to build, maintain, or expand its military capabilities, that latent power becomes manifest. Isoroku Yamamoto highlighted this transformation when, after the Japanese bombed Pearl Harbor, he is credited with saying "I fear all we have done is to awaken a sleeping giant and fill him with a terrible resolve."

In fact, the war between the Japanese and Americans neatly demonstrates the relationship between latent and manifest power. Clearly, as the Yamamoto quote demonstrates, the United States's latent power vastly overwhelmed the Japanese latent power. The successful attack on Pearl Harbor, however, showed that (at least in 1941), the manifest power of the Japanese was greater than that of the Americans. After the attack, the United States began the process of turning its latent power into manifest power as the Japanese attempted to use their advantage in manifest power to knock America out of the war before they could rally their latent capabilities. Ultimately, the Americans were able to stall the Japanese until they developed an advantage in manifest power, which led to an American victory.

While the amount of power matters, states tend to concentrate more on relative as opposed to absolute power. In other words, states are not acting to simply gain power; rather, "states pay close attention to how power is distributed among them, and they make special effort to maximize their share of world power" (Mearsheimer 2001: 34). So a state having 100 tanks is good only if every other state has 50 tanks. If, on the other hand, every other state has 200 tanks, then the 100-tank state would feel fairly vulnerable. This also implies that states view power from a zero-sum point of view, where the gains in power of state A would mean a loss in power for state B.

The above discussion highlights three critical aspects of power and how it operates in the international system. First, the anarchy of the international system forces states to concentrate on power and, in particular, political (aka military) power. Second, states have both latent and manifest power and both have an important effect on the behavior of states and the outcome of wars. Third, while states act to increase their power, they do so to gain a relative advantage over the other states in the international system. Given these salient facets of power, how does one measure the power of a state?

The power of states has been measured in any number of ways but one of the most common measures utilized in the quantitative literature is the Composite Index of National Capabilities (CINC) as collected by the Correlates of War (COW) project. In general, the CINC score attempts to take into account two critical aspects of political power. First, the measure is relative, meaning that the CINC for each state represents its share of world power. Second, the measure incorporates both latent and manifest aspects of power.

The CINC score is the combination of six separate components of state power: military personnel, military expenditures, energy use per capita, iron/steel production, urban population, and total population.

These represent the short- (military personnel and military expenditures), medium- (energy use per capita and iron/steel production), and long- (urban population, and total population) term aspects of state power. Obviously, military personnel and expenditures most closely resemble the manifest facet of state power. The energy use per capita and iron/steel production capture the economic power of a state, which is part of a state's latent power. Finally, total population and urban population measure the demographic portion of latent power.

Simply combining these components, however, would not take into account the relative nature of power in the international system. To account for this the CINC score takes each of the six components and looks at a state's relative share. For instance, the total population component for a state is its population divided by the world population. This means that, for each of the six parts of the CINC score, each state is measured relative to the international system. So if a state has 0.25 for total population, then that means that the state has 25 percent of the world population. To create the CINC score, the Correlates of War project simply averages a state's share of the components of power.

The CINC score, given its construction, has a number of characteristics. First, for each state it theoretically ranges from 0 (state has no power) to 1 (state has all of the power). Second, if you sum the CINC scores of all the states, in any given year, they will sum to 1. Third, simply because a state is increasing in its capacity does not mean that its CINC score will increase. For instance, imagine that a state increased its military expenditures by 10 percent but all of the other states increased their military expenditures by 20 percent, then the CINC score for the 10 percent state would decline (holding all other components constant). In general, then, the CINC has the advantages of capturing the relative nature of political power and incorporating the manifest and latent aspects of power. While it is important to understand how scholars view and construct measures of power, how does power affect the behavior of states?

Power and international politics

Power has always held a place of significance when discussing international politics. As far back as the Peloponnesian War in the fifth century BC, scholars relied on power to explain the onset of war. For instance, in his analysis of the conflict between Athens and Sparta, Thucydides (I, 23) argued that "the real cause I consider to be the one which was formally most kept out of sight. The growth of the power of Athens, and the alarm which this inspired in Lacadaemon [Sparta], made war inevitable." Roughly 2,000 years later, Machiavelli (*The Prince*, chapter 10) noted that a "prince will be able to take care of himself if he has a sufficient supply of men or of money to put an adequate army in the field, capable of engaging anyone likely to attack him." Fast forward another 500 years and one finds scholars today still focused on power. For example, Mearsheimer (2001: 2) explicitly argues that "the overriding goal of each state is to maximize its share of world power, which means gaining power at the expense of other states."

Even though power remains a central concern of scholars today after roughly 2,500 years of history and analysis, how power affects international politics remains hotly contested. For instance, are international systems more peaceful when there is a hegemon, bipolarity, tripolarity, or multipolarity? Are a pair of states (also known as a dyad) more likely to have conflict when their power is balanced or when one side has a preponderance? Does power make states more belligerent or do they simply have more varied concerns? While all of those questions are important, this chapter focuses on the last, i.e., does power make states more belligerent and why (or why not)?

Why power matters

Power has always been viewed as *the* key explanatory factor in the realist school of thought. This is not coincidental. While realists may disagree as to how power matters, there certainly exists a consensus as to the fact that it matters. The reason for such a consensus/non-consensus derives from the set of fundamental assumptions that rests at the core of realist[1] thought on the international system. In many ways, realists define politics as the use of power. Carr provides perhaps the clearest and most compelling explication of this view.

> Politics are, then, in one sense always power politics. Common usage applies the term "political" not to all activities of the state, but to issues involving a conflict of power. Once this conflict has been resolved, the issue ceases to be "political" and becomes a matter of administrative routine. Nor is all business transacted between states "political". When states co-operate with one another to maintain postal or transport services, or to prevent the spread of epidemics or suppress the traffic in drugs, these activities are described as "non-political" or "technical".

> But as soon as an issue arises which involves, or is thought to involve, the power of one state in relation to another, the matter at once becomes "political". (Carr 1939a: 102)

So for Carr, politics is the use of power or, perhaps more accurately, politics is the resolution of disputes over relative power.

Perhaps the most fundamental assumption of realism is that the international system is anarchic. Anarchy in this case does not mean chaos or lack of order; rather, anarchy is simply the absence of an overarching authority. The anarchy of the international system is often juxtaposed to the hierarchy of domestic politics, where the government acts as an overarching authority. The international system does not contain an actor capable of making and enforcing authoritative decisions. To word it slightly differently, no actor in the international system possesses a monopoly on the legitimate use of force.

The anarchy of the international system creates a self-help system, where states are solely responsible for their survival, i.e., no state has a duty to ensure the survival of any other state. While states may make alliance commitments or enter into international organizations, there is no guarantee that other states will live up to their commitments. As such, states realize that they are ultimately alone and can only rely on themselves. The self-help nature of the international system is important insofar as states want to continue to survive, which is assumed by all analysts of international politics.

In an anarchic international system containing a set of states seeking to secure their survival, one would expect power to occupy a unique position. In such a system, power is the ultimate arbiter of international disputes. While states may seek to resolve differences through diplomacy, or by other means, the threat of coercion always exists. The exercise of physical force to coerce opponents is the ultimate method as Poggi (1990: 9) noted: "violence – or the threat of it – appears as the facility of last resort in shaping and managing interpersonal relations." In terms of international relations, the ability to use violence to coerce an opponent is directly related to difference in capabilities (power).

The implication of the logic of realism is that rational states that wish to survive need to gather power to maintain their security.[2] As such, the drive for power is the best, and perhaps the only, way states can maintain their security in an inherently insecure world. Given this drive for security, what is the relationship between power and international conflict? Are powerful states inherently more likely to use that power? The answer to these questions rests, however, on another assumption of realism: rationality.

Rationally seeking power

Given the importance of power, it stands to reason that states act to maintain and expand their power resources. Realists generally assume that states are rational in their pursuit of power and security. When making policies, states examine their environment and enact the policy that will generate the greatest expected benefit with lowest expected cost. This does not mean that states never make mistakes. In fact, there is no guarantee that the expectations that states develop are accurate. What makes their actions rational is the method that they use to develop policies and not the outcome.

The rationality of states is both a simple and complex assumption. Rationality can be defined as "choosing the best means to gain a pre-determined set of ends" (Morrow 1994: 17) but this definition makes no assumptions as to the ends of states. In other words, it does not matter what a state is trying to accomplish; what matters is how the state chooses to achieve the end. As long as a state implements the policy that it believes has the best chance of achieving the chosen goal, the behavior is deemed rational. Does this mean that everything can be defined, *ex post*, as rational? No, although this is a common critique of the assumption of rationality.

Green and Shapiro (1994: 17), while generally critical of rational choice, offer a succinct description of how rational choice scholars perceive the assumption of rationality. "In sum, rational choice theorists generally agree on an instrumental conception of individual rationality, by reference to which people are thought to maximize their expected utilities in formally predictable ways. In empirical applications, the further assumption is generally shared that rationality is homogenous across the individuals under study." This conception is quite similar to Morrow's definition of rational choice. The Green and Shapiro view highlights the argument that rationality describes the method of choosing actions and not necessarily some psychological state. In this case, both the emotionless Spock and emotional Doctor McCoy can be rational actors as long as they use similar methods.

Even among scholars that use rational choice, the implications of the assumption of rationality differ. For instance, Ferejohn (1991) distinguishes "thin-rational" from "thick-rational." When assuming thin-rationality, actors need only efficiently use means to accomplish their goals. Thick-rationality, on the other hand, additionally assumes that actors have the same values/goals, i.e., power, wealth, and so on. Neo-classical economics offers examples of both thin and thick rationality. In terms of the consumer, neo-classical economics only assumes that they will maximize their utilities and they make no assumptions as to what gives the consumer utility, which is consistent with thin-rationality. In contrast, neo-classical theories of the firm assume that all firms will maximize profits. Since the theories about firms purport to know the ends (profit), this falls under the rubric of thick-rationality.

Perhaps the most critical aspect of rationality is the belief that actors are goal-directed: they implement policies that they believe increase the odds of a preferred outcome and/or decrease the odds of a less desired outcome. In most cases the desired ends of actors are deduced. For instance, it may be assumed that states want to survive, gain more power, or prevail in a crisis. In addition, the ends of the actors are assumed to be fixed and exogenous. This simply means that the ends do not change during the course of an interaction. While this may seem to be an incredibly strong assumption, it merely implies that a state will not suddenly decide that it no longer wants to survive or that gaining more power is not important.

The consequence of these assumptions is that actors have a preference over outcomes and this ordering is presumed to be fixed. The preference ordering is both complete (actors can compare across all outcomes) and transitive (if outcome A is preferred to B and B is preferred to C, then A is preferred to C).[3] It is important to note that preferences can never truly be known but have to be inferred. By making the previous assumption, rational choice research is able to deduce how changes in the environment and/or available information alter the decisions of the actors. In other words, a behavior change cannot be caused by a change in preference, which leaves the environment and/or available information as the only explanatory factors.

The assumptions of rational choice are often misunderstood, so it is just as important to learn the assumptions as to learn what are not the assumptions. First, rational choice does not require that actors literally make the calculations; rather, they act as if they were making the calculations. Second, rational choice cannot explain why actors have certain preferences, only how they work to achieve their goals. For instance, Hitler may have been crazy in his choice of goals but he still may have worked rationally to achieve them (although that can still be debated). Third, rationality does not imply that all actors will make the same choices in identical situations. As noted above, actors can have different sets of preferences, which means that actors in identical situations can rationally make different choices.

Perhaps the most important non-assumption of rational choice deals with the fallibility of rational actors. Rational actors can make incorrect choices. Often rational individuals are forced to develop expectations or enter into a situation where the outcome is probabilistic. Either of these situations could lead to a poor outcome. In the first case, imagine a poker player who has an ace high straight. One could reasonably believe that hand is the best hand at the table and bet accordingly. It could end up that another player has a flush, which leads to a loss. The player with the straight was still rational, but their beliefs (or information about their opponent's hand) were faulty. If the player with the straight knew that their opponent had a flush and still bet the same way, then one could consider that irrational.[4] In this case, the player was not making a choice that maximized their chance of winning.

Rational actors can also enter into a situation where the outcome is a not-known (probabilistic). Keeping with the gambling example, imagine a game existed where the "house" flipped a coin. On heads, the house paid the player $100 and on tails, the player paid the house $50. The expected outcome of this game is that the house would pay the player $25 (50% chance of the player winning $100 plus 50% chance of player losing $50). While no round of the game will generate the expected outcome, over the long run the expectation is that the player will win $25 per round. So if the game were played 100 times, then we would expect 50 heads ($5,000 paid to player) and 50 tails ($2,500 paid to house). The ultimate outcome would be a net gain of $2,500 to the player, or $25 per flip ($2,500 gain divided by 100 flips). If someone plays the game once and ends up losing $50, does this make the choice irrational? No, because playing the game had a better expected outcome than not playing (winning $25 for playing versus winning nothing for not playing).

In terms of states and war, both expectations and probabilistic outcomes matter. In the decision to enter into armed conflict, states are required to create numerous expectations about the quality of both armed forces, domestic and international reactions, the response of allies, the odds that additional states will intervene, and so on. States risk under- (or over-)estimating any number of crucial parameters. This could lead them to enter into a war that they cannot win or to avoid a war that they could have easily won. Even if a state correctly estimates all of the relevant parameters, the outcomes of wars are not predetermined. Any number of unpredictable events can alter a battle and hence the course of a war. Ultimately, this means that states can rationally choose to start, or enter into, a war that they eventually lose.

States, and actors, may also have a tendency to act in ways that are not completely rational. Jervis (1968, 1976) illustrates a number of factors that limit the ability of individuals to consistently behave rationally. One of the most significant factors is that individuals fit incoming information to their pre-existing beliefs, i.e., actors tend to see what they expect (Jervis 1968). This tendency can lead individuals to misinterpret, place too much (or too little) significance on, or simply ignore new information. In addition, new information is often interpreted in the context of an actor's evoked set (the immediate concerns). For instance, on November 27, 1941, Washington warned General Short (at Pearl Harbor) of an impending "hostile action" from the Japanese. While Washington believed it was clear that "hostile action" meant an attack, General Short was more concerned with covert actions and interpreted it as "sabotage."

Rational choice has also been critiqued for its focus on method over substance. In other words, rational choice is "a method-driven rather than a problem-driven approach to research, in which the practitioners are more eager to vindicate one or another universalist model than to understand and explain actual political outcomes" (Green and Shapiro 1994: 33). This often leads to post hoc theoretical development where the models are tweaked until they reflect reality. For instance, according to Downs (1957), voters should only vote when they expect their vote will make a difference. Since it is highly unlikely for this to occur, it is irrational for citizens to vote. Given that reality has repeatedly shown that millions of Americans vote every year, the model was altered to account for the emotional "utility" that citizens gain from voting. This new addition to the model changes it enough to account for the voting observed in reality, although a parameter that allowed it to account for reality was added post hoc.

Power and war

How does the rational pursuit of power affect the risk of conflict? Under what conditions would a powerful state enter into, or start, a war? The empirical record (Bremer 1980; Eberwein 1982; Geller 1988; Kohler 1975; Small and Singer 1970, 1982) has repeatedly found that powerful states (major powers) tend to be more belligerent than less powerful states (minor powers). One can account for this belligerence by looking at either the opportunity or willingness of major powers. In terms of opportunity, the power of major powers simply makes them more able to wage wars both close to home and further afield. Major powers also have more at stake in the international system which may increase their willingness to engage in armed conflict.

The opportunity to engage in war is simply based on the possibility of interaction. In other words, states that do not interact in the international system cannot fight because war is a type of interaction. In fact, Most and Starr (1989: 29) argue that "one way of looking at the environment is to see it as creating and constraining opportunities for activity." The power capability of a state is directly related to its ability to project power abroad. Bueno de Mesquita (1981: 41) notes that "combat over a long distance (a) introduces organization and command problems; (b) threatens military morale; (c) invites domestic dissension; and (d) debilitates soldiers and their equipment." Thus, the only states that have the capacity (opportunity) to fight at a distance are the most powerful states in the international system. So even if major powers are no more willing to engage in war than minor powers, we would still expect that on average major powers will fight more often than minor powers.

Aside from the increased opportunity, however, major powers may also have an increased willingness to become involved in war. According to Most and Starr (1989: 35), willingness "deals with the variety of (socio-) psychological, perceptual, informational and other processes by which humans perceive their environment." The interaction of these factors leads actors to view some actions as more acceptable than others. This perception may or may not reflect reality. In fact, "the willingness to choose war may be based upon real (relatively accurate) perceptions, or distorted and selective perceptions of security and insecurity, threat, hostility, fear or anxiety" (Most and Starr 1989: 35). So what makes powerful states more willing to engage in conflict?

In general, the more powerful the state, the more it has at stake in the international system. For instance, the most powerful state in the international system (the hegemon) has a strong stake in the maintenance of the status quo because "the international system is organized to the dominant country's advantage, reflecting its power preponderance" (Lemke and Kugler 1996: 8). The structure of the system also affects the other major powers in the system. Those that benefit from the structure are status quo powers that will act to defend the system, while those disadvantaged are revisionist powers that attempt to alter the system. While less powerful states are certainly affected by the structure of the system, it is to a much smaller degree. This ultimately means that the more powerful states have a greater stake in the structure of the international system which makes them more willing to engage in conflict to defend or change it.

The combination of both an increased willingness to fight and the capability to fight (high opportunity) makes major powers more belligerent. While this argument can explain the empirical reality that major powers are actually involved in more wars than minor powers, how does this happen? The German rise from the ruins of the First World War to its initiation of the Second World War highlights the effects of both opportunity and willingness. In addition, it develops a more dynamic image of the role of power in causing international wars and shows how context matters.

Germany and the Second World War

At the end of the First World War, the Treaty of Versailles imposed incredible restrictions on Germany. By the later half of the 1920s, the German economy was in ruins and few expected a quick (or even a slow) recovery. The 1930s, however, delivered explosive growth for the German economy as well as its military capabilities. The invigorated Germany eagerly used its renewed capabilities in a bellicose foreign policy that further strengthened the state. What role did Germany's power play in its expansion and the crises that ultimately led to the Second World War?

The perceived strength (weakness) of the German state in the 1920s and 1930s weighed heavily on the leadership. Gustav Stresemann, a liberal politician who served as Chancellor and Foreign Secretary during the Weimar Republic, noted in a private memorandum that "once Germany rebuilt its internal strength, it could once again form alliances and challenge its enemies" (Copeland 2000: 123). Unlike Hitler, Stresemann was not perceived to be a warmongering politician. In fact, Stresemann won the Nobel Peace Prize in 1926 for orchestrating the reconciliation between Germany and France. So was the peaceful nature of the German foreign policy of the 1920s simply a reflection of its inferior military capabilities? The short answer is "no" in that the original goal of rearmament was "the restoration of the Reich's position as a major European power" (Deist 1981: 49) and not the territorial expansion of the German state.

The 1930s saw both the rise of Hitler and the re-emergence of German military prowess. In fact, shortly after he gained power, Hitler initiated a rearmament plan that called for a 21-division peacetime army by 1938 (a mere year before the invasion of Poland). The aim of this military program was to "build up an army, which should be capable of waging a war on several fronts with 'a good chance of success'" (Deist 1981: 37). As the army implemented Hitler's plan, however, they quickly concluded that 21 divisions was too small. Early in 1935, the Commander-in-Chief of the army (General Werner von Fritsch) pushed for an increase in the peacetime army from 30 to 36 divisions that was quickly approved by Hitler in March 1935.

In the German case, the rearmament was initiated in conjunction with future plans for territorial conquest (often known as the search for *lebensraum* [living space] or the *Drang nach Osten* [drive to the east]). As the army increased in size, the military emphasized a defensive posture. The defensive, however, was only a short-term stance for when the military improved its capabilities Germany would have "an army which is ultimately capable of fighting a decision-seeking offensive war" (as quoted in Geyer 1985: 137). Ludwig von Beck, who was the Chief of the General Staff, epitomized German military thinking when he argued in a December 1935 report ("Considerations on Increasing the Offensive Capacity of the Army") that the most successful defense was an offense (Copeland 2000: 128). The key to the new offensive capabilities of the army rested in its armored divisions and not necessarily numerical superiority.

The German rearmament proceeded far enough that by 1936 Hitler began to cautiously push for territorial revisions. In fact, Hitler produced, in August 1936, a Four-Year Plan that directed the military to prepare for an offensive war within four years. The plan required the efforts of the entire state, which Hitler made clear on September 9, 1936 when he "publicly declared his intention to gear the economy entirely to rearmament" (Deist 1981: 51). Within both the political and military leadership, a consensus was forming that argued for a German-initiated war to occur as the rearmament created a favorable balance of power. Hitler faced some resistance from the military but "they accepted Hitler's view that Germany should strike after peaking in power . . . [only the military] came to disagree on exactly *when* that peak would be reached" (Copeland 2000: 130).

Germany continued its dual pursuit of rearmament and aggressive foreign policies in the second half of the 1930s. January to September 1939 marked the perceived peak of German military power and, not coincidentally, saw the most bellicose actions. In March of 1939, Germany completed its annexation of Czechoslovakia and on April 5 Hitler ordered the army to prepare for operations against Poland which could occur any time after September 1. Late May saw Hitler accelerate the plans for offensive war as France, Britain, and Russia increased their military capabilities. German forces invaded Poland on September 1, marking the opening stages of the Second World War.

While the invasion of Poland is seen as the beginning of the Second World War, the rise of Germany throughout the 1930s was marked by increasing belligerence and territorial expansion. For instance, 1935 saw the coal-rich Saar Basin, taken by France after the First World War as reparations, vote to return to Germany. In the following year, Germany abrogated the Treaty of Locarno and occupied the Rhineland. Two years later (1938), German tanks entered Austria, forcing its political union with Germany (known as the *Anschluss* [political union] and/or the *Blumenkrieg* [flower war]). Later in 1938, Hitler forced the other European powers to accept German annexation of almost 25 percent of Czechoslovakia.

The German rearmament and its relationship to the Second World War clearly shows a connection between power and war. When Germany was perceived as being weak, its leadership and military purposely avoided conflict. As the military regained its former strength, the belligerency of the leadership increased. When German power was perceived to have peaked (in relation to the other major powers in Europe), Hitler waged his offensive war. The case also highlights two additional relationships: the rationality of the plan and the possibility of reverse causality.

Tracing the plans to rebuild the German army also indicates that the political and military leadership used cost–benefit analysis to maximize the odds of German victory. Germany crafted a plan to not only maximize the number of troops but also the type (armor). In addition, the German government successfully integrated the economy into the process. While the political and military leadership may have disagreed over the details of any given plan, there existed little discord in the goal of maximizing the benefits and minimizing the costs.

The case of Germany also highlights the possibility that the relationship between power and war may be reversed. In other words, previous research has indicated that powerful states (independent variable) are more likely to become involved in war (dependent variable). Germany, however, began its rearmament program in the belief that it would become involved in a future war. In this case, the desire to initiate an offensive war (independent variable) caused Germany to increase its power (dependent variable). In either case, however, it seems clear that a powerful Germany was more likely to become involved in a war than a weak Germany.

In addition, the German case seems to indicate that the power of a state acts as a context in that it can alter the willingness of a state to engage in armed conflict. The weak Germany saw a completely different environment as compared to the strong Germany. Where the weak Germany concentrated on threats, the strong Germany looked for opportunities. This change in focus was directly linked to the power of the German state and how it altered the German perception of the international system, i.e., the context.

Power transition theory

The rise of Germany also highlights how changes in power can affect the onset of war, which will be examined in more detail in chapter 8. Power transition theory argues that the international system contains a single hegemonic power and a group of major power contenders. Most of the major powers are satisfied with the international system, although this is not universally the case. Eventually a dissatisfied major power will rise and challenge the hegemon for control of the international system. This pattern of hegemonic wars fought between the two strongest states in the system is a recurring and predictable pattern.

The strongest empirical case for power transition theory is the rise of Germany and its challenge to British hegemony. The German challenge to the British begins roughly in the second half of the nineteenth century and ends with the defeat of Germany in the Second World War (from this perspective, the First and Second World Wars could be grouped as a single conflict). While Germany was defeated, the reigning hegemon (the United Kingdom) lost its position to the United States, which has been the hegemon since the end of the Second World War.

Power transition theory emphasizes not just the amount of power but how the amount of power changes across time. Without changes in the distribution of power, the hegemon can maintain its control indefinitely. Unfortunately for the hegemon, the power of states is not constant. States experience any number of changes that affect their power, i.e., population growth, economic development, technological innovation, and so on. In addition, states have the capacity to influence these processes, although dedicating resources to spur economic growth means fewer resources for the military. As such, it is often a trade-off between the long-term and short-term prospects of a state.

While most of the major powers have the opportunity to split their resources between long-term and short-term projects, the hegemon has fewer choices. Hegemons generally craft the international system to both maintain their position and accrue as many benefits as possible. This often requires the hegemon to concentrate on short-term projects meant to maintain the status quo structure of the international system. The resources used to maintain the international system limit the amount of resources available for long-term projects. This need to sacrifice the long-term for the short-term ultimately weakens the hegemon (in the long term) and opens the system to states that want to challenge the hegemon's control.

Power transition theory, however, requires more than a simple change in power to trigger a hegemonic war. The rising challenger not only is gaining in power relative to the hegemon but is also dissatisfied with the current international system. In other words, hegemonic wars occur when a dissatisfied state gains enough power to credibly threaten the hegemon's control of the international system. As the hegemon's power advantage declines, the risk of war increases. In fact, it is in the hegemon's interest to initiate a war sooner rather than later because its advantage will only decrease over time.

Power transition theory also emphasizes the role of dissatisfaction in causing wars. In other words, the states that want to alter the international system are those states most disadvantaged by the status quo. It makes little sense for the hegemon to initiate conflicts that risk upsetting the current structure of the international system. In addition, the major power allies to the hegemon additionally accrue benefits that they would not want to risk in a war. This does not mean, however, that the hegemon and its allies would not fight to defend the status quo. States that are dissatisfied with the international system are much more likely to challenge the hegemon and its allies. In particular, dissatisfied major powers are most likely to initiate conflicts meant to alter the status quo. The German case highlights this as they actively built their power with the expectation to use it to alter the status quo. The rise of Japan offers additional insight as it moved from a dissatisfied minor power to a dissatisfied major power.

The rise of Japan

Early in the nineteenth century, Japan was essentially a closed and isolated state. Starting around 1853, the outside world forced Japan to open up, which was quite a traumatic experience for the nationalistic Japanese. For instance, Yamagata (the builder of the modern Japanese army) was only fifteen when "foreign warships visited his secluded country and forced her rulers to sign humiliating treaties.

Over the next decade and a half, the foreigners returned again and again; some desecrated the imperial country by becoming residents, and barbarian ships even shelled the fortifications of Yamagata's own Choshu domain" (Smethurst 1974: 4). The painful opening up of Japan educated a generation of Japanese youth in the role that power plays in international politics. While differences of opinion existed in this generation, they were absolutely united in their desire to "build a strong, rich, and emperor-centered Japan capable of defending itself again the Western threat" (Smethurst 1974: 4). One of the most important tasks was transforming the feudal Japanese army into a modern one.

Even before the forced opening of Japan to the outside world, the concept of *fukoku kyōhei* (rich nation, strong army) dominated the thoughts of their leadership. Dazai Shundai, a Confucian scholar and economist who lived from 1680 to 1747, argued that "national wealth (*fukoku*) is the basis of national strength (*kyōhei*)" (Samuels 1994: 36). As Yamagata and others rushed to develop both the Japanese economy and military, *fukoku kyōhei* was never far from their minds as exemplified in the Meiji saying *wakon yōsai* (Japanese spirit, western technology).

Before the eighteenth century, the indigenous arms production capabilities severely lagged behind those of Europe. For instance, in the 1780s a Japanese samurai (Hayashi Shihei) made an attempt to build artillery but the only gunpowder he found in the entirety of Japan was 150 years old (Samuels 1994). This sparked the samurai to write his *Kaikoku Heidan* ("Treatise on the Affairs of an Insular Country") which urged the Japanese to modernize their arms manufacturing capabilities. Ironically, shortly after the treatise's publication, Japan received numerous visits from technologically advanced states that pushed for a series of concessions. As a result, the late Edo period experienced a renaissance in arms manufacturing.

The Meiji restoration built upon the renaissance in arms manufacturing and mobilized Japan for military confrontation with the West. The Meiji government's first set of actions simply consolidated their control and, within a decade of the restoration, the state dominated the Japanese arms industry. By 1877 military spending was roughly two-thirds of government investments, and it averaged over fifty percent throughout the 1880s. The late nineteenth century saw Japan involved in a number of military actions (1877 Satsuma rebellion, Sino-Japanese War of 1895, Russo-Japanese War of 1905) that continually stimulated arms production. For instance, the Tokyo arsenal employed 500 workers during the Satsuma rebellion but, by the

Russo-Japanese War (28 years later), employment had expanded to over 5,000.

The policies of the Meiji government not only modernized the Japanese military but also developed and nurtured an indigenous arms production capability. As Kozo Yamamura observed:

> Meiji Japan's sustained efforts to build a "strong army" and its decision to wage war with China in 1895 and Russia in 1904 contributed in substantive ways to building the technological foundation for Japan's successful industrialization . . . the "strong army" policy and the wars provided at critical junctures the demand necessary for assuring the survival and for aiding the growth of often financially and technologically struggling firms. (As quoted in Samuels 1994: 88)

This process did not end after the Russo-Japanese War; rather, the government began to focus on diffusing the newly acquired expertise. This work actually began in the late nineteenth century with the privatization of the arms industry. For instance, the state sold the Ishikawajima shipyard to Hirano Tomizō in 1876 and the Hyogo shipyard to Kawasaki Shōzō in 1878. The government additionally transferred skilled labor into the private sector. In fact, Samuels (1994: 91) notes that "between 1907 and 1910, some 25,000 workers left the arsenals, taking their know-how to private firms in related areas."

Often the diffusion of technological expertise resulted from the Japanese backwards-engineering western technology. For instance, in Britain, C. A. Parsons invented the marine steam turbine engine in 1894. Four years later, the Japanese Imperial Navy purchased one of Parson's new engines and within three years Mitsubishi's Nagasaki shipyard backwards-engineered the new design. The Japanese also diversified their knowledge by acquiring the US Curtis engine in 1906. Ultimately this process led to the development of a completely indigenous turbine engine (Kanpon turbine) which was used throughout the navy in the Pacific War (1941–5) with America.

The arming of Japan with modern weapons was not sufficient to build a strong army. Concurrent with the armament programs was a parallel effort meant to educate the population and endow them with a strong sense of nationalism. Yamagata was at the forefront of this effort and he began by breaking the monopoly that the warrior class (samurais) held on military service through instituting universal male conscription starting in 1873. This essentially broadened the military's social base as it instilled military values (such as unity, cooperation, and hierarchy) in the population. Despite the ability to conscript the entire male population, Japan only drafted a small percentage of the eligible males (average of 12–16 percent before 1937).

Yamagata recognized the limitations of universal conscription and worked to supplement it with an independent martial and reservist organization (1889). The numerous exemptions for the wealthy and educated limited its reach. In fact, most of the exemptions went to the village ruling class, who learned to distrust the military. Katsura implemented a solution that eliminated all exemptions and forced graduates of middle or higher schools to serve a single year in an officer candidate system, after which they returned home as second lieutenants. The new law required the poorer villagers to serve three years before they could return home as enlisted men. This new system "aimed to identify the military's elite, the officer corps, with the village's, the landlord class, and thus increase army prestige and at the same time reinforce both military and village order" (Smethurst 1974: 7).

The new system encompassed a much larger portion of society and over time would socialize virtually the entire nation with military values. Tanaka Giichi succinctly made the case when he wrote to General Terauchi Masatake in 1913:

> if we think toward the future and correctly guide the reservists, who will number three million in another six or seven years, and the nation's youth, we can control completely the ideals of the populace and firm up the nation's foundation. By continuing to promulgate educational orders like the recent one, we can permeate education and the local government with the ideal that good soldiers make good citizens. (As quoted in Smethurst 1974: vii)

The reservist system was so successful that the landlord-officers built local military organizations (where they were the leaders) which performed community services. The new conscription laws combined with Japanese military victories fulfilled the visions of Katsura and Yamagata. In particular, "the local societies raised military prestige, reinforced the respect villagers naturally felt for their local leaders, strengthened unity and productivity, and slowed the growth of dissident movements" (Smethurst 1974: 8).

As a result of all of these efforts, the rise of the Japanese military capabilities was concurrent with a rise of Japanese bellicose nationalism. Thus it is not surprising that the late nineteenth and early twentieth centuries saw the Japanese involved in numerous conflicts (1877 Satsuma rebellion, Sino-Japanese War of 1895, Russo-Japanese War of 1905). By the middle of the twentieth century, the ascent of Japan was complete in that it had a unified country not only capable of protecting its homeland from foreign encroachment but also capable of projecting its influence in the Pacific region.

The rise of Japan has some striking similarities to the rise of Germany. In particular, both states increased their power with the expectation that they would challenge the status quo even if it meant armed conflict. In this way, dissatisfaction generated the willingness to use violence which stimulated domestic programs to increase capabilities (opportunity). In other words, both states had the willingness to use force to change the status quo, but realized that they did not have the opportunity. As such, both states generated rational plans to create the opportunity.

Conclusion

How do the experiences of Germany and Japan inform our understanding of the role of power in the onset of war? First, powerful states appear quite willing and able to use it to gain advantage in the international system. Second, the following arguments about the relationship between power and war may have the causal direction reversed, i.e., states expect to fight in the future and so they build their power to meet the expected need. Third, domestic politics matters in that even the most authoritarian states feel the need to rally the population.

Both the German and Japanese cases confirm the quantitative research that discovered a correlation between power and war: states use their power to coerce other states in the international system and this occasionally leads to war. Germany clearly understood its inferior position in the late 1920s and early 1930s and so consciously chose less belligerent policies. As Hitler rebuilt the German military, German foreign policies became increasingly belligerent (reoccupation of Saar Basin in 1935, reoccupation of Rhineland in 1936, *Anschluss* of Austria in 1938, annexation of 25 percent of Czechoslovakia in 1938, and invasion of Poland in 1939). A similar pattern of increasing belligerence occurred as Japan rose from minor to major power (Satsuma rebellion of 1877, Sino-Japanese War of 1895, Russo-Japanese War of 1905, and ultimately the Greater East Asia Co-Prosperity Sphere of the 1930s).

Aside from simply confirming the quantitative studies, the cases seem to indicate that willingness to engage in conflict preceded opportunity. For instance, Germany felt aggrieved by its treatment at the end of the First World War and sought to recapture what it had lost. Hitler and the military leadership purposely timed their most aggressive actions to coincide with their peak in power (relative to the rest of Europe). In the Japanese case, their forced opening by western powers in the nineteenth century stimulated their desire to secure their position both at home and then abroad. The policies of the Japanese political and military leadership were geared toward increasing their capabilities so they could force the foreigners out of Japan and then of the rest of Asia.

The fact that the willingness to use force came before the opportunity implies that the common explanation has the causal direction reversed. Previous arguments conclude that states become powerful which gives them the willingness and opportunity to use coercive diplomacy. For both Germany and Japan, they became powerful *because* they wanted to use coercive diplomacy. This implies that the correlation between powerful states and war may not be generated by power but by the factors that lead a state to want to become powerful. This provides some evidence for the view of Morgenthau (1948: 5), who argued that the key interest of states is "defined in terms of power." Despite such a desire for power, in both the German and Japanese cases power was a means to an end (security). This, in turn, confirms the argument of Waltz (1979: 126) who pointed out that "in anarchy, security is the highest end."

Perhaps most intriguingly, the Japanese case demonstrates not only a passing concern of the political and military leadership for domestic attitudes, but also that the government specifically initiated domestic policies to generate support. In some ways, Yamagata exemplifies this attention to domestic politics as constructed policies that indoctrinated the citizens with military values: as Tanaka Giichi wrote to General Terauchi Masatake in 1913, "good soldiers make good citizens" (as quoted in Smethurst 1974: vii). The unification of the Japanese people around belligerent nationalism gave the Japanese leadership the latitude needed to expand abroad. In this sense, the domestic context directly affected the ability of the state to initiate conflict.

The concern the Japanese leadership showed about winning domestic support clearly deviates from traditional realist assumptions that states are unified, rational actors. Waltz (1979: 97) succinctly makes this point when he argues that "the functions of states are similar, and distinctions among them arise principally from varied capabilities." The Japanese elites, however, seemed to believe that an ideologically unified Japan would act as a source of power for the Japanese state.

Just as a leader in a democracy would rally domestic support for their policies, the Japanese elites created institutions (mainly related to conscription) that socialized the Japanese population into a belligerent nationalism. This emphasis on domestic politics leads into the next chapter which examines the role of democratic institutions in the behavior of states.

2 LIBERAL PACIFISM

And the establishment of a Palestinian democracy will help to bring an end to the conflict in the Holy Land. Much has changed since June 24, 2002, when President Bush outlined a new approach for America in the quest for peace in the Middle East, and spoke the truth about what will be required to end this conflict. Now we have reached a moment of opportunity – and we must seize it. We take great encouragement from the elections just held for a new Palestinian leader.

Condoleezza Rice, January 18, 2005

In the past, in the era of colonialism, colonialist countries talked about their so-called civilizing role. Today, [some countries] use slogans of spreading democracy for the same purpose, and that is to gain unilateral advantages and ensure their own interests.

Vladimir Putin, April 26, 2007

Late in the Peloponnesian War the Athenians, the first direct democracy in history, were debating an attack against Syracuse (another democratic city-state). In an attempt to dissuade his fellow citizens from the risky move, Nicias spoke against the planned attack by highlighting the perils associated with such a massive undertaking. Nicias believed that he could dissuade the Athenians from the enterprise by arguing that the resources required to win were unbelievably large. The Athenians citizens, however, did not respond as Nicias hoped:

With this Nicias concluded, thinking he should either disgust the Athenians by the magnitude of the undertaking, or if obliged to sail on the expedition, would thus do so in the safest possible way. The Athenians, however, far from having their taste for the voyage taken away by the burdensomeness of the preparations, became more eager for it than ever; and just the contrary took place of what Nicias had thought, as it was held that he had given good advice, and that the expedition would be the safest in the world. (Thucydides 1982, Book IV: 24)

Ultimately the Athenians voted for the expedition, which became an unmitigated disaster that, in no small way, led to their defeat. The case of the Athenians offers a cautionary tale for the purported peacefulness of democracies. The Athenian citizens were neither turned off by the prospects of conflict nor able to discern the truth in Nicias' argument.

Contrast the experience of Nicias with that of President George W. Bush, whose effort to continue the war in Iraq after the 2006 congressional election was resisted by the newly elected, Democratic Party-controlled Congress. Just as the American president was planning his troop surge, the Congress was planning an emergency funding plan that set deadlines for the withdrawal of American troops. Both President Bush and Congress succeeded in that the surge went forward and Congress passed a funding plan that contained deadlines (although that bill was ultimately vetoed by the president). Regardless of the success, or failure, of Congress, this situation stands in stark contrast to Athens where the leaders faced virtually no resistance from the legislature in their bellicose policies.

The experiences of President Bush and Nicias raise two important questions. First, does domestic politics affect the foreign policy of states? Realism has traditionally argued that states are functionally equivalent, which implies that differences in the domestic structure of states should have no effect. Yet the Japanese case examined in the previous chapter seems to show that even in autocratic states domestic politics matters. If domestic institutions matter, then this leads to the second question. Are democracies systematically more peaceful (known as democratic, or liberal, pacifism)? The empirical record has been quite mixed in that some studies have found statistical evidence just as others fail to uncover any evidence.

In general, democratic institutions can decrease the use of force but the effect is conditioned by two critical contexts. First, while the theoretical argument assumes that democratic citizens are dovish, it is not universally the case that a majority of citizens in a democracy always want peace. In situations where the population is more hawkish, one would not expect democratic institutions to moderate the behavior of the government. In fact, it may have the opposite effect. Second, in order for democratic institutions to affect the behavior of states, the government itself needs to have a certain level of efficacy. In other words, we would expect democracies that have difficulty controlling parts of their population of state to additionally have problems in controlling the more hawkish portions of the society. In order to understand how these contexts matter, this chapter first examines liberal pacifism from a more theoretical perspective and then delves into two cases that highlight the importance of context.

Theoretical basis for liberal pacifism

Anarchy plays an important role in realism. The lack of an overarching authority acts as a permissive cause of war in that it forces states to fear for their security and operate in an exclusively self-help manner. This vision of anarchy parallels the views of Hobbes, although when Hobbes wrote of anarchy he was referring to the state of nature that would exist domestically without a government. Life in this state of nature is "solitary, poore, nasty, brutish, and short" (Hobbes [1651]1985: chapter 13: 62). Anarchy is a constant state of war and is so awful that man is even willing to accept a Leviathan (authoritarian government) to remove himself from the state of nature. As such, citizens should rarely, if ever, revolt against the government because even the worst government is better than the best state of nature.

In the constant state of war of Hobbes's anarchy, each individual fears all other individuals and must rely only upon themselves in order to secure survival. Mearsheimer (2001: 32) makes similar arguments about the international system in that "in a world where great powers have the capability to attack each other and might have the motive to do so, any state bent on survival must be suspicious of other states and reluctant to trust them." The solution of this dilemma, according to Hobbes, is for individuals to sacrifice their rights and live under the rule of a Leviathan that would at least guarantee them survival. Such a solution, however, does not occur in international politics (at least not yet) because no state has the power to act as an international Leviathan.

Locke, however, offered quite a different view of both man in the state of nature and the state in the anarchy of the international system. For Locke, even the state of nature (anarchy) does not provide man (or the state) an excuse to break natural laws, which give every man the rights to life, liberty, and property. Locke certainly did not believe that everyone will respect those rights, which is why it is everyone's duty to punish those who violate the natural laws. The right to punish violators derives from the fact that in the state of nature no institution exists to enforce these rights.

This condition of man offers a stark contrast to the Hobbesian state of nature that *is* a state of war. In his Second Treatise, Locke makes this abundantly clear: "Men living together according to reason, without a common Superior on Earth, with Authority to judge between them, is *properly the State of Nature.* But force, or a declared design of force upon the Person of another, where there is no common Superior on Earth to appeal to for relief, *is the State of War*" (Locke and Peardon 1952). In this conception, a state of war is actually a violation of the state of nature. This does not preclude the use of force; rather, it limits it to the defense of natural law against those who work to violate it. Under this situation wars can be judged as just and unjust, but such a division would have no meaning for Hobbes.

One would expect that states following the prescriptions of Locke would behave in a distinct manner. According to Doyle (1997: 220), the foreign policies of liberal states will be virtually identical to the realist, unitary, rational actor except that "they are rational legal egoists, bound to abide by the law but also to exercise prudent advantage when they doubt that others are upholding the law." Thus, these states will compete in the international system, attempting to secure every advantage for the state, but these interactions are bounded by a respect for the natural law. Once a state breaks that natural law, however, it not only becomes justifiable to attack it but almost morally required.

Wendt (1999) contrasted the Lockean and Hobbesian views of the international system. States in a Hobbesian system viewed one another as enemies whereas states in a Lockean system view each other as rivals. At the core of the Lockean system is the right of sovereignty, which places limits on the actions of even the most powerful states. Wendt (1999: 280) makes this clear when he argues that "a powerful state may have the material capability to defend its sovereignty against all comers, but even without that ability a weak state can enjoy its sovereignty if other states recognize it as a right." This implies that even during war Lockean states will limit their violence. In particular, Wendt (1999: 283) points out that wars between Lockean states "tend to be limited, not in the sense of killing a lot of people, but of not killing *states.*"

The difference between Locke and Hobbes derives from fundamentally different assumptions about the nature of the state and the state of nature. These two views generate varying predictions as to the international system. Yet how does the construction of the domestic institutions affect the behavior of states? Both Locke and Hobbes concerned themselves with domestic politics; where Hobbes argued for the utility of authoritarian states, Locke emphasized the importance of more open (liberal) states. How then would the liberal political institutions affect their behavior in the international system?

What makes a democracy a democracy?

Before detailing the effects of democratic institutions on the risk of international conflict, it becomes important to describe the characteristics of a democracy. While it may seem intuitive and easy to define democracy, the literature has quite varied techniques. For instance, should one concentrate on the institutions of states, the norms, or both? Is it more important that citizens hold the right to vote or is it the checks and balances that mark a democracy? Is it more important to look at civil rights, political rights, or economic rights? Carr (1939a: 41) forwards perhaps the most succinct, and glib, definition when he noted that "democracy, it has often been said, substitutes the counting of heads for the breaking of heads."

Dahl (1971) offers one of the more influential views of democracy (or what Dahl calls polyarchy). Democracies, according to Dahl, continually respond to the preferences of their citizens, which are considered political equals. This implies that each citizen has the opportunity (Dahl 1971: 2):

- to formulate their preferences;
- to signify their preferences to their fellow citizens and the government by individual and collective action;
- to have their preferences weighed equally in the conduct of the government, that is, weighed with no discrimination because of the content or source of the preference.

These three are necessary, although not sufficient, conditions for a state to be democratic. Note that Dahl does not specify specific institutions; rather, he concentrates on the outcome of the political institutions. As such, democracies will have varying institutional ways of satisfying the above conditions.

To define a polyarchy, Dahl concentrates on two dimensions: public contestation (liberalism) and the right to participate in elections and office (inclusiveness). This leads to four ideal regime types. States that are low in both liberalism and inclusiveness are called closed hegemonies. In contrast, regimes that are high on both dimensions are the polyarchies. Competitive oligarchies are high on liberalism but low on inclusiveness. Finally, inclusive hegemonies are low on liberalism and high on inclusiveness. While no state has ever existed which is an ideal of one of these types, modern states can generally be classified under one of these four groupings.

Przeworski (1991) offers a slightly different view of democracy in which the outcome of the political process is more important than the structure of the domestic institutions. In particular, Przeworski (1991: 10) argues that "democracy is a system in which parties lose elections." Losing matters because any state can have a sham election where the government-backed party "wins." What marks democracies as different is that every election results in at least one party losing and the losing is neither a social disgrace nor a crime (Kishlansky 1986). This ultimately means that "in a democracy all forces must struggle repeatedly for the realization of their interests" (Przeworski 1991: 14).

Linz (1978), while similar to Dahl and Przeworski, offers a slightly more complex definition of democracy. For Linz (1978), democracies are marked by their use of free and fair elections that lead to peaceful changes in government. More broadly, Linz defines democracy as:

> legal freedom to formulate and advocate political alternatives with the concomitant rights to free association, free speech, and other basic freedoms of person; free and nonviolent competition among leaders with periodic validation of their claim to rule; inclusion of all effective political offices in the democratic process; and provision for the participation of all members of the political community, whatever their political preferences. (Linz 1978: 5)

While certainly a longer definition than that of Przeworski or Dahl, Linz once again references the political institutions and processes. In addition, Linz emphasizes the point that in a democracy a group is not discriminated against based solely on its political preferences.

The purely institutional view of democracy offered by Dahl, Przeworski, and Linz, however, cannot differentiate the various social and economic characteristics. For instance, Luebbert (1991) differentiates liberal democracies from social democracies. Liberal democracies have traditionally rested on a center-right coalition that was essentially a coalition of the middle class. In contrast, social democracies relied on an alliance between the urban working class and the middle peasantry. While both social and liberal democracies are classified as polyarchies by Dahl, these two states rest on two fundamentally different social and economic structures. As such, we would expect differences in terms of their domestic policies.

The link between society and political institutions is not necessarily new. De Tocqueville ([1840]1956), in his analysis of democracy in America, equated political democracy with equality. For de Tocqueville the movement toward democracy started first in society with the idea of equality and only later altered the political institutions. In his examination of France, de Tocqueville ([1840]1956: 30) makes this clear when he argues "that the democratic revolution has taken place in the body of society, without that concomitant change in the laws, ideas, customs, and manners, which was necessary to render such a revolution beneficial." Ideally, however, a state would have both a society that values equality and political institutions where "the impulses of the social body might there be regulated and made progressive" (de Tocqueville [1840]1956: 32).

In general, the literature has defined democracy based on the institutional characteristics of the state and the outcome of political competition. A democracy allows for the free contestation of political offices where all legal citizens have the right to both vote and hold office. In addition, the repeated competition forces political parties to fight to maintain their control of the government, yet this competition is bounded by laws and norms. This makes losing an election a likely outcome but a loss does not preclude continued participation in the political system.

Liberal states and liberal pacifism

Before describing why democratic states may be more peaceful, it is critical to clarify that liberal (or democratic) pacifism (the subject of this chapter) is different than the democratic peace. Liberal pacifism argues that democracies are more peaceful *in general*. This means that they are less likely to fight other democracies *and* less likely to fight other non-democracies. In contrast, the democratic peace argues that democracies are less likely to fight one another but are more than willing to fight non-democracies. So the question for this chapter is what would make democracies less likely to fight both democracies and non-democracies.

While the bulk of the literature concentrates on the political institutions and norms of democracies, these states are similar on multiple aspects. For instance, liberal (democratic) states generally maintain an open economy that generates both wealth and international trade. According to Schumpeter, the development of open, capitalist states mitigates the social forces that motivate imperialism. In such a state, the citizens become rational materialists that have little to no interest in international war, which Schumpeter believed was the result of imperialism. Since only war profiteers and military aristocrats can gain from these wars and no capitalist democracy would contain a majority of these individuals, it stands to reason that these states would eschew war (destruction of wealth) for peace (generation of wealth).

The development of capitalist democracies does not guarantee peace in that these states may occasionally view war as profitable. While Schumpeter did not originally make this case, his later work (*Capitalism, Socialism, and Democracy*) notes that "almost purely bourgeois commonwealths were often aggressive when it seemed to pay – like the Athenians or the Venetian commonwealths" (Schumpeter 1950: 128). Schumpeter addresses these aberrant cases by appealing to the probabilistic nature of the international system. In fact, Schumpeter (1950: 128–9) notes that "the more capitalist the structure and attitude of a nation, the more pacifist . . . [but] owing to the complex nature of every individual pattern, this could be fully brought out only by detailed historical analysis."

Rummel (1983) found relatively strong support for Schumpeter's argument in that states with political and economic freedom have fewer conflicts. According to Rummel's (1983) analysis, free countries, such as the polyarchies of Dahl, only accounted for 24 percent of the conflict as compared to 61 percent for the non-free states. The results, however, were far from conclusive. The analysis only examined 1976 to 1980, thus excluding the bulk of the Cold War and the entire era of colonialism. The Cold War years are critical because western democracies had a tendency to intervene (often militarily) in the domestic politics of minor powers. In addition, the years of colonial expansion offer the opportunity to discover if the economic incentives of imperialism outweighed the peace-generating incentives described by Schumpeter.

Aside from the tests, Rummel (1979) made a theoretical contribution to the literature on democratic pacifism. According to Rummel, since wars can have dramatic effects on the citizens of a state, they will generally be pacifist. Since democratic institutions allow for the organization of interest groups, the policy outcomes of democracy will track the preferences of the citizens. In terms of war and peace, this implies that democracies will mimic their population and act peacefully in the international system. Aside from these institutional constraints, Rummel also argues that citizens within a democracy have a compatibility in their basic values. This generates a mutual understanding that makes democracies even less likely to attack one another.

The evidence for Rummel's argument that democracies are more peaceful in general is quite mixed, although a consensus has developed around the argument that democracies are *not* more peaceful in general. Chan (1984), Weede (1984), Maoz and Abdolali (1989), and Morgan and Schwebach (1992) all failed to find any evidence that democracies were more peaceful in general.[1] On the other hand, Geller (1985) noted that states with free elections are more constrained and that constraints negatively correlated with international conflict. This relationship, however, does not maintain when the models control for domestic conflict. Some of the strongest evidence comes from Bremer (1992), who examined all pairs of states from 1816 to 1965. The statistical analyses revealed that "the presence of a democracy in a dyad significantly reduces its war propensity" (Bremer 1992: 329). Despite the work of Bremer (1992), the general consensus is that no consistent evidence has been found to confirm the liberal pacifism arguments, although the theoretical development has continued.

A second institutional perspective

Bueno de Mesquita, Smith, Siverson, and Morrow (2003) argue that the incentive of leaders to remain in power affects how states form and implement their foreign policies. States obviously vary in how leaders are chosen and removed and it is these differences that will alter their foreign policies. Bueno de Mesquita, Smith, Siverson, and Morrow (2003) chiefly examine two aspects of a state's institutional structure: winning coalition (W) and selectorate (S). The selectorate is simply the citizens of a state that have a government-granted voice in the selection of the leadership. In addition, members of the selectorate have the opportunity to become members of the winning coalition. The winning coalition is the "subset of the selectorate of sufficient size such that the subset's support endows the leadership with political power over the remainder of the selectorate as well as over the disenfranchised members of the society" (Bueno de Mesquita, Smith, Siverson, and Morrow 2003: 51). So in the United States the selectorate would be the voting population (citizens, over 18, and no felony convictions) and the winning coalition would be the majority or plurality that elected a president.

The ratio of the size of the winning coalition to the selectorate (W/S) has important implications for both domestic and international politics. In terms of domestic politics, when the ratio is small (i.e., monarch, junta, and closed hegemonies), the leader has an incentive to provide private goods to members of the winning coalition to maintain their loyalty. In these states, the leader only needs to be concerned with a small portion of the population, which makes it relatively cheap to provide them with selective benefits (government contracts, tax breaks, mining rights, and so on) to keep their loyalty. In states where the ratio is large (i.e., democratic states), leaders do not have the resources necessary to provide private goods to all members of the winning coalition. In these cases, the leader has the incentive to provide public goods, i.e., those that benefit all members of society equally. How does the size of the winning coalition and selectorate affect the foreign policies of a state?

According to Bueno de Mesquita, Smith, Siverson, and Morrow (2003), states with large winning coalitions tend to put more effort into their wars, which increases their chance of victory. This occurs because these leaders are more likely to be removed from power if they lose the war. In addition, leaders in small winning coalition states are hesitant to transfer resources away from the private goods that maintain their grip on power. This implies that autocracies (small W/S) are less likely to initiate wars against democracies, although they are quite willing to initiate wars against other autocracies. A democracy, however, will only initiate a war when the chance of victory is quite high, which is more likely to be the case when facing an autocracy as opposed to another democracy. Regardless, the threshold for initiating a war is so high for democracies (needing a large expectation of victory), they should be more peaceful in general, which is exactly what Benoit (1996) found in his statistical analyses.

Audience costs

Another explanation for democratic pacifism revolves around audience costs (Fearon 1994). Audience costs occur when a democratic leader makes a promise (for instance when President George H. W. Bush said "no new taxes") which they fail to uphold (when President George H. W. Bush raised taxes). When this occurs, the leader incurs a cost, which in the case of President Bush quite possibly cost him a second term in office. Elected leaders can avoid these costs by simply following through on their promises, i.e., taxes would have been a non-issue for President Bush in 1992 if he simply had not raised taxes.

The possibility of incurring audience costs, however, can actually benefit a leader. When negotiating on the international stage, a leader who has greater potential audience costs generally is seen as having stronger resolve. For instance, if a leader promises not to cede a piece of territory, then it can be assumed that they are quite resolved in maintaining control over that territory because giving it up would incur tremendous costs (Schultz 1998, 1999). The ultimate outcome of high audience costs is that these states can better signal their resolve which, according to Blainey (1988), decreases the risk of war.

The audience cost argument can be easily related to democratic pacifism. In general, leaders in a democracy have to routinely risk their jobs in a general election. As such, these leaders need to closely follow the feelings of their citizens/audience, especially when compared to autocratic leaders where the feelings of the audience have virtually no effect on their tenure in office. This means that, on average, leaders in a democracy can generate more audience costs which can better signal resolve and decrease the risk of war (Schultz 1988, 1999). While the audience cost argument was first used to explain the democratic peace (the dyadic argument), Schultz (1999: 243) correctly notes that signaling arguments "are fundamentally claims about democratic states." As such, they are making claims that democracies should be more peaceful in general.

The case of Israel and Hamas offers an intriguing look into the relationship between domestic politics, democratic institutions, and international conflict. In this case, everything appears to be pushing the two sides into conflict: highly salient issues of contentions, contiguous, previous conflicts, territorial disputes, and so on. As a result, the history between Hamas and Israel is full of bellicose relationships but in 2006 Hamas won a free and fair election and took control of an arguably democratic government. The question then becomes, do the democratic institutions make conflict between Israel and Hamas less likely?

Israel and Hamas

The conflict between Israelis and Palestinians stretches well back into history. It has most recently focused on the territorial issues associated with the Israeli annexation of the West Bank and the Gaza Strip. Even before the Israeli occupation of these lands after the 1967 Arab–Israeli

War, the land was associated with contention and violence. During the reign of the Ottoman Empire (nineteenth century), the Palestinians were granted a degree of autonomy. When the British took control of the land in 1917, the Balfour Declaration argued that the "Jews who wish for a State shall have it . . . [but] shall we choose Palestine or Argentine? We shall take what is given us, and what is selected by Jewish public opinion" (Reich 1995: 18–19). Ultimately, the British chose the Land of Palestine.

On November 29, 1947 United Nations General Assembly Resolution 181(II) officially partitioned the Land of Palestine into three sections: one Jewish state, one Arab state, and one internationalized sector that included Jerusalem. The Arab states rejected this resolution which ultimately led to a conflict in which the Israelis took control of all of the lands. The Arab–Israeli War in 1967 continued the territorial expansion of Israel as it took control of the West Bank, Gaza Strip, and the Golan Heights. The Palestinians have created numerous organizations (mainly terrorist) in an attempt to retake control of the land.

Sheikh Ahmed Yassin created Hamas from the Gaza wing of the Muslim Brotherhood in 1987 during the first *intifada*. Hamas has routinely used terrorist attacks against military and civilian targets which has led Canada, the European Union, Israel, Japan, and the United States to label Hamas a terrorist organization. In addition, Australia and the United Kingdom list the militant wing of Hamas as a terrorist organization and Jordan has banned the group. Finally, to make Hamas even more threatening to Israel, their charter (written in 1988) argues for the destruction of the Israeli state.

As noted above, the long history of violence between the Israelis and Palestinians (and Hamas) provides an intriguing case for the examination of liberal pacifism. The international community has recently pushed the Palestinian Authority to enact democratic reforms in an attempt to move toward a settlement between the Palestinians and Israelis. For instance, American President George Bush, on July 18, 2004, argued that "in order for there to be a Palestinian state, it is essential for its leaders to be open to reform and be dedicated to their people" (*Le Figaro* [www.lefigaro.fr], retrieved February 6, 2005). The assumption associated with the movement to induce a Palestinian democracy is that a democratic Palestinian Authority would be a peaceful Palestinian Authority.

Those urging for democratic reforms got their wish in the January 2006 legislative elections. The elections were both peaceful and fair. The Carter Center observed the elections and concluded that the Palestinian Central Elections Commission (CEC) and their staff operated "confidently, effectively and impartially, resulting in a process that compared favorably to international standards" (Carter Center 2006).[2] The free and fair legislative election, however, produced a victory for a terrorist organization in that Hamas received a plurality of 43 percent of the vote. The electoral system additionally exaggerated the Hamas victory by rewarding the group 56 percent of the seats in the legislature.

According to the arguments of democratic pacifism, it should not matter who is elected. In fact, a number of Palestinians were quite worried that an elected Hamas would be a tamer Hamas. For instance, Ayesh Hussein, 35, noted that "We're accustomed to Hamas being fighters, a party that pressures Israel. But now it will join politics and will become politicized."[3] This change in Hamas, however, was exactly what the international community hoped for as they pushed for democratic reforms of the Palestinian Authority which would neatly square with democratic pacifism.

Even after being elected, however, Hamas refused to alter its charter that calls for the destruction of Israel, even though they did not emphasize that aspect of the charter during the election. One would not necessarily expect Hamas to turn dovish if the opinion of their voters was belligerent. Amal Saad-Ghorayeb, a political science professor at the Lebanese American University, argued that "these people voted overwhelmingly for Hamas, and did so partly as a referendum for resistance, saying that resistance will pay greater dividends than negotiation."[4] This does not mean that Hamas refused to deal peacefully with Israel. In fact, Ziad Daiah, a Hamas representative in Ramallah noted: "We are not interested in the Oslo-type peace process that went on for 10 years and wasted time. But if Israel will start new negotiations, with direct benefits for Palestinians in a useful time frame, we will accept that."[5]

Even though Hamas won the elections, the opposition Fatah party continued to push for more conciliatory policies toward Israel. For instance, in the face of Hamas opposition to a two-state solution, Fatah pushed for a binding referendum on the issue. If passed by a majority of Palestinians, it would effectively bind the Hamas-led government. The tension between Hamas and Fatah continued to increase and ultimately led to the deaths of about 200 Palestinians before they signed a deal to end the nascent civil war on February 8, 2007. Overlapping with the conflict between Hamas and Fatah was renewed fighting with Israel.

On June 9, 2006 an Israeli military operation accidentally killed eight Palestinian civilians on a crowded Gaza Strip beach. This led

Hamas to withdraw from a 16-month ceasefire on June 10 and begin Qassam rocket attacks, although the ceasefire itself was not completely devoid of Qassam attacks. The Israelis responded by apprehending alleged Hamas members Osama and Mustafa Muamar in the Gaza Strip on June 24. The following day Hamas managed to capture Israeli Corporal Gilad Shalit. Israel continued the escalation on June 29 by capturing 64 Hamas officials. In spite of a lull in attacks, which generally coincided with the cessation of hostilities between Israel and Hezbollah, fighting between the Israelis and Hamas flared up once again, starting on April 24, 2007, as Hamas renewed their rocket attacks.

The Hamas-led violence against Israel did not occur within a vacuum. Being the elected government of the Palestinian people, Hamas should, according to democratic pacifism, respond to the views of the population. This link, which is generally argued to generate an incentive for peace, was maintained but only increased Hamas belligerence as the population supported their violent actions. For instance, Ali Issa, 43, a farmer, noted that: "I am happy and I am unhappy. I am unhappy because the Israeli reaction will be tough. But I am happy because of the retaliation for the blood of our people."[6] The conflict with Israel also had the effect of unifying the Palestinian factions in that Abbas, the leader of Fatah, was "being pulled, and [was] pulling Fatah, closer to Hamas in the face of the Israeli threat, when he originally wanted to pull Hamas closer to Fatah."[7]

Ironically, the election of Hamas and the subsequent conflict with Israel may have made the organization less moderate. In particular, the violence "weakened Palestinian moderates and pushed the Palestinians to a temporary unity that is closer to the extremist stance taken by those living abroad" (Erlanger 2006b: 4). This means that any effect that public opinion had on the government would not be pushing Hamas toward a less bellicose stance. The problem actually became more acute as the conflict with Israel jeopardized Hamas's ability to provide services to the population.

> The haplessness of even Hamas has been evident in this latest crisis. The new leaders of the Palestinian Authority can't pay salaries or provide social benefits because they can't defeat the economic embargo that their election provoked. But the Hamas government has been unable to persuade Hamas militants, who take their orders from abroad, even to discuss a diplomatic resolution with Israel.
>
> Instead, with Israeli troops already in Gaza and bombing its power plants and ministries in "Operation Summer Rains," Hamas is putting at risk its cherished hold on power and its power center in Gaza itself,

its own little Hamastan. But the Hamas leaders in exile – in particular Khaled Meshal, Mousa Abu Marzouk and Muhammad Nazzal – have little interest in domestic issues.

"The farther you are from the real problems on the ground, the more radical and inflexible you tend to be," said Ali Jarbawi, a dean at Birzeit University here. "That was true of Arafat in exile, and it's true of Meshal in Damascus." (Erlanger 2006b: 4)

As the violence intensifies, the difficulty of the moderates becomes even more acute. The moderates will have to either maintain their position and become marginalized or simply match the changes in public opinion by becoming more belligerent.

Hamas did manage to moderate its voice as the violence with Israel continued. In July 2006, Prime Minister Haniya argued that "solving issues can't be through military escalation or expanding their scope, but through stopping the aggression, and respecting the will of the Palestinian people and answering to their just nationalist demands."[8] This more moderate tone, however, came at a steep cost. Abu Muhammad, a Qassam Brigades field commander in Jabaliya, noted that Prime Minister Haniya and his supporters "lost their position as leaders of Hamas when they joined the government . . . New leaders were named in the movement, and they are more senior than the government leaders, even Haniya."[9] This sentiment was reiterated by Giora Eiland, a former director of Israel's national security council, who argued that "recently there was the illusion that Hamas, while not a perfect partner, was at least a group that could implement decisions . . . But it has become apparent that the political leadership of Hamas is much less influential than Khaled Meshal and leaders of the military wing."[10]

Feldman reflects the growing belief that democracy is not a panacea for the problems of the Middle East and, in particular, for the Israeli–Palestinian conflict.

More important still, the fact that Hamas and Hezbollah owe much of their present standing to elections calls into question the viability of Middle Eastern democracy as a peaceful practice. In choosing these Islamists, Palestinians and Lebanese Shiites were in effect endorsing not only their political aims but also their commitment to violence, which was never hidden during their campaigns. (The same is true, to a lesser degree, of voters in Iraq who opted for the Shiite alliance.) It was possible that once in power, the politicians at the helm of Hamas and Hezbollah would distance themselves from violence or at least refrain from initiating it. That would have been a reasonable strategy if they wanted to persuade the voters that they could actually govern and use the resources of the state to improve their constituents' lives. We now know definitively that the leaders have rejected this path.[11] (Feldman 2006: 9)

Despite the rejection of the path of peace, the effects of governing may still alter the policies of Hamas and Hezbollah. It may be the case that in the short run these groups have trouble changing their standard operating procedure, but over the long term the exigencies of running a government will moderate the political leadership.

In fact, by August of 2006, Prime Minister Haniya appeared to be softening his stance. In particular, he announced that Hamas has "no problem with a sovereign Palestinian state over all our lands within the 1967 borders, living in calm . . . But we need the West as a partner to help us through."[12] In addition, Atran (2006) wrote about his discussions with another Hamas official who argued that:

> "You can't expect us to take off all of our clothes at once . . . or we'll be naked in the cold, like Arafat in his last years." This official said that if Hamas moved too fast, it would alienate its base, but if his government continued to be isolated, the base would radicalize. "Either way, you could wind up with a bunch of little Al Qaedas."[13]

In other words, Hamas understands the need to moderate but it needs time to adjust its policies and not alienate the Palestinians who elected it.

Liberal pacifism and state strength

The case of Hamas highlights an important aspect of the role of domestic politics in international relations. Huntington (1968: 1) aptly makes the point when he notes that "the most important distinction among countries concerns not their form of government but their degree of government." In other words, states have varying abilities to rule their own territories and the difference between capable and incapable states is more important than the difference between democratic and non-democratic states. Whether differences in state capacity are more important is somewhat beside the point but the case of Hamas clearly demonstrates that capacity matters.

While it remains debatable as to the amount of moderation that Hamas experienced as a result of its election, there is certainly evidence that Haniya, and his allies, were beginning to soften their views. The problem that they ran into was the extremist views of both a large portion of the voters and the exiled Hamas leadership in Syria. Erlanger (2006b) noted this dilemma when he wrote that:

> Power, however, has proved a trap for Hamas, accentuating its divisions and causing new fractures. While Hamas has been fighting with Fatah in Gaza, trying to consolidate its control over the security forces, it has been unable to control its own leaders in exile in Syria or its military wing, which operates with little regard for the Hamas prime minister, Ismail Haniya.[14]

If the Hamas government had had a greater capacity to rein in its more militant wings, then more moderate policies could have been enacted. Unfortunately, the Hamas-led government needed the support of the militant wing and thus the moderation of Hamas has been minimal. The role that state capacity plays will be additionally examined in chapter 5.

Another important aspect of the relationship between Hamas and Israel was the relative lack of economic interdependence. Clearly Hamas depended upon Israel to forward its revenues, which the Israelis stopped as Hamas took power. The results were quite dramatic in that the Hamas government could no longer "pay salaries or provide social benefits because they can't defeat the economic embargo that their election provoked."[15] Ultimately, in July, Javier Solana attempted to organize relief money, but it only further undermined Hamas because the money was sent through the opposition, Fatah.

To get a better sense of the role of democratic institutions requires a case where the state capacity was greater than that of Hamas. The development of the European Union offers an interesting juxtaposition to the case of Hamas and Israel. While peace in Western Europe almost appears preordained, the history of the region is one of continual conflict. After the end of the Second World War, there was no reason to suspect that a long peace would not only develop but also lead to economic union. So how would the arguments of liberal pacifism explain the peace of Europe and why did it work in Europe but not between Hamas and Israel?

Europe, democracy, and peace

Since the end of the Second World War, the democracies of Western Europe have experienced one of the longest periods of peace in their collective history. While any number of factors could have contributed to this peace, it appears that democratic institutions/norms played a critical role. Even ignoring the democratic institutions of the individual states, the supranational organizations created by the Europeans since the end of the Second World War all have democratic structures. Thus, if democracies are more peaceful domestically (Hegre, Ellingsen, Gates, and Gleditsch 2001), then a supranational democracy should also be peaceful. In other words, as the European states slowly create a pan-European democracy, it becomes more able to mediate disputes and to make, and enforce, authoritative decisions.

The movement toward the European Union began at the end of the Second World War as the European states began their respective recoveries. The scale of the devastation caused many to question the utility of the territorial state as the main organizing concept. Some argued that the "state" needed to be abandoned for "a comprehensive continental political community" (Urwin 1995: 7). Cognizant of the difficulties associated with unifying such a diverse group of states and peoples, the late 1940s saw the emergence of a more functionalist approach to unification. The key was to start with economic issues where a consensus already existed and then expand over time.

Many of the early economic organizations focused on free trade. For instance, shortly before the Second World War ended, Belgium, the Netherlands, and Luxembourg formed the Benelux Pact to integrate their respective economies. In addition, the United States helped create the Organization for European Economic Cooperation (OEEC) in 1948 to promote economic integration. In the following year (1949), a Council of Europe was created to act as a European Assembly.[16] By 1950, the stage was set for the development of perhaps the most successful of these early institutions: the European Coal and Steel Community (ECSC).

The European Coal and Steel Community was an agreement between states (France, West Germany, Italy, Belgium, the Netherlands, and Luxembourg) six Western European to integrate their coal and steel industries. Aside from the explicit economic characteristics, the ECSC was a specific attempt to reassimilate Germany into Europe through economic integration. Urwin (1995: 47) notes that the ECSC was "the first significant step toward European union that went beyond the merely consultative and intergovernmental in character." Despite the early success of the ECSC, the states of Europe maintained their hesitancy to move beyond economic issues.

By the late 1950s, the Europeans realized that a true movement toward integration required more than simple economic institutions focused on a distinct industry. This eventually led to the creation of the European Economic Community (EEC) and Euratom in 1957.[17] The EEC, aside from being more expansive, looked more like a "state" in that it contained an executive branch (Council of Ministers), a legislature (the European Parliament), and numerous judicial branches. With such a structure, the organization was meant to form policies, implement them, and then adjudicate disputes. Despite the success, the idea of European integration was failing in that it still excluded Britain and a number of other important states.

The British had been unwilling to commit to an integrated Europe but by the late 1950s they began to view their isolation as problematic. Unfortunately, the de Gaulle regime in France was unwilling to work with the British and this led to a deterioration in intra-European relations (especially with France). The British decided, however, to join the European Free Trade Association (EFTA) with Austria, Denmark, Norway, Portugal, Sweden, and Switzerland in 1959. The EFTA was less comprehensive than the EEC in that it only built a free-trade area. This period also saw the intervention of the United States as it created the Organization for Economic Cooperation and Development (OECD) to focus on issues of economic development. The significance of the OECD was that it allowed non-European members.

By the end of the 1950s, Europe was essentially divided into two groups (EEC and EFTA) and the key to further movement toward integration was some form of reconciliation. The first half of the 1960s saw continued French resistance to the British inclusion in the EEC, just as the rest of the members of the EEC pushed for British inclusion to check the influence of the French. This dispute led to a seven-month boycott of the EEC's Council of Ministers in 1965, which in turn eventually led to the Luxembourg Compromise in 1966 that gave each state a veto if a policy would affect their vital national interest. Despite the compromise, the French vetoed British application for membership once again in 1967.

After a series of meetings and the resignation of de Gaulle in 1969, Britain, Ireland, Norway, and Denmark signed the Treaty of Accession in 1972. The newly enlarged European Communities (EC, formerly EEC) originally had difficulties in forming coherent policies, given the numerous new voices (and states with veto power). Within the EC, the European Parliament (EP) most promoted integration, which the Council of Ministers generally opposed. The EP fought with the Council of Ministers throughout the early 1970s to extend its power. The EP scored a partial victory in 1974, when the Council of Ministers capitulated and allowed for the direct elections of the Members of the European Parliament (ultimately held in 1979).

The first real use of power by the EP occurred in 1982 when it refused to pass a budget supported by the Council of Ministers (known as "the 1982 budget revolt"). Despite the refusal, the Council of Ministers remained the dominant force in the EC. In 1984, a Draft Treaty for European Union was overwhelmingly approved by the EP. The goal of the Draft Treaty was to produce political integration along with economic integration, which was done through increasing the power of the EP and decreasing the power of the Council of Ministers. While progress was slow on the political integration, the European Council passed the Single European Act in 1986 which planned on fully integrating the European Market by 1992.

The political integration of Europe had to wait until the early 1990s with the Maastricht Treaty (1992). The treaty rested on three main pillars: a reformed and strengthened EC, more cooperation in foreign and security policies, and a codification of collaboration in judicial and policy matters. A separate protocol of the Treaty led to the creation of the Euro (single European currency). In many ways, the Maastricht Treaty was the culmination of European integration and was the first time that it took the form of political integration. So, did the process of European integration contribute to the peace between the major European powers?

Perhaps the most noteworthy point to make with the integration process was the bounds that existed in the resolution of disputes. For instance, the French outright hostility to British entry into the EEC/EC was resolved by a process of negotiation and working within the framework of the "law." These boundaries were set not by any sovereign state but by a supranational organization. The states were under no obligation to follow the rules but they did. In fact, the first French veto of British membership was done without consultation which led to the boycott that eventually got the French to begin to compromise. This sort of working within the boundary of the laws is exactly what occurs in the domestic realm of democracies.

The struggle between the Council of Ministers and the European Parliament was also settled in a democratic manner, even though the Council had the power to act outside the "law." While the Council certainly resisted the EP, it was eventually forced to concede, in part because the direct election of its members endowed the EP with democratic legitimacy, i.e., it spoke for the people of Europe. It became clear in the reform talks of the 1980s that the European Parliament was going to gain more influence. In many ways, the pendulum had switched from support for an intergovernmental organization to that for a supranational organization.

Conclusion

As noted earlier, the statistical research into the efficacy of liberal pacifism has produced mixed results at best and disconfirming evidence at worst. For each study that shows a lack of support, however, a new theoretical explanation for liberal pacifism arises. In some ways, the basic logic of liberal pacifism (democracies are answerable to a public that does not want to pay the costs of war) has an intuitive appeal which may explain the enduring nature of the theory. The two cases examined in this chapter (Israel versus Hamas and the European Union) offer a slightly different take on liberal pacifism.

The case of Israel and Hamas clearly shows that citizens are not necessarily peace-loving and provides an important context. The individuals who voted for Hamas did so with the expectation that they would continue the use of violence against Israel to compel changes in its policies. In such a situation, the "peace" effect in liberal pacifism not only fails to generate peace but may lead to an increase in violence. In other words, just as a peace-loving population would act as a check against a belligerent leader, a war-accepting public would act to make the state's policies more belligerent. This essentially means that one of the fundamental assumptions of liberal pacifism is incorrect (or at least not universally accurate).

The discovery of a bellicose population does not necessarily disprove liberal pacifism; rather, it shows the conditionality of the effect. Democratic institutions are permissive in that they can increase or decrease the belligerence of a state's foreign policy. In order to determine the ultimate effect, an understanding of the public is required. Democracies where the citizens are accepting of the use of force should act in a more belligerent manner than democracies where the citizens are unwilling to support the use of force. In some ways, American President George W. Bush discovered this the hard way: when public opinion turned against the Iraq war, it placed significant constraints on the administration.

The cases also clearly demonstrate the role that state capacity plays in the effect of democratic institutions. While the election did not immediately moderate Hamas, the latter clearly became less bellicose over time. Unfortunately, Hamas's inability to rein in the more militant parts of its organization quickly halted that moderation. In order to maintain its tenuous grip on power, Hamas was forced to keep a relatively hostile attitude toward Israel even if it was against the long-term interests of Hamas and/or the Palestinians. In contrast, the

European case had two highly capable actors. At the level of the individual state, the governments were certainly able to enforce unpopular policies (if needed). In addition, the supranational institutions (like the ECSC, EEC, EC, and EU) have proven able to make binding decisions that the individual states follow even if it is against their perceived interests.

In general, then, liberal pacifism matters, although it requires two critical components. First, the population needs to conform to its underlying assumption about its pacific views. Violations of this assumption, which may not occur that often, absolutely eliminate the chance that democratic institutions would significantly enhance the prospects of peace. Second, the state needs to be capable of enforcing its decision even when the population disagrees with the policy. A democracy with limited capacity has little chance of generating support for peaceful policies or of keeping private citizens from acting to sabotage peace.

PART II   THE INTERACTION OF STATES

3 THE BALANCE OF POWER

And anyone who has well fortified his city and has well managed his affairs with his subjects in the manner I detailed above (and discuss below) will be besieged only with great caution; for men are always enemies of undertakings that reveal their difficulties, and it cannot seem easy to attack someone whose city is well fortified and who is not despised by his people.

Machiavelli, *The Prince* (Chapter X)

Worse still, the new French philosophy of war, by its preoccupation with the moral element, had become more and more separated from the inseparable material factors. Abundance of will cannot compensate a definite inferiority of weapons, and the second factor, once realized, inevitably reacts on the first.

Liddell Hart, *The Real War 1914–1918* (1930: 40)

When the Athenians attacked the Melians during the Peloponnesian War, the balance of power clearly favored the Athenians. Athens had an empire that spanned the Greek world with unrivaled naval supremacy. Melos, on the other hand, was a single city-state that could not even count on Athens' enemies for aid. Despite such forbidding odds, the Melians resisted and, as the balance of power indicated, were defeated by the Athenians. Given such an obvious outcome, why would the Melians fight? Did they simply refuse to accept their inevitable loss or were factors other than power more important to their decision? Perhaps more importantly, how does one measure the relative power of states?

Often when discussing power, scholars are simply referring to military power. Carr (1939a: 109) makes this point when he argues that "the supreme importance of the military instrument lies in the fact that the *ultima ratio* of power in international relations is war. Every act of the state, in its power aspect, is directed to war, not as a desirable weapon, but as a weapon which it may require in the last resort to use." For Carr, and realists in general, the nature of the international system, especially the continual risk of armed violence, forces states to obsess over balances of power. It remains the prerogative of states to address matters aside from power but they do so at their own risk, a risk that most states refuse to take.

As the Carr quote implies, power matters, but generally matters in a relative, as opposed to an absolute, sense. In other words, 1,000 tanks will only make a state secure if its enemies have fewer tanks. In their analysis of wars, Reiter and Stam (2002) consistently found that states with an advantage in terms of capabilities were more likely to win the war. It seems fairly intuitive that more powerful states defeat less powerful states in wars but it highlights a puzzle. Given the advantage of power, why would less powerful states ever enter into a conflict that they expect to lose? Are these states irrational or do most wars occur when the capabilities are balanced (or at least perceived to be balanced)?

In general, power certainly matters when looking at the onset of war. How power matters is not nearly as apparent. This chapter addresses this issue by first defining power and then describing two influential theories about the effect of power balances on the risk of war. The first argues that wars are less likely when a preponderance of power exists, i.e., an asymmetry. The second theory makes the case that peace is more likely when power is balanced. In order to better understand these arguments, the chapter additionally examines two cases. In the one case a preponderance of power existed (Germany versus Denmark in the Second World War) and in the second case a balance of power existed (Germany versus France in the First World War).

Power preponderance and peace

Blainey (1988) observed that when two states enter into a war, they both have optimistic assessments as to the outcome. In other words, no state decides to fight a war it believes it will lose. Since wars generally have both winners and losers, at least one state in a conflict has overestimated their capabilities. When the two sides of a potential conflict cannot agree as to the distribution of capabilities, the opportunity for war exists. In fact, if the two sides agree as to the distribution of capabilities (or the odds that either side would win a war), then the states should rationally come to a negotiated solution.

Imagine, for instance, that states A and B are competing over 100 resources. If a war occurred over these resources, assume that the winner would take an amount equal to their power ratio, i.e., if they have 80 percent of the power they would receive 80 percent of the resources. Each year of a war, however, destroys 10 resources. So if state A wins after a single year, it would receive a portion of 90 resources instead of 100. In addition, assume that the odds that either state would win the war is directly related to its power (relative to its opponent). Now if we assume that the two states are at parity, then the odds that state A wins are 50 percent, which means that the odds of a state B victory are also 50 percent. Given these chances, the expected benefit of a year-long war for both states is 45 resources, i.e., 50 percent chance of gaining 90 resources. The question then becomes, when will these states reach a negotiated agreement and when will they fight?

For the sake of the argument, let us first assume that both states know their own capabilities as well as their opponents'. In other words, there is complete information as to the outcome of the war. In this scenario, both states would be willing to accept a pre-war bargain where they receive at least 45 resources, i.e., the amount that they expect to gain in a war. Under these conditions, the odds of a negotiated solution are relatively high. For instance, state A could offer to split the resources 51/49. While state B would certainly want more than 49, it is still more than it would expect to win in a fight. State B could counter-offer with a 49/51 distribution, which would be better for B and would still offer state A more than it would expect to receive in a war. As long as both sides are willing to offer the other side at least 45 resources, war will be avoided.

The chances of a negotiated solution decrease when the two sides disagree as to the distribution of capabilities. Even though we have assumed that the distribution of capabilities is 50/50, states A and B do not have to have accurate information or to have accurately assessed the distribution of capabilities. What if state A believes that it has 60 percent of the power and state B also believes that it has 60 percent? First, this means that both states believe that they will receive 54 resources in the case of a war that lasts one year (60 percent of 90 resources). Second, this implies that neither side would accept a negotiated solution were they offered less than 54. Third, the most that either state would offer the opponent is 46 because offering any amount higher implies that the offering state would get less than 54. Since the

46-resource offer is much less than the expected 54 resources, it is unlikely that a negotiated solution would be possible. In this case, unless the two sides change their assessment as to the distribution of capabilities, war is likely.

Even if war occurs, the "negotiations" do not simply end. While the states may not be sitting around a bargaining table, the two sides are continually updating their beliefs about the distribution of capabilities. In other words, wars help resolve disagreements over the distribution of capabilities. So imagine that, at the end of the first year of the war, both states A and B lower their estimated capabilities down to 55 percent. With this new assessment, both sides now believe that at the end of the second year of the war they will get 44 resources (55 percent of 80). This new set of beliefs actually creates space for a negotiated solution (44/46, 45/45, or 46/44). While this does not make a negotiated solution a guarantee, it at least makes it a possibility.

As seen from the above example, the Blainey perspective argues that wars occur when states disagree as to the distribution of capabilities. The process of war conveys information to both sides of the conflict as to the "real" distribution and, when the beliefs converge enough, a negotiated solution become possible. This sort of process neatly explains a seeming paradox of the First World War: why did Germany unconditionally surrender to the Allies having never fought a major battle on German territory? The answer is that it became obvious in 1918, especially with the American entry into the war, what would be the ultimate outcome of the First World War. Since both sides had the same assessment as to the outcome of the war, continued fighting served no purpose and a negotiated solution arose. How does Blainey's theory illuminate the debate over power preponderance versus power parity?

The logic of Blainey's argument implies that war is more likely when parity exists as opposed to situations of preponderance. If wars occur because states cannot agree as to the distribution of capabilities, then this is much more likely when a pair of states are at parity (50 percent/50 percent) as opposed to preponderance (75 percent/25 percent, for instance). While this does not preclude states at severe disadvantages from overestimating their relative capabilities enough to cause a war, the point is that it is more likely to occur when states are closer to parity. That being said, Blainey's key insight is the role that a lack of information plays in generating international conflict.

Blainey's argument in some ways addresses a key problem in studying the onset of war. In particular, theories that assume rational leaders need to explain "what prevents leaders from reaching *ex ante* (pre-war) bargains that would avoid the costs and risks of fighting" (Fearon 1995: 380). All wars end and the vast majority end with a negotiated solution. This implies that rational leaders should figure out what the post-war settlement will be and reach that solution before the war. In this case, everyone is better off because they have the same outcome but do not have to pay the costs associated with war. Blaney's solution to that problem is that the two sides simply do not agree as to the ultimate outcome of the war. The process of fighting a war brings the expectations in line with one another until a negotiated solution can be reached.

Fearon (1995) builds upon the logic of Blaney and creates a "rationalist" explanation for war. According to Fearon, there are three ways in which rational leaders can enter into a conflict. The first argument rests on the incentive of leaders to misrepresent their strength in order to increase their bargaining position. As such, the *"private information* about relative capabilities or resolve" (Fearon 1995: 381) prevents a mutually acceptable negotiated solution from occurring. Second, leaders could overcome the incentive to misrepresent, but one or both states "would prefer war due to *commitment problems,* situations in which mutually preferable bargains are unattainable because one or more states would have an incentive to renege on the terms" (Fearon 1995: 381). Finally, and admittedly least convincing to Fearon, the two sides could fail because of issue indivisibilities, i.e., some issues cannot be divided (for instance, right of return of the Palestinians).

Power parity and peace

The power preponderance and peace argument implies that states engage in conflicts that are relatively risky. If wars occur when power is balanced, then each side has an equal chance of winning. Given the stakes involved in international war, why would a rational state take on that risk when the odds of a favorable outcome are essentially a coin flip? Would it not make more sense for a state to initiate a conflict when it has a preponderance of power, when it knows that it will win? In this case, power parity will act as a deterrent to conflict.

While the concept of balance of power remains at the core of realist thought, it has intriguingly been used in vague and often contradictory ways. Haas ([1953]1961) found eight separate meanings in his survey of the literature that range through its use as a policy, concept, and even propaganda. In addition, Zinnes (1967) discovered eleven different meanings and Wright (1965) counted both nine and fifteen separate uses in the literature. Despite the variety of definitions, balance of power is perhaps most accurately described by the nineteenth-century British prime minister Palmerston (as quoted in Doyle 1997: 162) when he noted that " 'Balance of power' means only this – that a number of weaker states may unite to prevent a stronger one from acquiring a power which should be dangerous to them, and which should over-throw their independence, their liberty, and their freedom of actions. It is the doctrine of self-preservation."

Despite the difficulties in defining balance of power, difference also exists in the consequences of a balance of power. The balance of power has been purported to generate stability (continued existence of the anarchic international system) in the international system (Waltz 1979). The balance of power could also generate geopolitical counter-poise, which is simply when states act to balance power with power (the enemy of my enemy is my friend) (Doyle 1997: 163). The conse-quence of geopolitical counterpoise is a patchwork set of alliances where a state fights those it borders and allies with the states that border its enemies. Perhaps the earliest version of this argument comes from Kautilya and his concentric circles of alliances. Geopolitical counterpoise can also lead to equipoise which is the formation of two of more balanced coalitions of states (Mowat 1923).

The balance of power also has consequences for individual states. It has often been argued that a balance of power generates a status quo bias in that states will survive. This could imply that major powers will not be eliminated in the course of major power wars or it could be more expansive and relate to the survival of all states. Niou and Ordeshook take the balance of power a step further and argue that the "balancing will lead to a continuous reproduction of the status quo, implying a peace in which no actor experiences a loss of resources or power" (Doyle 1997: 167). This belief is reflected in the earlier works of both Pecquet (1757) and Leckie (1817).

The evidence for the classical balance of power remains mixed. Doyle (1997) examined eighteenth-century Europe for evidence of state balancing. This period in Europe provided almost an ideal test case in that:

> The troubles of the sixteenth- and seventeenth-century wars of religion had by and large been settled in favor of the status quo, yet the nine-teenth- and twentieth-century wars of nationalism and liberalism had yet to materialize. For the first time the European state system operated as a strategically interdependent whole, rather than as separate "north-ern" and "southern" systems, as it had earlier. The measure of power

was more stable than it would be when the industrial age stepped up the pace of change. After a long seventeenth century of warfare, state institutions had become centralized and coherent. There were few, if any, "alliance handicaps" – barriers other than security and power calculations to changes in alliances through external balancing. All of the assumptions [of the balance of power theory] were in place: international anarchy, coherent states as rational positionalists, and a multipolar distribution [of power]. (Doyle 1997: 175–6)

Despite these conditions, the interaction of the major powers of Europe did not perfectly act in the manner predicted by the balance of power theory. On the positive side, the major powers designed policies to balance against their enemies and they survived the entire period (although the minor powers were often partitioned). That being said, the classic balance of power system imposed massive costs in terms "of a large investment in arms, the destruction of small powers, and a series of devastating great power wars" (Doyle 1997: 193). If the balance of power affects the actions of states, then what are the implications for dyadic balance of power?

According to the balance of power theory (Claude 1962; Wright 1942; Waltz 1979), wars occur when one side has a preponderance of power, and it is implicitly understood that the stronger state initiates the conflict. While much of the research is cast at the systemic level of analysis, which will be discussed later, a number of works have looked at the balance of power in terms of dyads. Bueno de Mesquita (1981) found partial evidence for this argument in that his research discovered that the initiators of interstate wars were generally twice as strong as the targets. In addition, Siverson and Tennefoss (1984) found that fewer conflicts between major powers (presumably more equal in power) became militarized.

Mearsheimer (2001) reiterates the balance of power theory in his work on "offensive realism." While much of his analysis looks at the systemic distribution of capabilities, he often extends the logic of his argument to the dyadic level of analysis. For instance, Mearsheimer (2001: 341) notes the "power asymmetries among the great powers are more commonplace in multipolarity than bipolarity, and the strong become harder to deter when power is unbalanced, because they have increased capability to win wars." This dovetails with previous work on the balance of power that emphasizes the role of deterrence in keeping peace when balance of power exists.

So how do states incorporate power into their decision-making processes? To answer this question, the following case examines the

German decision to attack Denmark during the Second World War and the Danish decision to capitulate. This is clearly a situation where a preponderance of power existed between the two states. Blainey and the power preponderance theorist would argue that the asymmetry of power would lead to Danish capitulation and no German attack. The power parity theorist would predict a German attack with the Danes resisting. In reality, both sides are half correct in that Germany attacked (supporting power parity) and the Danes capitulated (supporting power preponderance).

Germany, Denmark, and the Second World War

Often the northern front of the Second World War is overlooked but the Baltic and Scandinavian regions played a crucial role early in the conflict. As early as 1928, Hitler wrote about the importance of the region: "What the Mediterranean Sea is to Italy . . . the eastern coast of the Baltic Sea is to Germany" (as quoted in Hiden 1992: 16). Even earlier, General Hans von Seeckt argued that "maintaining sea access to Sweden is a matter of importance to Germany, that to Russia can be a question of survival" (as quoted in Hiden 1992: 17). Control of the Baltic gave Germany access to critical natural resources such as Estonia's oil shale production. In addition, it gave the Germans a chance to cut the flow of resources to their enemies.

Any attempt by Germany to secure the Baltic Sea placed the Scandinavian states (especially Denmark) clearly in German crosshairs. Danish policy-makers never forgot this fact and their foreign policy had a single tenet:

> The independence of the country was at the discretion of the German army. As long as Germany could be persuaded that an independent Denmark was in its own interests or at least not contrary to them, Denmark could remain tranquil. The chances of avoiding a German attack and occupation (or incorporation) did not depend on the Danish armed forces and could not be secured by an alliance with any other great power, much less by an alliance with the other Nordic countries. (Nissen 1983: 9)

Denmark was in the ultimate self-help situation and, unfortunately for Denmark, its military capabilities were simply incapable of helping.

To make matters even worse, the Danish possessions in the Atlantic (Faroe Islands, Greenland, and Iceland) were becoming increasingly important to both the United States and Great Britain.

While neutrality in the Second World War seemed like the best policy, the structure of the Danish economy made that difficult. In particular, Denmark was reliant on foreign trade to such an extent that by 1936 the country was exporting $81.34 per person (Nissen 1983: 17). In contrast, Britain exported only $46.06 per person, Germany $28.42 per person, and the United States a lowly $18.62 per person. This reliance on exports was even more problematic because 52 percent of Danish exports went to the United Kingdom and an additional 20 percent went to Germany. So a neutral Denmark had to balance two demands: to remain sovereign (which depended on Germany) and to remain economically viable (which greatly depended on the United Kingdom).

Up until the 1930s, the Nordic countries conducted their foreign policies in association with the League of Nations. The rise of Germany saw the Nordic states withdraw from collective security toward neutrality. German attitudes toward Denmark were not (yet) bellicose. In fact, the "Nazi government ordered the German minority in northern Schleswig to remain passive, since its long-term plan envisaged not only a revision of the frontier, but also the incorporation of the whole of Denmark, and perhaps more than that, into a greater German Reich" (Nissen 1983: 45). So while on the surface German policies appeared peaceful, they were simply waiting for the most opportune time to act.

Denmark, in the 1930s, acted to minimize any and all possible conflicts with Germany. The Danes feared that the Germans would use any provocation, no matter how small, to turn a latent military domination into an actual military occupation of Danish territory. The Danish government went as far as to "influence the press to refrain from provoking the leaders of the Third Reich and organized Denmark's defenses in such a way that it must have been clear that it did not intend to resist a deliberate German attack" (Nissen 1983: 45). While some in the United Kingdom viewed Denmark as a "military vacuum," the truth of the matter is that in the 1930s the Danish straits and territories were already controlled by Germany.

In the period before the invasion of Poland, Germany attempted to secure the status quo in northern Europe through offering (on April 29, 1939) bilateral neutrality pacts with Denmark, Norway, Finland, Estonia, and Latvia. While a neutrality pact would serve their interests, the states of northern Europe had no illusions as to their dire diplomatic straits. Nurek recounts the feelings of the Scandinavian countries:

> The head of the department of commerce in the [Swedish] Ministry of Foreign Affairs, Gunnar Hagglof, presented the view of his government: "Great Britain in reality left the Baltic Sea by signing the Naval Treaty with Germany in June 1935 and I know what Hitler said about it after the signing: 'The Baltic is now a bottle which we can close. The British cannot exercise control there. We are masters of the Baltic.'" (Nurek 1992: 33)

It was within this environment that Denmark signed a neutrality pact with Germany on May 31, which supposedly secured the Danes the right of free trade with all countries. This was critical to both the Danes and the United Kingdom because this meant that any war would not disrupt their bilateral trade.

As important as Denmark and the Jutland were to the British, a study completed on May 1, 1939 by the Committee of Imperial Defense concluded that an attack by Germany against Denmark was not a *casus belli*. The report notes that: "the strategic and economic issues involved in an isolated act of German aggression against Denmark are not of sufficient importance to warrant regarding it as a *casus belli*. In the event of general hostilities, we could not afford her direct military assistance and her ultimate fate would depend on the outcome of the war" (Nurek 1992: 42). In addition, the British informed their ambassador in Moscow that Denmark was to be excluded from the list of states for which Britain wanted a Soviet guarantee against German aggression.

When war finally broke out in September of 1939, all of the Nordic countries (including Denmark) immediately declared neutrality. The states met in Copenhagen on September 18 to discuss matters, in particular, the need to maintain trading relations with all of the belligerents. Germany was quite content to consent to the neutrality of the Nordic states because it allowed Germany to continue its vital import of iron ore from Sweden. In addition, the British felt that the interior coasts of Norway, Sweden, and Finland were not strategically important, so it concentrated on other areas. The Soviet Union, however, believed that the status quo was unacceptable and this ultimately led to its invasion of Finland.

The Soviet invasion of Finland marked the beginning of the end for Nordic neutrality. In fact, Haikio (1983: 73) argues that "the Soviet advance into Finland unleashed a race for northern Europe among the great powers." In terms of Denmark, this meant that the latent military domination by the German army ran the risk of becoming a military occupation. By the spring of 1940, Germany was planning its invasion of both Denmark and Norway. On March 1, Hitler ordered the execution of Operation Weserubung which required the occupation not only of northern Jutland but also of all Denmark. The goal was to secure German access to the iron ore coming out of Sweden. Despite the German preparations for invasion, however, "neither Norway nor Denmark . . . made any attempt at political or military mobilization or to increase military preparedness" (Haikio 1983: 92).

On April 9, German troops marched into Copenhagen. In conjunction with the military actions, the Germans sent the Danish government a note stating the German aims were to thwart Allied actions and requested the cooperation of the Danish government. In addition, the note detailed a 13-point occupation program that dealt with ending the resistance, controlling the media and the economy. In response to the German actions, the Danish government capitulated "without resistance within a few hours" (Haikio 1983: 94).

The Danish capitulation to Germany after the invasion roughly conforms to Blainey's theory. In this case, both the Germans and the Danes knew the outcome of a military confrontation. As such, it behooved the Danes to minimize the costs of the invasion and not resist the Germans. Blainey's theory, however, has a more difficult time explaining the German decision to invade because, if there was agreement as to the outcome of a conflict, then Germany would not have had to invade. So why did Germany invade?

This anomaly can be explained by the Soviet invasion of Finland. Before the Soviet attack against Finland, the Germans were quite content to maintain the status quo in northern Europe. Once another major power intervened, it changed the calculus in that Germany could no longer be sure that the British would stay out of Norway and Denmark. It was this threat (British intervention in northern Europe) that forced the German hand. So in some ways, the German invasion of Denmark was to pre-empt the British and not to fight the Danes.

Germany versus France in the Second World War

While both the Germans and Danes agreed as to the outcome of a potential military confrontation, the French and Germans had vastly divergent views as to the outcome of their potential military confrontation. The French, deriving confidence from their victory in the First World War, built a state-of-the-art trench (called the Maginot Line) that they believed would halt any German attack. The Germans, attempting to avoid a repeat of the First World War, merged new military technologies (tank and airplane) with a new tactic (*Blitzkrieg*) in an attempt to bypass the Maginot Line. As a result of these factors, the French and Germans had divergent beliefs as to the distribution of power. According to Blainey, it is the beliefs that matter in that states make decisions based on their beliefs which may or may not match the underlying reality.

The origins of the Maginot Line derived from both the military and psychological needs of the French. In terms of the military, the eastern border of France (the Alsace and Lorraine areas) was critical to French industry. For instance, Alsace provided the bulk of French potash and the entire region contained numerous, and economically critical, industrial goods. Psychologically, the French nation suffered tremendous loss in the First World War and could not simply leave the land undefended. Sergeant André Maginot represented this view as he spoke to the French Parliament as they debated the Treaty of Versailles:

> We are always the invaded . . . We are always the ones to suffer, we are always the ones to be sacrificed. Fifteen invasions in less than six centuries give us the right to insist upon a victor's treaty that will offer something more realistic than temporary solutions and uncertain hope. They do more; they make it our duty to do so. After all we have suffered, we have the right to demand certainties. This treaty does not provide certainties, either in respect of the reparations due to us, or in the respect of security. Without proper guarantees of both, it is going beyond the possibilities of human nature to expect our people to rebuild the regions that remain exposed to the risks and calamities of a new invasion. (As quoted in Rowe 1959: 17)

The solution for the French nation, the French political leaders, and the French military was to defend their eastern border, to create such a defense as to make a German victory impossible.

Given the veritable stalemate of the trench warfare of the First World War, French military thinkers attempted to learn from that war and develop the ultimate trench. In an interview given to the *Daily Express* in 1928, French Minister of War Paul Painlevé described the new defensive system: "We have based the defenses on the lessons of the last war. Our scheme is a combination of two plans. The first is a sort of continuous front line, an organized trench system of concrete and steel, whilst the second is a series of regional strongholds" (quoted in Rowe 1959: 45–6). Painlevé's description highlights two aspects of the proposed fortification. First, it was based on the assumption that a new war with Germany would be fought like the last war, i.e., trench warfare. Second, the French defense would be static, i.e., unable to move.

The Maginot Line, however, did not need to hold the Germans indefinitely. The fortifications only had to halt the Germans long enough (even a surprise attack) so the French could mobilize the rest of their army (about three weeks), although the French clearly believed that the Maginot Line would be "a great rampart against which future German armies would hurl themselves and be repelled" (Overy 1989: 128). Even if the Germans decided to avoid the Maginot Line and attack through Belgium, the French believed that the combination of Belgian and British forces could slow the Germans enough to allow a complete French mobilization. In fact, General Giraud noted in 1939 that "the German Army will break itself upon our defenses" (quoted in Rowe 1959: 99).

The French were not alone in their belief in the Maginot Line. After Germany incorporated a number of Czechoslovakian territories in 1938, they were able to examine Czechoslovakian fortifications modeled after the Maginot Line. According to a Czech newspaper, "the Germans . . . after investigating the Czech fortifications, believe the Maginot Line to be the most impregnable [sic] in the history of warfare" (quoted in Rowe 1959: 97). In fact, the German Army Chief of Staff (General Franz Halder) wrote in his diary on September 29, 1939 that the "techniques of [the] Polish campaign [are] no recipe for the West. No good against a well-knit army" (as quoted in Mearsheimer 1983: 102). The German army was so convinced that an invasion against France would fail that the three commanders of the planned attack (Bock, Leeb, and Rundstedt) held a secret meeting on November 5, 1939, to discuss ways to dissuade Hitler from attacking France.

Aside from the Maginot Line, the French army possessed additional advantages over the Germans. In particular, the French had more and better tanks than the Germans as Deighton (1981: 231) noted: "by 1939 the French Army had the best tanks in Europe, far more sophisticated than anything the British or Germans could field." On top of this advantage in quality, by 1940 the French army had a numerical advantage – 2,342 tanks for the French against 2,171 for the Germans (Deighton 1981: 232–3). French armor, however, was not put in a position to exploit its advantages. Whereas the Germans saw armored units as shock troops capable of operating in isolation from infantry, the French tank battalions were assigned to "infantry units or kept in a general reserve" (Deighton 1981: 235).

The prospect of a war of attrition against the West forced the German military leadership to develop alternative plans. Manstein and Guderian began to examine ways to utilize the German Panzer Corps in the impending attack. After having his Nineteenth Panzer Corp assigned to Army Group A, Manstein related his idea to concentrate the Panzers in order to break through the French forces and make a deep, strategic penetration. Manstein summarized his (and Guderian's) view of the upcoming operation in a memorandum sent to the OKH: "For the A Gp it is, however, important, after dashing through Luxembourg making maximum use of the element of surprise, to break through the fortified Belgian positions before the French are able to form up their defense forces and to entirely defeat in *Belgium* those French elements initially to be expected for encounter" (as quoted in Mearsheimer 1983: 121). By quickly breaking through the French front and pushing forward, Manstein and Guderian hoped to defeat the French both quickly and decisively. Their plan was a deviation from the original German army plan of September 1939, which called "for an attack on France [like] the one that failed in 1914" (Deighton 1981: 43).

The adoption of *Blitzkrieg* gave the German military commanders more faith in their ability to win a war in the West. While they did not think victory was inevitable and clearly understood the risks, the German army felt confident, where they had earlier felt uncertain. Mearsheimer has a lengthy quote from a memorandum written by General Halder before the attack that highlights this perspective.

> The mission assigned to the German Army is a very difficult one. Given the terrain (Meuse) and the ratio of forces on both sides – especially with regard to artillery – this mission cannot be fulfilled if we employ those means which were relevant in the last war. We will have to use exceptional means and take the resulting risk.
>
> Whether the panzer divisions of the forward wave appear on the Meuse in full combat power is less important to me than the necessity of demonstrating resolute daring in pursuit of the retreating enemy and in making the initial crossing to the western Meuse bank decisive . . .
>
> I am absolutely aware of the fact that these units, when dashing forward, will have hours of severe crisis on the western Meuse bank. The *Luftwaffe* will relieve them by fully bringing to bear its superior combat power. Without taking this risk we might never be able to reach

the left Meuse bank. But I am convinced that, in this operation, too, our panzer leaders will have an advantage, due to the energy and flexibility, combined with the effect of setting personal examples. Against an enemy proceeding methodically and less trained in commanding panzers, they will be able to exploit the severe psychological burden imposed by the appearance of German panzers on a unit which lacks battle testing. Assuming that all possibilities for an adequate allocation and a carefully considered disposition of our forces have been exploited, I cannot accept the argument that our mobile forces, organized and armed as they are, do not meet the necessary requirements for such a task. (Mearsheimer 1983: 128–9)

In the parlance of No Limit Texas Hold 'Em poker, the Germans were going all in and believed that the French would fold.

Balance of power and war

The German invasions of Denmark and France highlight both the strength and weakness of the power preponderance and power parity theories. The power preponderance leads to peace argument would predict that Germany would attack France but not Denmark. In contrast, the power parity leads to peace argument would predict that Germany would attack Denmark but not France. History has shown that Germany invaded both Denmark and France, which offers support (and contrary evidence) to both theories. What, then, do the cases ultimately demonstrate about the relationship between power and war?

Perhaps the most consistent aspect of the two cases was that Germany only attacked when it was confident in its victory. While this is less important in the case of Denmark because it was always clear that the Germans would win, the decision to invade France was greatly influenced by Germany's belief in the prospects of victory. It was clear from the beginning that the German military did not want to repeat the trench warfare of the First World War and they balked at invading France when they held this belief. With the development of *Blitzkrieg* in the winter of 1939–40 as a viable option, the prospects of repeating the pitfalls of the First World War dimmed just as the potential for victory increased. Armed with their new belief in victory against France, the Germany military fully supported Hitler in his planned attack.

This dynamic offers support to both the power preponderance and power parity arguments. In terms of the power parity argument, the French capabilities clearly deterred the Germans in late 1939. The

German military feared having to attack the "impregnable" Maginot Line. Only when the Germans felt that the French defenses were inadequate did they attack. The case also supports the arguments of Blainey in that when the Germans attacked both the French and Danes, they believed that they would win. The German faith in their impending victory led to the attack, and the French belief in their imminent victory led them to resist.

The German attack on Denmark also provides evidence for both the power preponderance and power parity arguments. Denmark clearly did not deter the Germans and, in fact, actively attempted to look vulnerable. With such a pitiable defense and massive German advantage, the power parity argument would predict a German attack. The invasion, however, was not in response to the actions of Denmark. Before the Russians invaded Finland, Germany was quite content to accept the status quo of a latent German dominance of northern Europe, which was only possible because the Germans had such a large military advantage. This clearly conforms to the expectations of Blainey and the power preponderance arguments.

The behavior of Germany in these two cases ultimately conforms more to the expectation of the power preponderance theory. While Germany invaded and occupied Denmark contrary to theoretical expectations, the action was in response to Russia and the United Kingdom. Without outside interference, it appears that Germany would have been content to maintain the status quo with the Danes. In terms of the invasion of France, the German military clearly wanted to avoid war with France when they believed that they would lose. The military changed its tune only when a victory through the use of *Blitzkrieg* became an option. So in the French case, war occurred when both sides believed that they would win.

Aside from Germany, the response of both France and Denmark additionally conforms to the expectations of Blainey and the power preponderance theory. The Danes had no illusion as to the outcome of a military confrontation with Germany and believed that their best defense was to maintain their vulnerability. After this failed and the Germans invaded, the only option was capitulation. The French, on the other hand, with both the Maginot Line and their conventional forces felt confident in their capacity to resist a German attack. As such, they resisted, although, once the outcome became obvious, they surrendered.

Despite the support for the power preponderance argument, the cases clearly demonstrate a role for an aspect of the power parity theory: deterrence. The Maginot Line clearly deterred the Germans through the winter of 1939 as they had little confidence in their capacity to overcome the French defenses. The lack of deterrence also encouraged the German attack against Denmark, although it is unclear whether the Danes could have mustered enough forces to deter the Germans. The best hope for the Danes would have been an assurance from the British which was clearly not in the offing. In any case, deterrence clearly played a role in that it affected how Germany perceived its chance of victory.

4 THE DEMOCRATIC PEACE

The same interests, the same fears, the same passions, which deter democratic nations from revolutions, deter them also from war; the spirit of military glory and the spirit of revolution are weakened at the same time and by the same causes. The ever-increasing numbers of men of property who are lovers of peace, the growth of personal wealth which war so rapidly consumes ... that coolness of understanding which renders men comparatively insensible to violent and poetical excitement of arms – all of these causes concur to quench the military spirit.

de Tocqueville, *Democracy in America* ([1835]1956: 273)

War does not arise because consciously wicked men take a course which they know to be wrong, but because good men on both sides pursue a course which they believe to be right, stand, as Lincoln stood when he made war, for the right as they see it. It is a case not of conscious and admitted wrong challenging unquestioned and admitted right; but of understanding of right.

Normal Angell, *The Great Illusion* ([1909]2007: 124)

The earlier chapters have shown that domestic politics matters in how both democratic and non-democratic states make their policies. These chapters do not, however, clearly demonstrate the pacific nature of democratic regimes as opposed to their autocratic counterparts. As noted before, the evidence that democratic states are dovish is mixed at best in that it fails to show a compelling relationship between democratic institutions and peace. This does not disprove the democratic peace, which posits that democracies are more peaceful with one another. Again it is important to differentiate democratic pacifism from the democratic peace. As examined earlier, democratic pacifism argues that democracies are less likely to have conflicts with both democratic *and* non-democratic states. From this perspective, democratic states are peaceful in general. The democratic peace, in contrast, argues that democracies are less likely to fight one another but are more than willing to fight non-democracies. In fact, it may be the case that democracies are so willing to fight non-democracies that they are not more peaceful than non-democracies (in general). In this case, democracies fight just as often as non-democracies but, when they fight, it is more likely to be with a non-democracy.

Unlike the evidence for democratic pacifism, the democratic peace represents the strongest empirical relationship yet found in international politics. Despite the success of the democratic peace research program, it has not been universally acclaimed. Critics have argued that the democratic peace is simply the effect of Cold War alliance patterns or, more generally, that democracies simply have nothing to fight over. In addition, many have noted that the democratic peace seems strongest among developed states that are highly interdependent. In this case, the relationship may only work in the developed (wealthy) world. All of these critiques, however, simply reinforce one of the running themes of this book: context matters. It may be the case that democracies are less likely to fight one another but this effect can be magnified by its context, such as the Cold War or the wealth of the states.

The problem with the democratic peace is that the empirical relationship is exceptionally strong but the community has failed to center on one explanation for the results. In other words, there are multiple theories that all predict the democratic peace. In this case, how does one choose among the plethora of theoretical explanations? In addition, the possibility that context affects the relationship makes it even more difficult to uncover the root cause(s). To develop a better understanding of both the democratic peace and the effect of context, this chapter examines three cases: 1971 India–Pakistan war, the Fashoda Crisis, and the recent flair of violence between Hamas and Israel. It is important to note, however, that the democratic peace does not predict that war will never occur between democracies, so the investigation of cases of conflict puts the theory at a disadvantage. This does not dispute, however, the consistent quantitative evidence that the democratic peace has generated in the scholarly literature.

In general, democratic structures seem to provide states with the opportunity to find diplomatic solutions to their disputes. Yet it is less clear that democratic citizens push their governments to seek peace as opposed to war. In fact, the cases seem to show that the public is often more hawkish than the government. That being said, democracies do have domestic norms that push for peaceful resolution of disputes, which move democracies toward peace even when disputes arise. These norms, however, take time to develop and newly democratized states may lack such constraints. As such, the effects of the democratic peace may be contingent on the length of time a state has been democratic. Finally, the cases, and theory for that matter, hint that the effect of the democratic peace may be more pronounced between wealthy states (particularly those that trade with one another) but this argument is left for chapter 5.

What is the democratic peace?

The most common conceptualization of the democratic peace contends that pairs of democracies are less likely to experience militarized international disputes (Small and Singer 1976; Chan 1984; Maoz and Abdolali 1989; Bremer 1992; Russett 1993; Ray 1995; Oneal and Russett 1997, 2001; Russett, Oneal and Davis 1998; Bueno de Mesquita et al. 1999; Cederman and Rao 2001; Hewitt and Young 2001; Russett and Oneal 2001; Reed and Clark 2002; Sobek 2003). The first, and perhaps most critical, component of that statement is the use of the term "pairs." The democratic peace is a dyadic theory and makes no claim that democracies are more peaceful in general (the democratic pacifism argument). As such, the unit of analysis is the dyad, i.e., a pair of states. The second important aspect of the theory is that it is probabilistic in that it argues that democracies are "less likely" to have militarized conflicts. As a result, the existence of jointly democratic conflicts does not necessarily disprove the democratic peace. Finally, the democratic peace addresses both wars and militarized interstate conflicts. In other words, the democratic peace does not argue that all democracies will agree with one another all of the time; rather, the democratic peace argues that disagreements between democracies are less likely to escalate to militarized conflicts and/or wars.

The democratic peace has often been criticized as an empirical finding in search of a theory. While democratic peace scholars often draw upon Kant for their theoretical underpinnings, the literature did not really develop until researchers (starting mainly in the late 1970s and early 1980s) found a consistent relationship between joint democracy and peace. Since then, the literature on the democratic peace has developed along two parallel courses. First, a number of researchers have concentrated their efforts on further confirming the evidence, i.e., are democracies really more peaceful with one another? The second path has attempted to deepen the theoretical roots of the democratic peace, i.e., why are democracies less likely to fight one another? This does not mean that researchers have not attempted both paths at once; rather, these represent the two key questions that the democratic peace research program has attempted to answer.

Structural versus normative

Scholars have attempted to explain the democratic peace with one of two broad theoretical frameworks: structural and normative (see Russett and Oneal 2001 for a review of the democratic peace arguments and literature). The structural explanation argues that democratic institutions constrain leaders in a democracy so that they are less able to engage in conflict. When two democracies meet in the international system, these constraints provide democratic leaders with time to arrive at a diplomatic solution. The normative explanation argues that democracies develop internal norms of behavior (bargaining culture and peaceful resolution of disputes) that are socialized in their citizens. When democratic leaders meet in the international system, these norms trigger and allow for non-violent solutions to their disputes.

The structural explanation of the democratic peace generally relies on two main constraints and, in some ways, derives from the arguments of Kant, who emphasized the effect of both a separation of power and the regular election of leaders. One of the key institutional aspects of a democracy is the regular election of their leaders who are consequently more apt to reflect the interests of citizens. Since it is the citizens who pay the costs of war, especially in terms of casualties, it is assumed that democratic publics will want to avoid international conflicts. This means that leaders in a democracy need to be extremely careful when involving the state in a conflict in which the electorate is going to pay the price.

Aside from regular elections, the second main constraint in democracies is the separation of power between the executive and legislature. This separation of power institutionalizes a set of checks and balances that limit the actions of the government. For example, in the United States the president, while commander in chief, cannot completely ignore the demands of Congress, which controls the budget. This implies that a president needs more than simply the approval of the

executive branch to engage in an international conflict, which ultimately leads to American presidents being more cautious in their
use of military force (at least when compared to non-democratic
leaders).

The normative explanation of the democratic peace rests less on the
institutions that democracies share and more on the norms that develop
within democratic societies. While the norms are not identical across
all democratic states, it appears that two norms are exceptionally
common: belief in the peaceful resolution of disputes and a bargaining
culture. When disputes form between citizens in a democratic society,
these norms are going to constrain their behavior in ways that
minimize interpersonal conflict. While violent interactions still occur,
these are going to be minimized by the norms. Since the leaders in a
democratic society come from the population, they are going to reflect
societal norms. As such, when two democratic leaders interact in the
international system, they are going to rely on the same norms as their
respective domestic societies, i.e., the belief in the peaceful resolution
of disputes and the bargaining culture.

Since the democratic peace is a dyadic theory, it is important to
show how these theories explain behavior between states. It is simply
not sufficient to develop a theory that argues that democracies are
more peaceful in general and therefore more peaceful with one another.
The democratic peace, in many ways, describes an emergent behavior
that is not predictable on the characteristics of its component parts. If
one wants to argue that democracies are dovish, peace-loving societies,
then that is a state-level theory (democratic pacifism). The democratic
peace specifically describes the behavior of democracies interacting
with one another. So the real question is how the structures and norms
of democracy generate peaceful interactions in jointly democratic
dyads but not in mixed dyads (those that contain one democracy and
one non-democracy) or in jointly autocratic dyads.

The Fashoda Crisis: the effect of democratic structures

The Fashoda Crisis offers a unique look into the operation of the
structures of democratic states in the midst of an international confrontation. The underlying cause of the Fashoda Crisis was the colonial competition between France and Britain in late nineteenth-century

Africa. The British had a strategic interest in the land currently occupied by Egypt and the Sudan, especially given their need to keep the Suez Canal open to their shipping interests. The French, on the other hand, felt threatened by British control but also saw the area as a useful bargaining chip in the ongoing division of Africa among European states.

The proximate cause of the dispute was the joint arrival of both a French (July 10, 1898) and British (September 19, 1898) military expedition at Fashoda. Despite arriving first, French claims over the territory were weak. In essence, they disputed the British claim that Fashoda fell under its sphere of influence and was thus "effectively occupied" by Britain even before the British or French troops arrived. France felt that either Egypt or Turkey, which technically had suzerainty over the region, should choose between the British and French. The British firmly disputed French arguments, setting the stage for a military confrontation between two democracies.[1] Ultimately the French were forced to accept a humiliating diplomatic defeat (March 21, 1899) and a war was avoided. How, then, did the democratic structures influence this outcome?

Obviously diplomacy worked in this case, but it is important to note that it took slightly over six months. This is even more striking, given that during this entire process both sides had military forces occupying the same territory. On top of this, during the whole period the British government was preparing for war. On October 15, 1898, Britain assembled the Channel fleet and deployed it to Gibraltar on October 28. In addition, October 28 saw the British deploy the Mediterranean fleet to Malta and activate their reserve fleet. Despite this tinderbox of events, diplomacy not only was given time to work but ultimately prevailed.

With the increasing pressure of British belligerence, Delcasse, the French foreign minister, worked hard to reach a diplomatic solution. Delcasse sent Baron de Courcel to England to meet with the British prime minister (Lord Salisbury) in the hope that England would offer France a face-saving concession (in particular, France wanted a small outlet into the Bahr al-Ghazal). The negotiations collapsed and Britain demanded that the French forces leave the Fashoda area before negotiations could begin over colonial boundaries.

Behind the scenes in both Britain and France, divisions arose as to the proper courses of action. Where Lord Salisbury wanted to avoid war, a solid portion of his government was pushing for a preventative war against France. In fact, Chamberlain noted the following to a German colleague in early November, 1898:

> I am afraid Lord Salisbury himself has not got the strength of mind to bring about the necessary crisis and choose the right moment to strike like Bismarck did at Ems. You may be certain, however, that all of my colleagues, even Mr. Arthur Balfour, are of the same opinion as I am, namely that Lord Salisbury's policy "peace at any price" cannot go on any longer, and that England has to show to the whole world she *can act*. (Pakenham 1991: 552)

While Salisbury still had allies in the Cabinet, he ultimately appealed to The Queen who argued that "A war for so miserable and small an object is what I could hardly consent to" (Pakenham 1991: 552). With the backing of The Queen, Lord Salisbury was able to rein in the belligerence of the British Cabinet.

Just as Lord Salisbury was facing down the hawks in his government, Delcasse was facing a similar problem in France. Earlier in the crisis, Delcasse had ordered Marchand's number two (Baratier) back to Paris to report on the military situation in Fashoda. Delcasse hoped that the British had a superior position which would allow for a face-saving retreat. Unfortunately for Delcasse, when he met Baratier on October 27, he reported that the French troops were recently resupplied, had high morale, were in good health, and could easily repulse any British assault. In fact, the British forces were facing a mutiny of their native troops and were on the verge of collapse. Baratier assured Delcasse that France would not suffer the dishonor of seeing their flag hauled down by the British. Delcasse's response was, however, quite unexpected: "*Vous ne comprenez pas bien l'honneur de la France*"[2] (Pakenham 1991: 553). Baratier left the meeting enraged and feeling betrayed.

Baratier was able to find support among Delcasse's political allies in the *Parti colonial*. As soon as Delcasse discovered the subterfuge, he ordered Baratier back to the Sudan (Fashoda). With the departure of Baratier and the support of new allies (such as the industrialist Félix Faure), Delcasse was able to defeat the colonialist challenge. In addition, Charles Dupay was able to form a new French government on November 2, 1898, committed to the de-escalation of the Fashoda Crisis. Two days later, Lord Salisbury announced that the French would be leaving Fashoda, effectively ending the crisis.

While the internal turmoil of both the French and British governments appears problematic for the structural argument of the democratic peace, it actually highlights the importance of the separation of power in democratic states. First, as both Salisbury and Delcasse were dealing with their domestic issues, diplomacy was given the opportunity to continue. The infighting clearly gave both sides more time to decide upon a course of action, which was ultimately diplomacy over war. Aside from simply creating time for diplomacy, the separation of power, especially in Britain, helped diffuse the more belligerent members of the government. Remember that it was ultimately with the weight of the queen's opinion that Salisbury was able to prevail. In general, then, one cannot say that democratic structures determined the peaceful outcome of the Fashoda Crisis but it was the case that they operated in the way predicted by the democratic peace.

The structural explanation of the democratic peace does not, however, find complete support in the case of the Fashoda Crisis. Where the democratic peace argues that the citizens of a state would act as a source of peace and caution, we find the exact opposite in both France and Britain during the Fashoda Crisis. In both France and Britain, the public not only seemed willing to accept a war but also appeared to be actively stoking the flames of conflict. To be fair, the British public was being egged on by jingoistic press, such as the *Daily Mail*, but even the *Upper Nile* noted that "war with France was not exactly desired in England, but it would be accepted without hesitation if the occasion arose" (Layne 1994: 31). The situation in France was similar with a split public where "for every patriot who identified national honour with the defence of the army and the refusal to climb down over Fashoda, there was another patriot who regarded the whole business of Fashoda as a red herring" (Pakenham 1991: 554). This is clearly not the universally dovish citizenry described by the democratic peace.

In general, however, the Fashoda Crisis highlights the effect of democratic institutions on international politics. In both France and England, the separation of power increased the amount of time available for diplomacy. In addition, it allowed voices of peace to be heard and ultimately to influence the outcome of the crisis. It is important not to conflate the outcome of the crisis with support for the democratic peace. A single case could never prove or disprove the democratic peace. It could have been the case that the hawks on both sides of the English Channel won control of their respective governments and war would have resulted.

The Fashoda Crisis offers a slightly alternative view of the causal mechanisms of the democratic peace: the role of information. Blainey (1988) argues that wars occur when the sides disagree as to the distribution of capabilities. The rationalist explanations for war (Fearon 1995) expand upon Blainey's argument and emphasize the role of information, where increases in the availability of information decrease the risk of war. In many ways, democratic institutions help states transmit accurate information. For instance, the role of the public in democracies is assumed to generate peace because they place a check on the government. Yet in the Fashoda Crisis, it was not immediately clear that either government was limited by popular pressure.

The public can play a role not by directly pressuring the government to pursue peace but by forcing the government to display their preferences and capabilities. In both France and England, the citizens were not clamoring for the states to step back from the precipice of war but were, to a significant degree, pushing the states closer to war. As Gat (2005: 75) notes: "it was the public opinion in both Britain and France that proved most bellicose, chauvinistic, and unsympathetic to the other." This is not necessarily bad because this sentiment was obvious and could be observed by both governments. So when the British government threatened the French with war, it was seen as a real threat and not a bluff. This ability of the public to create more clarity in the interaction of states would, according to the rationalist explanations of war, lead to more negotiated settlements and fewer wars. This implies that citizens in a democracy do not necessarily have to be dovish to decrease the risk of war. What really matters is that the preferences of the citizens are clearly demonstrated for both domestic and foreign governments.

While this offers additional insight into the democratic peace, this role of citizens is not isolated to the interaction between democracies. The clarity that the public brings will be obvious to both democratic and non-democratic states. What this implies is that a single democracy in a dyad would decrease the risk of war, although this dyad would still have a higher risk than one with two democracies. This matters because the democratic peace is a dyadic theory and does not necessarily argue that democracy is more peaceful in general.

Democratic norms

While democratic institutions may decrease the risk of international conflict, democracies tend to possess similar domestic norms. Domestic (and international) norms are not rules that proscribe the behavior of states; rather, they are "patterns of activities that permit some degree of certainty and predictability, that rest on expectations of how others (and oneself) are supposed to behave" (Starr 1999: 93). Norms, while fairly consistent across time, can change as actors alter their expectations. For instance, 50 years ago the norm was for men to open doors for women but, with the women's movement, this norm has progressively weakened.

Norms can develop both domestically and internationally. The repeated interaction of states in the international system generates internationally accepted norms of behavior. Despite the development of these norms, it is not expected that all states follow all norms all of the time. The norms do, however, increase the predictability of foreign policies. For instance, one could argue that a norm has developed, since the Second World War, which bans the use of nuclear weapons (Tannenwald 2005). Does this mean that no state will ever use nuclear weapons? No, but it does mean that states expect that nuclear weapons will not be used even during international conflict.

Domestically, the repeated interaction of citizens and the state creates mutual expectations of behaviors (norms). These norms can differ between individual states (United States as compared to the United Kingdom) or between different types of states (democracies as compared to autocracies). Democracies, for instance, it is often argued, develop norms that prescribe peaceful resolutions to political disputes, i.e., it was expected that Al Gore would not use violence to contest the results of the 2000 presidential election. These domestic norms, however, can also affect the behavior of the states in the international system and this is at the core of the normative argument of the democratic peace.

The normative explanations contend that democracies develop (and internalize) norms of peaceful resolutions of disputes (Dixon 1994). This implies that interactions within a democracy are bounded, i.e., citizens expect that political disagreements will not be resolved through violence. While violence certainly occurs, these are exceptions rather than the expectation. When a democratic state interacts with other states in the international system, it attempts to determine whether other states will interact in a bounded or unbounded way. In general, a democracy believes that the other democracies operate with the same norms, which means that interactions between democracies will be guided by the domestic norms and hence be bounded (Dixon 1994; Maoz and Russett 1993; Schmitter and Karl 1991). When a democracy encounters an autocracy, it assumes that the autocracy is not bound and hence does not use its domestic norms.

Since democracies interact on the basis of their domestic norms of peaceful resolution of disputes, it stands to reason that the risk of conflict will be lower. This effect only increases over time as democracies continue to have peaceful interactions (Axelrod 1984; Dixon 1994). The opposite is true for the relationship between democracies and autocracies, where the attachment to norms of non-violent conflict resolution is unclear in the autocracy. In these cases, a democracy reasonably assumes that the interactions are not bounded in the same way as the interaction between democracies. Ultimately, this leads to an increase in the risk of conflict between democracies and autocracies (Maoz and Russett 1992; Huth and Russett 1993).

The belief in bounded competition between democracies in the international system remains reliant upon "contingent consent." Contingent consent is the mutual agreement between democracies to interact on the basis of the non-violent domestic norms only as long as both sides agree to be bound. This agreement is exceptionally difficult for autocracies because they routinely demonstrate that they do not practice this norm domestically. As such, a democracy would have little faith in an autocracy's ability and/or willingness to remain bounded in their interactions.

These domestic norms may also be affected by economics. When looking at democratic pacifism, it was noted that Schumpeter believed that capitalism and the market would eliminate the incentive for imperialism. Part of his argument relied on the expectation that individuals concerned about gaining wealth will want to avoid conflicts, which tend to destroy wealth. Over time this turns into a norm against the use of violence which dovetails with the normative argument of the democratic peace. As such, it may be the case that context affects the strength of democratic norms. While poor democracies may have the democratic norms that decrease the use of violence, the norm may be stronger and better established in wealthy democracies.

Hamas and the dangers of democratization

The relationship between Hamas and Israel in 2006 offers additional insight into the effect of the public on international politics. As previously noted, in the run up to the Palestinian elections in 2006, both Israel and the United States had been pressuring the Palestinians to engage in more democratic reforms of their political institutions. In 2006, the Americans and Israelis got their wish and a general election was held in Palestine. The expectation was that incorporating Hamas into a democratic political process would both check their militaristic policies (through checks and balances) and moderate their views (the effect of democratic norms). When Hamas assumed control, it remained armed and unabashedly militaristic and the nature of its interactions with Israel (another democracy) did not notably change.

The democratic peace theory would generally expect an election to moderate Hamas since it would be answerable to a dovish public, but in this case the assumption of a dovish public once again fails, just as it did in the case of Fashoda. Amal Saad-Ghorayeb, a political science professor at the Lebanese American University, noted that the "people voted overwhelmingly for Hamas, and did so partly as a referendum for resistance, saying that resistance will pay greater dividends than negotiation."[3] In fact, some Palestinians were actually fearful that electing Hamas would moderate the group, as Ayesh Hussein argued: "Having Hamas in power and assuming such a position is bad . . . We're accustomed to Hamas being fighters, a party that pressures Israel. But now it will join politics and will become politicized."[4] Given the attitude of Palestinian voters, it is not surprising that an elected Hamas was not moderated.

While Hamas was not turned into a dovish party as a result of the elections, it does not mean that the electoral process had no effect. During the campaign, Hamas did not use its purported goal of destroying Israel as part of its party manifesto. In addition, Hamas candidates never ruled out the prospect of peace with Israel. For instance, as quoted in an earlier chapter, Ziad Daiah, a Hamas representative in Ramallah noted: "We are not interested in the Oslo-type peace process that went on for 10 years and wasted time. But if Israel will start new negotiations, with direct benefits for Palestinians in a useful time frame, we will accept that."[5] In this way, Hamas did not rule out peace with Israel but certainly indicated that it would not accept the peace that was accomplished by Fatah.

In the months after the elections, relations between Israel and the Palestinians deteriorated, as well as the relations between Hamas and Fatah. The abduction of Corporal Gilad Shalit of the Israeli Defense Force on June 25 fanned the flames on both sides. After the kidnapping, the Israelis made it eminently clear that they held the Palestinian government responsible, not simply the Hamas militants. The Palestinian population, while supportive of the abduction, was clearly worried about the Israeli response, as Ali Issa, 43, a farmer, succinctly noted: "I am happy and I am unhappy. I am unhappy because the Israeli reaction will be tough. But I am happy because of the retaliation for the blood of our people."[6]

While one may argue that elections had little effect in moderating Hamas (in contrast to the expectations of the democratic peace), it may also be the case that newly democratized states simply have not had time to develop the democratic norms that lead to moderation. The "dangers of democratization" literature (Mansfield and Snyder

1995, 2002) has consistently argued for this addendum to the democratic peace. If these democratic norms had not developed, then the contingent consent did not exist in the Israeli–Hamas interactions. This implies that their relationship would not be bounded in the same way as that of two mature democracies.

The election of Hamas seems to support this argument. After the election, it became clear that the Palestinians were not united by democratic norms. The divisions were exacerbated during the conflict with Israel. As Steve Erlanger notes:

> Power, however, has proved a trap for Hamas, accentuating its divisions and causing new fractures. While Hamas has been fighting with Fatah in Gaza, trying to consolidate its control over the security forces, it has been unable to control its own leaders in exile in Syria or its military wing, which operates with little regard for the Hamas prime minister, Ismail Haniya.
>
> The crisis touched off last week by the abduction of an Israeli soldier, and by Israel's invasion of Gaza in response, has made Hamas's divisions more apparent. At the same time, it has further weakened Palestinian moderates and pushed the Palestinians to a temporary unity that is closer to the extremist stance taken by those living abroad. (Erlanger 2006b)

Unable to control factions within its own government, Hamas inherited an almost untenable situation. It is not surprising, then, that a more militant faction capitalized on the situation and drove a wedge between the Hamas government and the Israelis.

The weakness of the Hamas government was even recognized by the Israelis. Giora Eiland, a former director of Israel's national security council and a retired major general who led an investigation into the June 25 raid, noted that "recently there was the illusion that Hamas, while not a perfect partner, was at least a group that could implement decisions . . . But it has become apparent that the political leadership of Hamas is much less influential than Khaled Meshal and leaders of the military wing." If neither Hamas nor Israel believed that Palestinian militants could be restrained by the Palestinian government, why would we expect the democratic institutions to have any effect?

While the Hamas case illustrates the need for a democracy to have the capacity to govern, it still may be true that new democracies have yet to develop the norms that lead to peaceful resolution of disputes. Mansfield and Snyder (1995, 2002) have consistently argued that peace found in the empirical tests of the democratic peace derives from the peaceful relations between mature (consolidated) democracies. It seems intuitive to expect that the democratic norms that purportedly generate the peace do not develop overnight; rather, these norms emerge only after years of democratic governance. If this is the case, then we would expect that newly democratized states do not have the contingent consent that bounds democratic interactions. While the statistical analyses are not conclusive (Thompson and Tucker 1997; Ward and Gleditsch 1998), significant evidence has been rallied to support this contention (Mansfield and Snyder 1995, 1997, 2002).

In some ways, the dangers of democratization argument rests on Huntington's view that the degree of government matters as much as the form of government. In states that move from non-democratic to democratic forms of government, the demands that the citizens will make upon the state are bound to increase. When the demands on the state exceed the capacity of the government to suitably address those demands, the result is not a democratic form of government (Huntington 1968). This does not mean that these states cannot have the institutional trappings of a mature democracy, i.e., elections, parliament, independent judiciary, and so on. In fact, the root of the problem is that these states have the exterior of a democracy but lack the internal capacity to rule like a democracy.

New democracies also do not necessarily have the democratic norms that are associated with consolidated democracies. Generally, norms within states take time to develop, especially the peaceful resolution of disputes and bargaining culture routinely associated with the democratic peace. For instance, after the removal of Saddam, the Iraqi citizenship did not instantaneously develop democratic norms. Given time, however, the norms within Iraq may change. As a democratic government arises, and stabilizes, in Iraq, the population will learn how to participate in a democratic environment. These experiences will eventually generate the democratic norms associated with the democratic peace. In the intervening period, however, one would not expect to see emerging norms have a strong effect on interstate behaviors.

Mansfield and Snyder (2002) also argue that incomplete democratic transitions create states that have an increased risk of engaging in international conflict. States transitioning away from authoritarianism toward democracy experience a marked increase in demands made upon state institutions. Unlike consolidated democracies that routinely address large numbers of demands from their citizens, democratizing states have yet to develop such capacity. To maintain the support of their citizenry, these states often resort to highly nationalistic ideologies that "can close the gap between popular demands and weak institutions" (Mansfield and Snyder 2002: 531). Such an ideology often exacerbates the in-group/out-group behavior, increasing the risk that the state will become involved in international conflict.

The dangers of newly democratic regimes highlight problems also found in partially democratic states, known as anocracies (Mansfield and Snyder 2002). These states contain a mix of both democratic and autocratic institutions. Anocracies, at least when compared to full democracies or autocracies, tend to be quite fluid in terms of their institutions. The mix of institutions and the accompanying uncertainty creates a dynamic political environment that is ripe for exploitation. The India–Pakistan war in 1971 offers a further glimpse of how a partially democratic state does not necessarily experience a partial democratic peace.

India–Pakistan war in 1971

In 1947, the modern Pakistani state was created. Unfortunately, the state was divided into West Pakistan (modern-day Pakistan) and East Pakistan (modern-day Bangladesh), which were separated by India. Unlike West Pakistan, the population of East Pakistan was predominately Bengali, who were politically dominated by West Pakistan. Between independence and 1971, the discontent of the Bengali population intensified as the political domination and economic exploitation by West Pakistan continued unabated. After the failed war against India in 1965, the Pakistani president (Ayub Khan) faced increased pressure from East Pakistan. In 1966, Sheik Mujib's Awami League (an organization geared toward achieving Bengali independence) adopted a six-point manifesto which was designed to be a charter for the economic and political autonomy of East Bengal. Under these six points, the Pakistani central government would be responsible for defense and foreign affairs but would not be given control of the Bengali economy, taxation, trade, or aid.

In 1968, as President Ayub Khan faced renewed pressure from the Bengali population of East Pakistan, he fell ill. Having attempted to reach a political compromise with Mujib through a new Pakistani constitution, Ayub resigned from office in 1969 and gave power to General Yahya Khan (commander in chief of the Pakistani army). Unlike Ayub, Yahya had no intention of reaching a political compromise that would involve a more equitable distribution of political and economic resources. On November 28, 1969, Yahya announced that a unified election would occur in late 1970 which could conceivably lead to an East Pakistani majority in the parliament. The elections ultimately took place on December 17, 1970, and resulted in Mujib's Awami League garnering 167 of the National Assembly's 313 seats (all but two seats in East Pakistan, and none in the West). In addition, Mr Bhutto's Pakistan People's Party captured 85 seats and the Islamic parties garnered little more than 10 percent of the total vote.

After the elections, Bhutto realized that he held a strategically important position because he could boycott the Pakistani government, making it unworkable. While it was unclear that the military would allow this to occur, Bhutto did attempt to devise some way in which he would be able to share power with Mujib's League. Toward this end, he demanded that a compromise on a new constitution be made prior to the summoning of the Assembly into session (which would force Mujib to violate one of his six points). In January 1971, Yahya seemed to support Bhutto's plan. On February 13, the date for the first meeting of the new Assembly was set (March 3) but Bhutto refused to attend the Assembly unless the constitutional issue was discussed first. Mujib, on the other hand, refused to even meet with Bhutto on the issue prior to an Assembly meeting.

The infighting between Yahya and Mujib highlights the precarious natures of the democratic institutions of Pakistan at this time. While elections had occurred, the Assembly had not met. In addition, underlying the dispute was the threat of violence. Given the incomplete nature of the democratic institutions, it would be difficult for democratic norms or institutions to affect the behavior of Pakistan. For instance, how could the Assembly check the executive when it was not meeting? How could other democracies assume that Pakistan would follow democratic norms when it was on the verge of using violence to solve a domestic political dispute? As the dispute continued, it became increasingly clear that the democratic institutions could not constrain the government (given its limitation) and democratic norms were not operating domestically.

On March 1, President Yahya announced that the Assembly meeting was postponed. Following this, Mujib declared a number of strikes in East Pakistan and implied that this region would become ungovernable unless the Assembly was allowed to meet. The president responded by calling the Assembly into session on March 25. While it was obvious that many within East Pakistan desired full-blown independence, Mujib remained unwilling to make such a demand. Mujib did, however, lay out a number of conditions that needed to precede his party's participation in the Assembly. Perhaps most importantly, this included the provision of "the immediate transference of power to the elected representatives of the people" (Jackson 1975: 30).

At this point, Mujib's hands were tied, largely because his domestic base of support would not allow him to depart from his six points. In addition, Yahya would no longer negotiate in good faith simply because he would have to give up his power if he conceded to Mujib's demands. Nonetheless, these groups met in mid-March and negotiated for eight days, largely over whether the Assembly should meet as one body or two. On March 22, Yahya's team of negotiators agreed to step down once the Assembly began meeting. Further, Mujib agreed to have the Assembly meet in two separate bodies to develop separate drafts of the constitution so that Bhutto would be appeased (representing West Pakistani opinion, Bhutto did not want Hindi or Bengali influence in West Pakistani affairs). This action by Mujib was later represented by the authorities as "virtually a constitutional formula for secession" (Jackson 1975: 32).

Despite the seemingly peaceful resolution of the dispute, the situation deteriorated on March 24 following shooting incidents in Chittagong and Rangpur (two East Pakistani cities) and a 24-hour curfew was imposed by the president. The next day, President Yahya abruptly flew from East to West Pakistan and 35 journalists in East Pakistan were confined to their hotel (prior to being deported on March 27). The West Pakistan-based military, headed by Yahya, began occupying East Pakistan and cracking down on pro-independence Bengalis. At this point, 40,000 West Pakistani soldiers were scattered throughout East Pakistan, opposing 5,000 Bengali police. At 1.00 a.m. on March 26, Sheikh Mujib was arrested at his house and, several hours later, the army cleared the remaining barricades that had been put up by Bengalis, killing many civilians in the process. Clearly, the norm of peaceful resolutions of disputes was not operating at this point.

On March 26, Yahya stated that Mujib wanted to create a "legal vacuum" in between stripping the military of its power and establishing the power of the Assembly, during which Mujib could do anything he wanted with impunity. Yahya believed that this, and Mujib's desire to have two assemblies, was unacceptable (although Mujib had suggested the latter in order to appease Bhutto). Meanwhile, Bengali forces were losing badly to the Pakistani army and were forced to retreat to the borders. At this point, there is no explicit evidence that India was supporting the East Pakistani forces, although the nucleus of the future Bangladeshi army was able to retreat to India.

Beginning in early April, India attempted to sway international opinion toward the side of the Bengalis. By the middle of April, it was apparent that the Pakistani authorities had prevailed "in the first round of the East Bengal crisis" (Jackson 1975: 44) but it was also clear that the Indian populace was firmly in support of East Pakistan. This issue was debated in the Indian parliament in late May and it was decided at that time that the provisional government in East Pakistan should not be recognized (and it would not be recognized until after the Indian–Pakistani war had begun). By the end of April, the Indian government had decided to support the Bangladeshi movement and to form, train, and arm Bangladeshi forces inside India who would receive further Indian military and political support once they returned to East Pakistan. This decision was made in the recognition that this could result in a third Indo-Pakistani war.

Early in May, the Pakistani line began to shift slightly and officials from international organizations, disallowed in East Pakistan following Yahya's crackdown, were allowed back into West Pakistan. Included here was the acceptance by President Yahya of a UN relief presence in East Pakistan. Yahya also made claims that political reconciliation was desired in this area, claiming on May 24 that he would provide amnesty for "law-abiding" citizens of East Pakistan to return to their homes, while also claiming that he would soon transfer power to the "people." Though no word was given on what would be (or had been) done with Mujib, "only those Awami League elected members who had revolted or were guilty of crimes would be disqualified from taking up their seats in the assemblies" (Jackson 1975: 51).

In early July, the "monsoon offensive" began, and it became clear that Yahya's attempts at reconciliation would not bear fruit. Additionally, due in large measure to India's diplomatic efforts and the reports of a team sent by the World Bank to evaluate the economic prospects of Pakistan (these reports were largely negative due to the impact of the fighting in East Pakistan), World Bank development aid for Pakistan was terminated. This decision had a domino effect on other suppliers of international aid who were wary of losing money in Pakistan. The United States, however, still seemed to be giving moderate support to West Pakistan, reinforced by Pakistan's assistance in opening up talks between the US and China.

Late July saw the UN Secretary General U Thant advocating the use of the United Nations as a peacekeeper to ensure that refugees were able to return safely to their homes while Bangladeshi insurgents were prevented from crossing the border. Pakistan (in the person of Yahya) backed this plan but India opposed it, as it was wary of the likelihood that U Thant's proposed actions would inhibit independence in the East. Indian public opinion saw this attempt at "repatriation" by Yahya as simply a ruse to entrench his own, preferred style of Pakistani government. Indian official opinion was more moderate, due in large measure to the fact that international opinion was almost completely behind West Pakistan.

India's freedom to reflect public sentiment, however, was enabled on August 9 by the signing of the Indo-Soviet Treaty of Peace, Friendship and Co-operation. Though the Soviet Union had, up until this point, tried to balance Indian and Pakistani influence as best it could, the Chinese and the US had firmly placed their support behind Pakistan. This created a dilemma for the Soviet Union, as an imbalance in South Asian power was generally undesirable – even more so, given that the current trajectory was shifting power in favor of a state with ties to the Soviet Union's two major challengers. The Indo-Soviet Treaty of Peace, Friendship and Co-operation stipulated that neither side would give support to a third party that might militarily harm the other signatory. The agreement also stated that a political agreement (presumably between the Awami League and Yahya's government), in line with Prime Minister Ghandi's preferences, was necessary to resolve the East Pakistan question and that a military solution was not acceptable. It is noteworthy that, despite this agreement, the Soviets continued to give economic aid to Pakistan.

Following the signing of this agreement, the incursions of the Bengali insurgents (who were initially called the *Mukti Fauj* but changed their names to the *Mukti Bahini* in July to mark their new air force and navy) into East Pakistan began to increase in intensity. This was leading to growing Bengali support for their cause, despite the amnesty for the Bengali refugees promised by Yahya. On the same day as the announcement of the Indo-Soviet agreement, it was revealed that Sheikh Mujib would be tried on camera for "waging war against Pakistan." This signaled that Yahya imposed limits on the kinds of agreements that would be made regarding East Pakistan, while also showing that an agreement with Mujib would not take place.

On August 23, Bengali insurgents sunk two Pakistani vessels in Chittagong Harbor and several more boats were destroyed soon after. The effect of this "sabotage" was to restrict the flow of soldiers and supplies to West Pakistani forces in East Pakistan. Also around this time, international support for the Bangladeshi cause surged. The political basis of a future Bangladesh, however, was in disarray. Many disagreed with the Awami agreement to "wage war until victory" that was signed in mid-July, and there were other differences amongst the political leaders now in India. India attempted to strengthen the political solidarity of these groups by supporting the idea that members from all relevant pro-Bangladeshi parties should have a say in the political objectives of the refugees, realized in a "Five-Party Consultative Committee" (Jackson 1975: 79).

From September to December, the major activity in the conflict was diplomatic, both in the United Nations and between the United States and the Soviet Union. During this time, India was compelled to shift its public stance from that of complete Bangladeshi independence to the Russian stance – i.e., a lack of commitment to any of the three potential outcomes: (1) independence of Bangladesh; (2) the provincial autonomy of East Pakistan within Pakistan; or (3) the re-integration of East Pakistan into greater Pakistan. India only stated at this point that a politically acceptable solution with the "already elected representatives" of East Pakistan would have to be reached. Yahya responded (basically to the Soviets) that he would not negotiate with Mujib or the Awami League. Mrs Ghandi retaliated by withdrawing India's earlier statement and again argued that the independence of East Pakistan was the only possible solution.

In early October, the Bangladeshi delegation at the UN stated that only complete independence from Pakistan would be acceptable. This was followed by a statement from the *Mukti Bahini* that they would sabotage any elections that took place, which they did through a number of political assassinations. At this time, Indian and Pakistani forces strengthened their positions along the border of East Pakistan in preparation for conflict. In late October, a final attempt at diplomacy was initiated by U Thant to allow for a mutual withdrawal of forces by India and Pakistan from the East Pakistani border. Throughout November and early December, Pakistan attempted various other strategies to end the confrontation (trying to diplomatically deter India, agreeing to allow US mediation, and seeking to escalate until the great powers had to step in), but with little success.

Though a number of small border skirmishes had taken place in September and early October (principally between Bengali insurgents and Pakistani forces), Indian forces only became overtly involved on October 30–31 when they crossed the border in order to stop cross-border shelling. The "drift to war" accelerated after November 20 as Indian tanks drove 8 miles over the border into East Pakistan (allegedly in response to Pakistani attacks against insurgents in India). Following this event, Mrs Ghandi stated before parliament that border-crossing by India into East Pakistan would be allowed as a consequence of such "offensive" acts. Nonetheless, the Indian involvement generally was carefully limited. Not surprisingly, the Pakistanis blamed these cross-border skirmishes on Indian aggression while the Indians blamed Pakistani aggression.

On December 3, 1971, the drift evolved into open war between India and Pakistan. India was much better equipped and trained than Pakistan, while additionally having an indigenous armament industry to rely on which Pakistan lacked due to its overreliance on western supplies (which had been cut off following the 1965 conflict between India and Pakistan). Though Pakistan still had some help from the Chinese, this was not enough to overcome India's advantage. In addition, Pakistani morale was low during the onset of war, largely due to the impact of the insurgency on East Pakistan. Additionally, Pakistan, which was only prepared for a single-front war against India on open plains via their eastern front, was not as strategically prepared. India, however, had prepared for a two-front war against Pakistan and China on both open plains in the west and mountainous terrain in the east.

In spite of its disadvantaged position and the fact that Pakistani defensive positions were set up in East Pakistan, the conflict was initiated by West Pakistan. Though specific Pakistani motivations in making this decision are unclear, there appear to have been three separate justifications: (1) it may have stemmed from Yahya's inability to control his subordinates, following a final, failed attempt at diplomacy in late November; (2) it could have stemmed from the mindset that the best way to "protect the east" was to "attack from the west," as captured Indian territory could then be traded for Indian concessions (this was the strategy taken in the 1965 war); or (3) it may have been that the Pakistanis were willing at this point to concede East Pakistan but wanted to obtain additional Indian territory in the west in the process (Jackson 1975: 112). Ultimately, by the end of the first week of fighting, it was apparent that the war in the west was deadlocked and that the UN would be unable to achieve a settlement between these states. Following this, the Indians moved forward in the east, eventually capturing Dacca (the current capital of Bangladesh) and the war ended in the west on December 17 at 8 pm, following a unilateral ceasefire by India which was respected by a defeated Pakistan.

This case again highlights the crucial role of democratic state capacity. The war between India and Pakistan was related, in no small way, to the inability of a democratic Pakistan to incorporate a predominately Bengali East Pakistan into a unified state. The political tension that formed as a result of the West–East divide led to the collapse of a democratic Pakistan. While Yahya worked to re-establish a democratic role, the anocratic (mixed democratic/autocratic) system allowed hardliners to hijack state policies. India's response was relatively muted, given the intensity of public opinion that was pushing for war. Clearly the norms of democracy had not yet developed far enough in India to encourage contingent consent which creates a per-missive environment for international conflict.

Joint democracy and war

The previous quantitative research and the three cases examined in this chapter point to three main conclusions. First, the assumption that citizens in a democratic state will consistently push for peace is not accurate. In all of the cases, a significant portion of the democratic populations actually took exceptionally belligerent stances. This does not mean that the emphasis on the population is not accurate. In fact, the bellicosity of the English population during the Fashoda Crisis helped force the French into conceding, which averted war. As such, it appears that having politically active citizens lowers the risk of war but does so by allowing democracies to send stronger signals to their opponents (Schultz 1999).

The cases also highlight the role of contingent consent in generating peaceful outcomes. Both in the case of Hamas versus Israel and that of India versus Pakistan, contingent consent did not appear to exist. In particular, Israel never trusted Hamas to moderate its desire to destroy the state of Israel and India did not believe that the military government in Pakistan was willing to grant real autonomy to the Bengali population in East Pakistan. In cases where contingent consent does not exist, it does not matter if the states practice democratic norms domestically.

Finally, the cases clearly demonstrate the role of state capacity. Democratic institutions can have a conflict-dampening effect but it will not mean anything unless the state has the capacity to enforce its deci-sions (domestically). So in the case of Hamas, the electoral process could have moderated its demands but the question is how would Hamas have been able to rein in the most militant members of the movement? Unless a democracy can act with one voice, it is highly unlikely that democratic structures will be able to reduce the risk of conflict. In addition, as was obvious with the Israeli reaction to Hamas, a unified state is required for contingent consent to operate successfully.

The chapter does not, however, address how economics affect the behavior of states. As noted in the chapter on democratic pacifism, it has been argued that wealth and trade will pacify states. While the evidence for democratic pacifism is at best mixed, it could be the case that wealth and trade matter in a dyadic sense. In other words, just as democracies are less likely to fight one another, so are states that trade. In addition, simply because trading states are less likely to fight one another does not mean that they are peaceful in general. So does trade decrease the risk of conflict? In addition, is there an interactive effect between trade and democracy?

5 TRADE AND PEACE

The principal feature of modern capitalism is the domination of monopolist combines of the big capitalists. These monopolies are most firmly established when *all* the sources of raw materials are controlled by one group . . . The more capitalism is developed, the more the need for raw materials is felt, the more bitter competition becomes, and the more feverishly the hunt for raw materials proceeds throughout the whole world, the more desperate becomes the struggle for the acquisition of colonies.

V. I. Lenin, *Imperialism* (1939: 82)

A purely capitalist world therefore can offer no fertile soil to imperialist impulses. This does not mean that it cannot still maintain an interest in imperialist expansion . . . The point is that its people are likely to be essentially of an unwarlike disposition. Hence we must expect that anti-imperialist tendencies will show themselves wherever capitalism penetrates the economy and, through the economy, the mind of modern nations.

Joseph Schumpeter, *Imperialism and Social Classes* (1951: 69–70)

The previous chapters paint the relations between states as essentially uncooperative but in reality, for the vast majority of time, most states are not at war. In fact, states often choose to interact with one another in a cooperative manner. Perhaps the most important of these interactions involves bilateral trade, where states exchange goods and services with one another in a mutually acceptable (and beneficial) manner. Ideally, trading relations create interdependencies that increase the costs of war and which would concurrently decrease the occurrence of armed conflict. Trade, however, may not be mutually beneficial as some states establish trading relationships that increase their relative power. In general, however, does bilateral trade decrease (or increase) the risk of war?

The debate over the role of trade in international politics has a relatively long lineage. A classic debate began in seventeenth- and eighteenth-century Europe as Enlightenment thinkers passionately argued for the expansion of free trade. Free trade would not only increase the wealth of the states involved in the transaction but would additionally spark freedom at home and abroad. In other words, free trade would initiate an inexorable march of freedom across the globe which would be concurrent with an expansion of peace. In many ways, this train of thought culminated in 1909 when Norman Angell wrote *The Great Illusion*, which essentially predicted the end of conquest among developed and interdependent states, i.e., Europe. Showing that history is no stranger to irony, only five years after the publication of the book, the most deadly war in the history of mankind (until then) began in the most developed and interdependent region of the world.

While questions about the role of trade remained important after the First World War, scholars generally did not claim that trade promoted peace. This changed after the end of the Second World War when the role of trade in promoting peace once again became part of the debate. With the emergence of the United States as a superpower/ hegemon, a new global economic system was established, based on the liberal principles that were seemingly discredited by the First World War. After the end of the Second World War, the international economic system truly became global as states increasingly embraced the principles of economic freedom which included open and free trade. As a result, a new literature developed that espoused the peace-generating effects of bilateral trade.

Despite the re-emergence of the "trade equals peace" argument, the debate still rages at both the theoretical and empirical levels. Just as some scholars argue that trade leads to peace, others contend that trade either has no effect or might actually generate conflict. In addition, statistical evidence has been rallied by both camps in an attempt to settle the debate. Unfortunately, the issue of trade and conflict is both complicated and convoluted. For instance, is it more important to examine trade flows or trade laws/institutions? Do asymmetries of trade have the same effect as trade symmetry? How does one measure trade? To address these questions, this chapter traces the debate about the role of trade and examines how interdependence affected the behavior of European states.

Trade and peace: the origins

The argument that trade between states acts as a source of peace has its roots in the Enlightenment. Scholars further developed these arguments when they pushed for free trade in nineteenth-century Europe. In many ways, the arguments culminated with Normal Angell's 1909 book entitled *The Great Illusion*. Unfortunately for Angell and fellow thinkers, the onset of the First World War greatly discredited this line of thought. A mere five years before the onset of what was the largest war in world history, Angell ([1909]2007: 139) noted that "the only feasible policy in our day for a conqueror to pursue is to leave the wealth of a territory in the possession of its occupants; it is a fallacy, an illusion, to regard a nation as increasing its wealth when it increases territory." Only after the end of the Second World War did a new batch of scholars emerge that continued to develop the theoretical link between trade and peace.

The debate over war, trade, and economics goes back to liberal and Enlightenment thinkers who wrote against the mercantilist policies of their seventeenth- and eighteenth-century states. In many ways, mercantilism is realist theory transplanted into economic policy. Mercantilists essentially sought to use economic policy to increase the power of the state. Doyle highlights three ways in which this occurred:

> mercantilists especially sought a favorable balance of trade (exports exceeding imports) as a way to encourage a steady inflow of gold . . . [they used] economic exchange . . . as a tool of political power through boycotts, bribery, and the manipulation of trade incentives . . . [and they shaped] the political-economic growth of a weaker, less developed economy through the opportunity offered to it in the form of trade and finance. (Doyle 1997: 131)

In other words, mercantilism made economics subservient to power politics.

Enlightenment thinkers began to view the consequences of numerous states employing mercantilist policies as continuous warfare. This conflict, however, was not limited to Europe but extended to colonial holdings (or the decision to seek colonies in the first place). As Rosecrance noted:

> in the age of mercantilism – an era in which power and wealth combined – statesmen and stateswomen (for who dares slight Elizabeth I or

> Catherine the Great) sought not only territory but also a monopoly of markets of particular goods highly valued in Europe...military force could be used to conquer territories or commodity-producing areas that would contribute to greater revenue and power in Europe. (Rosecrance 1986: 7)

In a world of mercantilism, according to the logic of the argument, it was easier to steal a commodity through the use of force than purchase it through trade.

Mercantilism essentially used economic policy to supplement the state. By expanding the economic capacity of the state through beggaring thy neighbor, the relative capabilities of the state increased. From this perspective, economic policy, like power politics in general, is a zero-sum game where the only way to gain was for your opponents to lose. This also implies that gains for its opponents are a loss for the state. Angell ([1909]2007: 119) summarizes this argument from the British perspective: "If she has dominated the commerce of the world, it is because her unconquered navy has dominated, and continues to dominate, all the avenues of commerce." So if another state, Germany for instance, wanted to increase its economic wealth, it was forced to both take from the British and engage the British navy.

While the role of economics in international politics has been hotly debated, Rosecrance (1986) takes it a step further and argues that the international system is split between the military-political and the trading worlds. The military-political world consists of states that act in a manner consistent with realism and mercantilism. Where realists often contend that states have little choice in how they act in the international system, Rosecrance (1986: 30) believes that states have more agency in that "the difference between states is that some rely primarily on military force and only incidentally engage in trade; others make their livelihood in trade and use defense only against the most remote contingencies." For realists, choosing to exist in the trading world is equivalent to state suicide, so what theoretical justification exists for such an action?

Perhaps one of the best places to start is with the work of Jeremy Bentham, who had a tremendous effect on the laws of Great Britain. Sir Henry Maine noted that "I do not know...a single law reform effected since Bentham's day which cannot be traced to his influence" (as quoted in MacCunn 1910: 7). Bentham's most stunning – at the time – argument dealt with the purpose of politics, which was to generate "the greatest happiness of the greatest number." This stands in stark contrast to both the realists' and mercantilists' policies which acted to minimize the amount of happiness of others and focus only on a small portion of the world population (and oftentimes only a portion of a state's citizenry).

Bentham does not ignore the role of security in politics. In fact, security plays a critical role in his political philosophy. As MacCunn (1910: 26) argues: "No one has made it clearer that without social security and the sense of security, the reasonable expectations on which men plan their lives would be at an end. Accumulation would cease. Even subsistence, he declares, would no longer be forthcoming, and society perish in want. This radical is nothing less than an apostle of security." The key for Bentham is that security is a means to an end, where the ends of greatest happiness are clearly the most important. To reach these ends, Bentham places his faith in good governance (and good laws).

John Stuart Mill carried Bentham's ideas further, and perhaps with an even greater optimism. For Mill, the ills of society are created by society, which implies that man can craft a solution. Individuals should follow the Greatest Happiness Principle (Mill [1863]2002: 239) which "holds that actions are right in proportion as they tend to promote happiness, wrong as they tend to produce the reverse of happiness." By striving toward producing happiness (utility), many of the ills of society can be redressed:

> Yet no one whose opinion deserves a moment's consideration can doubt that most of the great positive evils of the world are in themselves removable, and will, if human affairs continue to improve, be in the end reduced within narrow limits. Poverty, in any sense implying suffering, may be completely extinguished by the wisdom of society, combined with good sense and providence of individuals. (Mill [1863]2002: 247–8)

Bentham and Mill mark a change in the perception of the state and its role in society. Part of this change deals with the focus on absolute as opposed to relative gains, where the perspective launched by Bentham and Mill tends to value absolute over relative gains. Imagine for instance that American policy-makers had a choice as to two possible future worlds. In the first, the Chinese economy grows 50 percent and the American economy expands 10 percent. In the second world, the Chinese economy shrinks 10 percent and the American economy contracts 1 percent. What world would a rational American policy-maker choose? If the realists are accurate and relative gains matter, then the second world is more attractive even though the American economy is worse off. Bentham, Mills, and fellow liberal thinkers, however, would focus on the absolute gains and prefer the first world, even though America loses ground to China in a relative sense.

Given the mercantilist, beggar-thy-neighbor, policies of European states in the seventeenth, eighteenth, and nineteenth centuries, it comes as no surprise that liberal thinkers would push their states toward free trade. One of these influential liberals was Richard Cobden, who traveled to the United States as a young man early in the nineteenth century. Like Tocqueville, he was fascinated with American democracy but Cobden also saw the United States "as industrial and commercial rival formidable beyond all precedent . . . and it was this perception more than any other thing which shaped within him the conviction that the policy of England must be a policy of trade" (MacCunn 1910: 93–4).

The trade of Cobden was not the beggar-thy-neighbor policies of the mercantilist, but it was free trade. He saw the nineteenth century as a pivotal moment in human history as international trade grew exponentially and continually affected more aspects of the state and society. Speaking of free trade on January 15, 1846, Cobden noted (as quoted in MacCunn 1910: 95fn): "I believe that the speculative philosopher of 1000 years hence will date the greatest revolution that ever happened in the world's history from the triumph of the principle which we have met here to advocate." For Cobden, free trade was a historic revolution that states needed to embrace or risk falling irrevocably behind.

The focus of Cobden, and his political allies, was the repeal of the protectionist Corn Laws. The fight over the Corn Laws was not only about free trade, but became a symbol of the larger fight over political reform meant to open the political system. Howe (1997: 4–5) argues that "the repeal of the Corn Law was not simply the logical culmination of Liberal Tory economic reforms, but became indissolubly linked with the class politics of the 1840s . . . the merits of free trade were already incontrovertible, embodying a peaceful constitutional and social revolution." In this way, freedom in the economic realm became inexorably linked to freedom in the political realm.

Cobden realized that an industrial revolution had occurred in the United Kingdom and as a consequence the country would see a dramatic increase in the population. Cobden firmly believed that the only way to secure the needed supply of food was through free trade, which would both increase the availability of food and also decrease the price (making it more affordable to the laborers). MacCunn notes that:

in the face of an industrial population increasing like a rising torrent – at the rate of 1000 a day, he [Cobden] once said – it was essential to secure two things: one, that abundance of food supply without which labour could not be efficient; the other, a check upon monopoly prices of corn – monopoly prices which, by dearness of bread, would divert ultimately into the pockets of the landed interest an undue proportion of the wages of labour, thereby leaving less available for stimulating the demand in other commodities besides food. (MacCunn 1910: 98–9)

Clearly one can see the utilitarian roots in this argument, where Cobden was attempting to generate the most for the greatest numbers even if it harmed the landed elites. Free trade, according to Cobden, would remove the shackles from the British economy and allow it to expand to the benefit of all.

Freedom in the economic realm was not isolated from freedom in the political realm or international politics. While Cobden's proximate goal was to push free-trade policies in the United Kingdom, he ultimately wanted a global system of free trade. The expansion of free trade would stimulate a change in international politics where "traditional aristocratic diplomacy was to be superseded by the spontaneous pursuit of the common good by the peoples of Europe, inspired by the British example" (Howe 1997: 71). In other words, free trade would ignite a fundamental shift in the conduct of international politics and move it from a focus on relative gains to one on absolute gains (the common good). Despite these objectives, those outside of England saw traditional power politics at work as C. J. Fuchs (a German protectionist) noted that Cobden "well knew how to cloak the special interests of England in the garb of philanthropic cosmopolitanism" (as quoted in Howe 1997: 73).

Cobden and his supporters expected a complete reorganization of the world based on the liberal philosophy. MacCunn (1910: 103) points out that Cobden wanted "nothing less than a complete international division of labor, under which the production of the whole world would be maximized . . . but above all, it was to be not only the harbinger but the cause of peace, and breaking down of hostile barriers between nation and nation." For Cobden the emergence of free trade would bring about the trading world espoused by Rosecrance (1986: 24) where "the incentive to wage war is absent [because it] disrupts trade and the interdependence on which trade is based." As the amount of trade increased, states would become increasingly reliant on one another (interdependence). Interdependence would necessarily increase the costs associated with war, for harming one's trading partner harms oneself. Ultimately the costs of war would become so prohibitive that the incentive for war is minimized if not completely eliminated.

Angell ([1909]2007) built upon Cobden and others when he examined the underlying incentive for international conflict. In particular, Angell argued that states traditionally fight to expand their territory on the assumption that territorial conquest provides a material benefit for the state. This belief in the benefits of territorial conquest is an illusion in the industrialized world because the very act of conquest destroys the resources of the territory (either human or physical capital). In fact, Angell ([1909]2007: 139–40) states that "military power can do nothing commensurate with its cost and risk for the trade and well-being of the particular states exercising it." So war does not pay, which means that rational states should not use force to resolve their conflicts.

Aside from simply minimizing the benefits from territorial conquest, industrialization and free trade create an interdependent world that limits the effectiveness of physical coercion. With the mutual dependence that results from free trade comes mutual vulnerability, which places boundaries on the relationship. Angell makes this case when he argues that:

> To the degree to which we are really dependent upon someone, our physical power over him is limited; to the degree to which the service we demand of him is difficult, needing for its performance knowledge, tools, freedom of movement, he can use those things to resist the power we try to exercise over him. To the degree to which he is powerful to fill your need, he is powerful to resist you. Very simple forms of service like the pulling of a galley oar, the cutting of sugar cane, can be compelled by the sheer compulsion of the slave-driver's whip. But you cannot get your appendix cut that way. It is not much use threatening which you will visit upon the surgeon if he is clumsy: you may not have the last word on the subject. In that circumstance you come to voluntary agreement, bargain, contract, fees. (Angell [1909]2007: 163–4)

So as economies become more complex in that they rely on specialization that only a few individuals possess, the more difficult it will be to steal the wealth of a society through military coercion. In addition, specialized economies become more dependent on each other to provide the inputs for their outputs, which again decreases the benefits of physical coercion.

As noted earlier, the thinking of Cobden, Bentham, Mill, and other liberal writers culminated in Angell's 1909 book *The Great Illusion*. The outbreak of the deadliest war in human history a mere five years later in the most economically developed and interdependent part of the world tended to discredit the liberal thinkers. The interwar period, filled with conflict and German expansion, simply reinforced the view that *The Great Illusion* itself was an illusion. In fact, the interwar period saw a decrease in international trade as states resorted to a relative gains mentality. Stiglitz argues that these new trade policies produced the exact opposite effect, i.e., they hurt everyone and helped no one:

> The beggar-thy-neighbor policies of the 1930s are generally thought to have played an important role in the spread of the Great Depression. Each country hit by a downturn tried to bolster its own economy by cutting back on imports and thus shifting consumer demand to its own products. A country would cut back on imports by imposing tariffs and by making competitive devaluations of its currency, which made its own goods cheaper and other countries' more expensive. However, as each country cut back on imports, it succeeded in "exporting" the economic downturn to its neighbor. (Stiglitz 2002: 107)

These policies not only failed, but also represented the exact opposite of the goals of Bentham and other liberal thinkers. Rather than produce the greatest happiness for the greatest number, the trade policies in the 1930s generated the least amount of happiness for the greatest number.

The end of the Second World War marked another turning point in the international economic system as the United States emerged as a global hegemon. America established a set of international organizations meant to promote both development and free trade. The founding of a liberal economic order by the United States and the subsequent peace between the major powers once again turned attention back to the liberal theses as to the effects of trade and economic interdependence. The re-emergence of the debate over interdependence and international politics has revisited all of the old questions just as it has sparked novel debates.

Trade and peace: the revival

The end of the Second World War, the establishment of a liberal economic order, and the proceeding peace between the major powers has sparked a revival of interest about the relationship between trade and peace. The theoretical revival can trace its origins back to the original arguments put forth by the likes of Bentham, Mill, Cobden, and

Angell. The revival is unique in that it has coincided with the beha-
vioralist revolution, which has led to a greater emphasis on testing the
arguments. As such, a lot of the recent research aims to test the competing hypotheses about trade, interdependence, and peace.

One vein of the newer research revisits the debate over the utility of
military conquest, i.e., *The Great Illusion* of Angell ([1909]2007). Where
Angell made the case that all industrialized, modern economies no
longer have the incentive for territorial conquest, scholars such as
Rosecrance (1986: 22) have toned down the claims and simply argue
that "the choice between territorial and trading means to national
advancement has always lain before states." In this case, states have a
choice between living in the military-political world (quite similar to
the realist–mercantilist perspective) or the trading world (quite similar
to the liberal perspective).

The military-political and trading worlds are essentially ideal points,
where states tend toward one extreme but never completely abandon
the other. The modern international economic system, however, should
push states away from the military-political and toward the trading
world. The first reason is the rising tide of interdependence, which
means that "it becomes harder to solve national problems by military
means" (Rosecrance 1986: 31). Second, the costs and benefits of war
have changed in that war has become more destructive, which decreases
its benefits while raising the costs. In addition, states are having an
increasingly difficult time organizing conquered territories in ways that
produce revenue and resources for the conquering state (Rosecrance
1986: 38). Finally, the new liberal economic order has lowered the costs
of trade, making it more attractive and beneficial. All of these factors
combine to push states toward the trading and away from the military-
political world. As the proportion of trading states increases, the prevalence of war decreases.[1]

Recently, Boehmer and Sobek (2005) tested aspects of Rosecrance's
argument and found fairly robust evidence. In particular, they argued
that conflicts occur when states have both the opportunity and willingness to use force. As a state develops, the opportunity and willingness
move in opposite directions in that poor states have little capability to
use force but, since conquering new territory (since they are mainly
agrarian states) provides definite benefits, they have the willingness.
Wealthy states, however, have the capabilities to use force but, as
Rosecrance, Angell, and others note, conquering territory provides
little benefit. These relationships imply that both poor and wealthy
states will be less likely to initiate conflicts (the poor because they are
not able and the wealthy because they are not willing). The most

conflict-prone states are those in the middle (the developing states). These states are developing the capability to use force but also garner some benefits from territorial acquisition. Boehmer and Sobek (2005) test this argument with a series of statistical analyses and find strong support for their argument.

Gartzke (2007) reinforces the arguments of Boehmer and Sobek (2005) as well as the original thesis put forward by Angell (1909). For Gartzke (2007), the rise of a capitalist economic system greatly decreases the risk of conflict. Echoing Angell (1909) and Rosecrance (1986), Gartzke (2007: 166) notes that "land does little to increase the worth of advanced economies while resource competition is more cheaply pursued through markets than by means of military occupation." Yet that is not the whole story as Gartzke (2007: 166) tweaks the traditional theses by claiming that "development actually increases the ability of states to project power when incompatible policy objectives exist. Development affects who states fight (and what they fight over) more than the overall frequency of warfare." So Angell was accurate when arguing that development would decrease territorial conflict, but the same is not true for conflicts not over territory. Gartzke (2007) tested his arguments and found robust statistical evidence that corroborates his theory.

While scholars have looked at the effect of broad changes in the economic system, a veritable cottage industry of research has examined the role of trade/interdependence. As noted by previous authors, bilateral trade increases the mutual dependence of states, i.e., interdependence refers to "situations characterized by reciprocal effects among countries or among actors in different countries" (Keohane and Nye 1989: 8). Keohane and Nye (1989) highlight two aspects of interdependence that affect states: sensitivity and vulnerability. Sensitivity examines the responsiveness of policy, i.e., how quickly does the change in one state generate costs in another state? Vulnerability, on the other hand, looks at the availability of alternatives, where numerous alternatives decrease vulnerability. In general, "sensitivity means liability to costly effect imposed from outside before policies are altered to try to change the situation. Vulnerability can be defined as an actor's liability to suffer costs imposed by external events even after the policies have been altered" (Keohane and Nye 1989: 13).

When interdependence exists, actions by one state create costs (or benefits) for the interdependent state. Bilateral trade, for instance, creates interdependence, where the action one state takes toward trade (increasing tariffs) affects the other state. Interdependence does not imply that the vulnerabilities and sensitivities are equally balanced.

If state A exports paper clips to state B and imports food from it, for instance, this creates a situation of interdependence. In this scenario, however, the potential costs of severing that relationship are much greater to state A. As such, asymmetries in interdependence "are most likely to provide sources of influence for actors in their dealings with one another" (Keohane and Nye 1989: 11). In contrast, symmetric interdependence will not provide one side with leverage.

Reed (2003) offers a slightly different take on how interdependence affects the odds of conflict. While acknowledging that interdependence raises the cost of war, Reed (2003: 55) claims that "trade may enhance the probability that states settle their disagreements short of militarized conflict, because it serves to minimize distortion about the willingness of a target to give in to any specific demand issued by a dissatisfied challenger." In other words, trade provides each side in a dispute more consistent and accurate information as to the costs the opponent will incur, which provides a better chance of finding a mutually acceptable agreement short of violence.

Morrow (1999) and Gartzke, Li, and Boehmer (2001) have made similar arguments to Reed (2003), although Morrow (1999) is less convinced that trade affects conflict because it alters the perceived costs of war. In fact, even if high levels of trade reduce the resolve of nations to fight a war, it will still have no effect empirically. As Morrow argues:

> Relative resolve determines the willingness of a state to initiate a crisis. A prospective initiator considers the likely response of the intended target of its threat; if the latter is likely to yield the stakes without a fight, then the former is more likely to use a threat to make a demand on the latter. If two states have a high level of trade, and higher levels of trade reduce resolve, the two could be more or less likely to have a militarized dispute with each other, compared to a pair of states with a low level of trade. The threat of the loss of trade could either deter the prospective initiator or intimidate its target into making concessions, and so encourage the prospective initiator. (Morrow 1999: 485)

This does not mean that trade has no effect on the odds of conflict. High levels of trade allow states to send credible signals of resolve during crises, which reduces the risk of a conflict escalating to war. Reed (2003) confirmed the belief that bilateral trade allows for more credible signals, and works such as Russett and Oneal (2001) show that interdependence additionally decreases the risk of conflict.

While trade may increase the accuracy of information between trading partners, it also can have a dramatic effect on the perceived costs associated with any given conflict. While Keohane and Nye (1989) point out that interdependence may be asymmetric and a source of power for one side, Russett and Oneal (2001: 129) contend that while "the benefits of trade may not be symmetrical and may favor the side with the stronger economic power in the market [it is] always to some degree a mutually beneficial interaction; otherwise, it would not be undertaken." As such, this provides each side with an interest in the economic well-being of the other, which provides an incentive to avoid conflict. As Russett and Oneal (2001: 129) point out, "it is hardly in a state's interest to fight another if its citizens sell their goods, obtain imports (raw materials, capital goods, intermediate products, or consumer goods), or have financial investments or investors there."

While the bulk of research points to bilateral trade as a source of peace, Barbieri (1996) found some evidence that economic interdependence could actually increase the risk of conflict. In particular, it seems to matter whether the trading relations are symmetric or asymmetric. When the trading partners are mutually dependent, the risk of conflict is generally lower, although at extremely high levels of interdependence even symmetric interdependence increases the risk of conflict. When interdependence is asymmetric (one side is more dependent on trade than the other), however, Barbieri (1996) found that bilateral trade actually increases the risk of conflict. In many ways, this reinforces the Keohane and Nye (1989) contention that asymmetries create an opportunity to coerce. In general, Barbieri's (1996: 42) analyses find that "the greatest hope for peace appears to arise from symmetrical trading relationships, [although] extensive economic linkages, be they symmetrical or asymmetrical, appear to pose the greatest hindrance to peace through trade."

Pevehouse (2004) offers possible resolution of the Barbieri (1996) and Russett and Oneal (2001) conflicting results. In particular, Pevehouse (2004) argues that the effect of interdependence may not be consistent across different types of conflict. Looking at disputes at all levels of severity, Pevehouse (2004: 261) discovered that "both realists and commercial liberals have part of the story right – trade simultaneously makes the presence of small amounts of conflict more likely, yet seems to restrain the outbreak of rampant fighting." So trading partners may squabble over minor issues, which show up as low-level disputes, but their interdependence keeps them from escalating the dispute to war.

Keshk, Pollins, and Reuveny (2004) offer another perspective on the relationship between interdependence and peace. Whereas the bulk of the literature focuses on bilateral trade affecting the decision-making of states, Keshk, Pollins, and Reuveny (2004) argue that the causal direction is reversed in that peace generates trade. If correct, then all of the statistical analyses that discovered evidence for the trade-promotes-peace arguments are called into question. Keshk, Pollins, and Reuveny (2004: 1176) found support for their contention because "careful specification of a simultaneous model of trade and conflict, exercised under a number of different assumptions, [found] that political relations affect the flow of commerce between nations, and that when this effect is accounted for, the apparent impact of trade on conflict disappears."

The expansion of the liberal economic system since the end of the Second World War has also sparked a backlash by claiming that free trade is not the same as fair trade. The bulk of the literature that touts the peace-generating effects of trade assumes that free trade is both fair and mutually beneficial, but is that the case? In addition, the liberal institutions that maintain free trade should be impartial and above political influences, but often politics intervenes. Stiglitz makes this case when he describes one particular decision by the International Monetary Fund (IMF):

> The IMF is a political institution. The 1998 bailout was dictated by a concern to maintain Boris Yeltsin in power though, on the basis of all the *principles* which should have guided lending, it made little sense. The quiet acquiescence, if not outright support, to the corrupt loans-for-share privatization was partially based on the fact that the corruption was for a good purpose – to get Yeltsin reelected. IMF policies in these areas were inextricably linked to the political judgments of the Clinton administration's Treasury. (Stiglitz 2003: 166)

So the international institution charged with supporting the liberal economic order was undermined by the very state that wanted to create such an economic system.

The use of trade and liberal economic institutions for non-economic goals does not discount the peace-generating aspect of trade per se, but it does raise two critical points. First, what role does asymmetric interdependence have in promoting peace and/or conflict? On the one hand, interdependence should have the uniform effect of increasing the cost of war. If it increases the cost for one state more than the other, so be it, but both states still face increased costs. On the other hand, the state with the advantage could manipulate it to extract concessions, which may generate grievances and hence conflict. The second point is that trading relations may not be mutually beneficial, voluntary exchanges.

The anti-globalization movement has focused on the non-mutually beneficial nature of the liberal economic order. In fact, the spread of the liberal economic order has not benefited everyone, nor necessarily created the greatest benefit for the greatest number of people. Stiglitz highlights the competing perspectives:

> While the institutions seem to pursue commercial and financial interests above all else, they do not see matters that way. They genuinely believe that agenda they are pursuing is in the *general interest*. In spite of evidence to the contrary, many trade and finance ministers, and even some political leaders, believe that everyone will eventually benefit from trade and capital market liberalization. Many believe this so strongly that they support forcing countries to accept these "reforms," through whatever means they can, even if there is little popular support for such measures. (Stiglitz 2003: 216)

Thus, the elites pushing for the expansion of the liberal economic order are truly the progeny of Bentham, Mill, Cobden, and Angell. For them, free trade benefits all and, in terms of maximizing utility, is the best option. Perhaps the best example of this is the creation and expansion of the European Union.

The evolution of the European Union

In many ways, the development of the European Union reflects the evolution of a trading world described by Rosecrance (1986). In other words, the European Union is a set of states that have forgone military conquest in favor of the mutually beneficial exchanges of trade. After the devastation of the Second World War, the

> idea of unity resurfaced again, but this time as part of an argument that retention of the historic notion of the independent state as the foundation of political organization had been discredited and that it should be abandoned, to be substituted by a concerted effort at unifying state practices that in time might lead to a comprehensive continental political community. (Urwin 1995: 7)

The modern war had increased the costs of the military-political world enough to push states into a trading world.

The march to the European Union started with relatively simple and pedestrian organizations. The Benelux pact was formed in 1944 between Belgium, Netherlands, and Luxembourg in an attempt to unify their economies. In 1948, they abolished internal customs duties, although additional barriers to trade remained. While not particularly successful, the Benelux pact provided a framework for future economic agreements such as the equally unsuccessful Joint Nordic Committee for Economic Cooperation. This groundwork, however, set the foundation for the emergence of the European Coal and Steel Community (ECSC).

The European Coal and Steel Community was originally suggested by French Foreign Minister Robert Schuman in May of 1950. Schuman proposed a pooling of coal and steel resources with the ambition to (1) bring the European states together through the elimination of trade barriers; and (2) begin the rapprochement between France and West Germany. The ECSC would allow steel, which was cheaply produced in West Germany, to be exported to France. This economic interdependence would ultimately check German aggression. Despite dissent from the British, the Treaty of Paris was signed in June 1950 between France, West Germany, Italy, Belgium, Netherlands, and Luxembourg, forming the European Coal and Steel Community. Urwin (1995: 47) notes that the ECSC was "the first significant step toward European Union that went beyond being merely consultative and intergovernmental in character."

During the mid-1950s, the momentum toward economic integration continued, especially with the Spaak Report (Paul-Henri Spaak was president of the Council of Europe and the OEEC) unveiled in March 1956. The report proposed both a common market and the development of a nuclear energy committee. The ECSC Common Assembly overwhelmingly approved the report, which ultimately led to the creation of two treaties: the European Economic Community (EEC) and the European Atomic Energy Community (Euratom). The EEC was specifically designed to push Europe toward political integration through economic integration. In fact, the EEC included an executive institution (Council of Ministers), a legislative institution (the European Parliament), and judicial branches.

At the first meeting of the EEC, the European Parliament Assembly elected Robert Schuman as president. In addition, the Assembly laid out the long-term plan of the organization which was the establishment of a common market in Europe to maintain harmonious economic activity. In other words, it was the goal to eliminate all vestiges of mercantilist policies and move Europe from the political-military into a trading world as described by Rosecrance. This movement was not to take place immediately, but would slowly evolve over the course of 12–15 years.

The British remained relatively aloof from the drive toward economic integration, although this began to change as they participated in the European Free Trade Association (EFTA) in 1959. The British were joined in the EFTA by Austria, Denmark, Norway, Portugal, Sweden, and Switzerland. The goals for the EFTA, which simply consisted of creating a free-trade area, were relatively modest when compared to the EEC. With the creation of the EFTA and the EEC, Europe was essentially divided into two main groups. Into this milieu the United States entered, favoring the EEC which more closely matched American economic interests. In addition, the United States reformed the OEEC to focus more on international problems of economic strategy and development and allow non-European members. This new organization was renamed the Organization for Economic Cooperation and Development (OECD).

The fortunes of European integration began to wane as the conservative Charles de Gaulle took control of France. De Gaulle's opinion on integration was fairly clear as a quote in Urwin (1995: 112) highlights: "However big the glass which is proffered from outside, we prefer to drink from our own glass, while at the same time clinking glasses with those around us." The rise of de Gaulle occurred as French influence in the EEC increased, much to the chagrin of the other members. To balance French influence, West Germany, Italy, Belgium, Netherlands, and Luxembourg pushed for British membership of the EEC. The French, however, vetoed British membership in 1963. Tensions boiled over in 1965 with a seven-month French boycott of the EEC Council of Ministers' meeting. Ultimately, the members were able to overcome this tumultuous period with the Luxembourg Compromise of 1966, which gave each state a veto if a policy affected the vital interests of a state.

The second half of the 1960s and early 1970s saw continued debate over the expansion of the EEC (whose name was changed to European Community [EC] in 1967). In 1972, Britain, Ireland, Norway, and Denmark signed the Treaty of Accession, marking their official entry into the EC. Concurrent with the momentum to expand came an increasing emphasis on political cooperation. Etienne Davignon, former EC commissioner, wrote a report in 1974 that argued for a movement toward more political and economic cooperation. The Davignon Report was successful in creating more political cooperation, known as the European Political Cooperation (EPC). In addition, 1974 saw the creation of the European Council as part of the EC.

The European Council was designed to add a degree of authority that members believed was missing from the EC. In particular, Urwin

(1995: 175) notes that the European Council could "set new targets and lay down the guidelines for future progress, modify or abandon existing programmes, and resolve disputes between the members at the highest level." Despite the stated goals, the European Council simply enhanced the EC as an intergovernmental body and did not necessarily make it more supranational, i.e., rather than being able to override the views of the member states, the European Council simply served as an additional diplomatic arena.

The push to further the political integration of Europe picked up speed in the 1980s. In February of 1984, a Draft Treaty on European Union was overwhelmingly endorsed by the European Parliament. The treaty would have given more power to the supranational aspects of the EC (such as the European Parliament) at the expense of the intergovernmental aspects of the EC (such as the Council of Ministers). This first draft was vetoed by the European Council (run by the Council of Ministers). In June of 1985, the European Council met in Milan to discuss the issue of political integration. While no critical changes were implemented, a second conference was authorized to construct a set of reforms. This latter conference, according to Urwin (1995: 228), allowed for "the most decisive changes in the structure of the EC since its inception."

The Single European Act (SEA) was accepted in 1986 and was meant to create a single European common market. The integrated internal market was to be completed by 1992, leading to the free movement of goods, capital, and individuals throughout the member states. Unlike previous European institutions where unanimity was required, the SEA only required a qualified majority (the states maintained weighted voting). Finally, the SEA focused once again on a European political community in order to create a unified, European foreign policy.

The 1990s finished the slow process of integration. At a European Council meeting in Lisbon (1990) the decision was made to invite the EFTA states (Britain, Austria, Denmark, Norway, Portugal, Sweden, and Switzerland) into the EC. In December of 1992, the EC met in Maastricht to "finalize a treaty framework for EU incorporating political union and EMU, determine a timetable for their implementation, and launch the EC along a new security dimension" (Urwin 1995: 253). Despite some setbacks, in November of 1993 the European Union (EU) came into existence, an EU based on both economic and political integration.

The development of the European Union, despite its fits and starts, clearly shows how economic integration can lead to political integration. Starting with the modest goals of the European Coal and Steel Community, the European states were able to slowly build a consensus around economic integration. With the idea of economic integration firmly in place, the Europeans made more dramatic moves toward political integration. Throughout this entire process, disputes were resolved with the boundaries set by the supranational institutions, which have essentially maintained a 50-year (and counting) peace between the major powers of Europe.

Conclusion

The debate over the effect of trade has been contentious since the start. Depending on the perspective, the prescription for state policies could not differ more drastically. The realist–mercantilist argument points to the use of economic power to supplement political power, i.e., it is simply another method of coercion to be used as such. From this point of view, trade is meant to maximize state wealth and not the total welfare of society (be it within the state or outside). The liberals, however, concentrate on the joint benefits to be gained from economic interdependence. The free trade promoted by the liberals not only helps the state but the trading partner as well. This clearly generates more good for more people than the beggar-thy-neighbor policies of the mercantilists.

At the heart of the disagreement between the two perspectives rest fundamentally different views of the international system. The realists conceive international politics through the lens of Hobbes, where anarchy creates a perpetual state of war of state against state. In such an environment, the state is almost compelled to act in a self-help manner and to concentrate on relative, as opposed to absolute, gains. The liberals, however, take their cue from Locke who argued that the state of war was a perversion of the state of nature. As such, the need to constantly seek every advantage is mitigated, although not eliminated. This environment, however, does leave room for states to engage in behavior that enhances their absolute utility, even if it helps others a little more.

In many ways, the basis of the liberal argument lies in the effect of bilateral trade on bilateral relations. If trade decreases the risk of conflict, then states can successfully bypass the self-help system of the realist without losing their sovereignty. If, on the other hand, trade has no pacifying effect, then those states that implement liberal economic policies place themselves at risk from "realist" states. In general, the data does not provide conclusive evidence for either argument, although the bulk of the research indicates that states engaged in bilateral trade are less likely to engage in conflict. That being said, this relationship may be contingent on those states either being developed and/or symmetrically interdependent.

The history examined in this chapter clearly indicates that economic interdependence matters but it cannot consistently trump power politics. The outbreak of the First World War a mere five years after Norman Angell proclaimed that the benefits gained from territorial conquest were a great illusion seemed to validate the realist arguments at the expense of liberalism. Despite the refutation of history, Angell defended his original argument when he noted:

> The real cause was the method which both nations were adopting to achieve defense: self-preservation; a method under which each attempted to achieve defense for himself by forbidding it to the other; each claiming the right of defense by superior power, thus denying it to the other. Security for one was to be purchased at the price of the insecurity of the other. (Angell [1909]2007)

Here Angell is highlighting a critical claim of many liberals: realism (and power politics) is a self-fulfilling prophecy in that it encourages behavior that only decreases security. The key to having a truly secured, free-trade system would be to exit from the military-political world described by Rosecrance (1986).

The development and expansion of the European Union appears to nicely demonstrate the liberal argument in action. Early in the process, a consensus was developed that first pushed for economic integration but would eventually move toward political integration. This could only work as long as peace existed between the major powers of Western Europe, which was in no way guaranteed. In spite of the clashes of interest between members of the EEC and the vigorous anti-British campaign prosecuted by the French, the states of Europe refused to use physical coercion to resolve the disputes. The Europeans consistently resorted to bounded competition and negotiation when they fought for advantage. Eventually, the functional approach set in place after the Second World War paid dividends when the European Union emerged from the Treaty of Maastricht.

In general, it appears that interdependence offers states an avenue to escape from the military-political world and minimize their risk of war. This transition, however, is both difficult and not guaranteed. The late nineteenth and early twentieth centuries highlight a failed transition in Europe just as the second half of the twentieth century shows a success. The transition is not absolute in that Europe could revert back to the military-political world, given the right set of incentives. Trade and interdependence alter the costs and benefits associated with peace and war. These changes could be either ephemeral or enduring but are certainly not permanent.

PART III   THE INTERNATIONAL SYSTEM

———

6 THE SYSTEMIC DISTRIBUTION OF POWER

The post-1945 bipolar structure was a simple one that did not require sophisticated leadership to maintain it. The great multipolar systems of the 19th century collapsed in large part because of their intricacy: they required a Metternich or Bismarck to hold them together, and when statesmen of that caliber were no longer available, they tended to come apart.

John Lewis Gaddis, *The Long Peace* (1987: 222)

Any plan conceived in moderation must fail when the circumstances are set in extremes.

Prince Klemens von Metternich (1822)

If there is ever another war in Europe, it will come out of some damned silly thing in the Balkans.

Otto von Bismarck (1898)

History has seen the international system possessing any number of balances of power. One of the most intriguing distributions contained two main powers. The first major power was a wealthy democracy that possessed the most dominant navy in the international system. Opposing the democracy was a land-based oligarchy with an incredibly powerful army. The bulk of the other states in the international system had an alliance (implicit or explicit) with one of the two "superpowers," creating a precarious balance of power between the two sides. As a result, even minor conflicts between two small states had the risk of sparking a massive war, a fact forgotten by neither side. So, does this describe the Cold War (United States versus the Soviet Union) or classical Greece before the Peloponnesian War (Athens versus Sparta)? In some ways that is a trick question because the situation described above is an apt portrayal of both the Cold War and classical Greece before the Peloponnesian War.

The stylized description of both the Cold War and classical Greece neatly demonstrates that history repeats itself (at least in terms of context). Despite having similar starting points, however, these two systems could not have had more different conclusions. The Cold War ended in the peaceful collapse of the Soviet Union and the Warsaw Pact alliance system. In contrast, the confrontation between Athens and Sparta ended in a 27-year war that encompassed the entirety of Greece. What explains the difference in outcome, given the similarity in context? Does the structure of the international system offer any explanatory power or are wars best analyzed at the dyadic level of analysis?

While scholars have traditionally relied on the systemic level of analysis to explain the amount of conflict in the international system, the past 30 years has seen a slow and steady movement from systemic to dyadic analyses. As scholars argued that war was dyadic in nature, it was only natural that they would begin to look at the interaction of individual pairs of states. Despite this change, many still believe that the characteristics of the system affect the amount of war (perhaps to a larger extent than the characteristics of the dyad). The system, from this perspective, structures the interaction of states in ways that alter their perception of cost and benefit. As such, to understand the broad contours of war and peace requires an analysis of the system and not the dyad.

Even granting that the structure of the international system affects the amount of conflict, major debates are held as to how structure alters the behavior of states. For instance, the distribution of capabilities across states is often deemed the most important causal factor at the systemic level of analysis but no consensus has emerged as to the most peaceful system (hegemonic, bipolar, tripolar, multipolar, and so on). In addition, scholars have yet to settle on a definition of "peaceful." Is it a lack of war? Do only major powers count? Is peace really just stability, i.e., lack of change in the distribution of capabilities? Or does stability mean that no states are eliminated from the system?

In order to better understand the effect of the structure of the international system on international conflict, this chapter first looks at why, or how, the structure matters. Once that is established, a series of theories will be examined that put forward one type of system as being the most "stable." To get a sense of how well the theories describe reality, the chapter examines one period of bipolarity (the Cold War) and one period of multipolarity (Europe before the First World War). While these cases cannot prove one argument correct, they should highlight how bipolarity and multipolarity alter the behavior of states.

The international states system

Any system, according to Waltz (1979), can be defined by three characteristics: ordering principles, character of the units, and the distribution of capabilities. The ordering principle simply describes the type of order, which can range from hierarchy to anarchy. The character of the units examines the functions of the units, i.e., to maximize wealth, security, and so on. Finally, the distribution of capabilities details how system resources are divided among the various units. Given these three broad characteristics, how does one describe the international states system?

In terms of the ordering principle the international states system exists in a state of anarchy (at least according to Waltz (1979)). Anarchy does not, however, mean chaos. When used in this context, anarchy is simply defined as the lack of an overarching authority. Contrast the anarchy of international relations with domestic politics, which is a hierarchy with the government acting as the overarching authority. For realists, it seems quite obvious to describe the international states system as anarchic, given the lack of an obvious overarching authority. While international organizations such as the United Nations exist, they cannot and have not exerted overarching authority. In fact, many realists would argue that international organizations cannot enforce *any* decision without the backing of the states.

The character of the states in the international system is one of functional equivalency. In other words, all states have the same role and that is survival. The international states system is not differentiated like the human body where some cells carry oxygen while others digest food. States in the international system, while not identical on all qualities, share a single function and that is simple survival. When this is combined with anarchy, it creates a self-help system of like units individually seeking to secure their own survival. This makes security (ensured through power) the ultimate goal of all states. The choice of any state to ignore this fundamental reality is to risk its very survival.

Unlike the first two aspects of the international states system, the distribution of capabilities is not constant (Waltz (1979) argues that the international states system has always existed in a state of anarchy and states have always had the same function). The distribution of power between states changes across time, altering the concentration of power in the international states system. While there exists an infinite number of possible distributions of capabilities, Waltz (1979) concentrates his analysis on two broad categories: bipolarity (two main states) and multipolarity (three or more main states).

In general, these three aspects of a system, according to Waltz (1979), will both describe the international states system and explain changes in the amount of violence. If one wants to explain the amount of war in the international states system, which varies across time, then how does one utilize the ordering principle and the character of the units, which are constant? The answer is that they simply cannot be used to describe changes in the amount of violence. The only aspect of the international states system that varies is the distribution of capabilities, which is why Waltz utilizes it to explain the stability of various distributions of power.

Bipolar stability

Waltz (1979) argued that the most peaceful distribution of capabilities was bipolarity (such as the Cold War). Building on his argument that states constantly strive to survive in an anarchic international system through the pursuit of security, Waltz delineates two broad strategies: internal versus external balancing. Internal balancing is fairly straightforward in that states will use their domestic resources to sustain and increase their power. So if its opponent builds 100 tanks, then a state using an internal balancing strategy would build 100 tanks to match. External balancing, however, occurs when states seek to balance through alliances. So when its opponent builds those 100 tanks, a state can ally with a second state that pledges 100 tanks if a war occurs with the first state's opponent. In general, states have the option to use either internal or external balancing, although the structure of the system can severely curtail a state's options.

Waltz argues that internal balancing is inherently more stable than external balancing. In part this derives from the anarchic structure of the international system. Given the lack of an overarching authority, what assurances do states have that their allies will actually come to their aid? Who punishes states if they fail their allies? This credible commitment problem is difficult for states to overcome. Even during the Cold War, West Germany was not convinced that the United States would come to their aid in the event of a Soviet invasion. The solution was to place 3,000 American soldiers in West Berlin, which would guarantee American deaths on the first day of a war and continued American involvement in the conflict. This credible commitment problem does not occur with internal balancing because the state maintains complete control over the additional forces.

Systems where states rely on external balancing will be rife with miscalculations that can lead to conflict. These miscalculations occur because states can never have complete confidence in how allies will respond. Imagine, for instance, a three-state system (A, B, and C). In addition, states A and B have an alliance against C such that C could not win a war against the combined might of A and B. State C could, however, defeat A or B in a one-on-one war. In this case, the actions of state C are contingent on its expectation that A and B will uphold their alliance commitments. The expectations of state C may or may not be accurate. In an international system with multiple alliances of unknown strengths of commitments, miscalculations are apt to occur. Contrast this with a system of internal balancing, where these errors are much less likely, i.e., everyone generally assumes that a state's army will respond to the government (although this is not always the case). The key point, however, is that those systems that rely on external balancing will be less stable than those that use internal balancing. How, then, does this relate to bipolarity and multipolarity?

Waltz makes the argument that states in a system with a bipolar distribution of capabilities will utilize internal balancing, while states in multipolar systems will balance externally. Why? It all relates to the costs associated with internal balancing. For instance, in a system with two major powers (bipolar), the costs of internal balancing are relatively low. So if state B builds 100 tanks, then state A only needs to build 100 tanks to match. This changes when one adds a third state. Imagine that state A expands its forces by 100 tanks. State B then builds 100 tanks to match. How many tanks will state C need to balance? The answer is 200 because C cannot know for certain that A and B will not join forces to attack it. After state C expands its forces, however, state A is now down 200 tanks (it has to address the increases of both B and C), which it will then need to build. This cycle will continue until the states are simply unable to expand their forces due to the constraints of their resource endowments. Remember that this scenario only had three major powers. The more states in a multipolar system, the more costly internal balancing becomes.

Given the prohibitive costs of internal balancing in multipolar systems, these states are forced to rely on external balancing to address their security concerns. This would not be the case in bipolar systems where internal balancing is more cost effective. Any time one side expands its influence or power, it can expect its opponent to respond in kind (Richardson 1960). Since states in multipolar systems rely on external balancing, these distributions of capabilities will be less stable than their bipolar counterparts.

Waltz additionally argues for the stability of bipolarity because in these systems there exists a clarity of the enemy that is not true for multipolarity. As James (2002: 138) noted, "the most obvious advantage [to bipolarity] is the absence of coalitional dynamics among great powers." In a bipolar system, an agreement among the great powers only involves two states and would obviously be easier to achieve when compared to multipolar systems with three or more major powers. In addition, the clarity extends to minor powers, where it becomes obvious who they support.

Perhaps most ironically, bipolar systems should be peaceful because the major powers will have a series of recurring crises. These crises, which are resolved short of war, act as tests of resolve and proxy for armed conflict. The advantage of regularly occurring minor crises is that "rather than storing grievances, which could explode into world war, tensions are dissipated through third-party conflict in a series of contained environments" (James 2002: 139). In other words, bipolar systems have a series of small tremors that release pressure, whereas multipolar systems will store these tensions until they explode in a world war. Not all realists, however, believe that bipolar systems will be the most stable.

Multipolar stability

Just as Waltz (1979) argues that a bipolar system creates a clarity of the enemy, which decreases uncertainty and the risk of war, scholars of multipolar stability argue that such clarity will increase the risk of war. In multipolar systems, states have a flexibility in their diplomatic behavior that does not exist in bipolarity. Kegley and Raymond (1994: 51) note that in a multipolar system "anyone is a potential partner; no one is an implacable enemy, [which means that] the shifting equilibrium of forces in a multipolar balance of power encourages conciliation." In other words, states in a multipolar system cannot harm their enemies too much because they may soon be vital allies. This also implies that one cannot help one's allies too much because they could be tomorrow's enemies. This bounded competition both encourages states to avoid war (at least total war) and provides them the flexibility to do so. As Claude noted (1962: 62), "the world could do much worse than manage the power relations of states so as to keep the major contestants in a position of approximate equality. There is danger when power confronts power, but there is even greater danger when power confronts weakness."

The bipolar system of the Cold War eliminated the subtle dance of diplomacy that was the hallmark of multipolarity. The rigidness of Cold War alliances forced states to exchange their dancing shoes for boxing gloves as each side fought for every inch of advantage in an intense zero-sum game. The gain for one side was a loss for the other. This fact, or at least the two superpowers' belief of the "fact," made minor issues highly salient issues, turned minor crises into major threats to world peace. In a multipolar system, however, the flexibility of action would have kept minor issues and crises minor. Niou, Ordeshook, and Rose (1989), using a formal analysis, found that in a bipolar system, strict equality of power would lead to peace. Whenever one side gained a slight advantage, it would have an incredible incentive to use its edge in a war of conquest. Such an incentive would be mitigated in a multipolar world, where numerous balancing coalitions exist.

The second advantage of multipolar systems derives from the number of interaction opportunities. In particular, the greater the number of major powers, "the number, range, and diversity of mutually beneficial trade-offs among them rise; hence the prospects of armed conflict decline" (Kegley and Raymond 1994: 51). In many ways, increasing the number of major powers increases the number of cross-cutting cleavages, i.e., any given pair of major powers will contain issues of contention and consensus (Deutsch and Singer 1964). These cross-cutting cleavages prevent relationships from hardening as there is always a measure of cooperation in all relationships. Compare this to bipolarity in which the cleavages become cumulative (overlapping). As James (2002: 140) noted, "cross-cutting cleavages could help prevent division of the major powers into two exclusive coalitions. If and when warfare occurs, it is less likely to be all-inclusive."

Perhaps the most compelling argument for the stability of multipolar systems rests on the risk aversion of states. As the number of major powers increases, the ability of each state to accurately forecast the actions of other states (especially in war) becomes virtually non-existent. If one assumes that states are risk-averse, then they would be unwilling to push issues too far in the confused milieu of a multipolar system. Kegley and Raymond (1994: 52) note that "without a clear way to gauge the probability of success on the battlefield, they will negotiate rather than fight." This behavior, however, is contingent on the assumption that states are risk-averse.

Liska picks up on the argument that the characteristics of the states matter in how the systemic distribution of capabilities affects the amount of conflict.

> The relative simplicity of forces and relationships in a single-tier, two power situation is the optimum condition of equilibrium, or stability, when both powers are rational and conservative. Complexity, and unpredictability of political and military responses, may be the only deterrent to offensive thrusts by an expansionist power which is ruthless but rational and calculates its risks and probabilities of meaningful gains. (Liska 1962: 276)

In some ways, Liska (1962) is noting the conditionality of the relationship between polarity and international conflict. For some international systems, bipolarity works best in producing peace, but in others multipolarity is required.

Wilkenfeld and Brecher (2003) offer another take on the role of polarity in international politics. Similar to Waltz (1979), they argue that bipolar systems would exhibit the greatest amount of peace but polycentrism (two major powers with multiple decision centers) would be more conflict-prone than multipolarity. According to Wilkenfeld and Brecher (2003), each distribution of power has varying costs of decision-making and implementation, where polycentrism has the most unstable structure. When they tested their argument, they found consistent support for it. In particular, they noted that "crises during polycentrism were by far the most likely to be triggered by violence (53 percent), followed by multipolarity (33 percent) and bipolarity (24 percent)" (Wilkenfeld and Brecher 2003: 286).

Concentration not polarity

While most of the research has examined the international system in terms of the number of major powers (poles), this sort of measure leaves out a lot of information. For instance, imagine two multipolar systems with three major powers. In system 1, state A has 25 percent of the power, state B has 30 percent, and state C has 45 percent. In contrast, system 2 contains three states where each has 33 percent of the power. Simply looking in terms of polarity these systems would be identical, but are we willing to make that assertion? The alternative would be to move away from polarity and toward a measure called concentration.

Power concentration does not examine the number of major powers in the system but looks more at the distribution of power across the states in the system. In general, concentration provides a single measure of how much power varies between the states in the international system and it can vary from 0 (complete equality) to 1 (complete preponderance). Historically, the level of concentration has been low during periods of equality between the major powers such as the Concert of Europe era (Singer, Bremer, and Stuckey 1972). In contrast, the level of concentration was highest when a single power dominated the system, such as in the twentieth century right after the end of the Second World War.

While concentration may not be a better measure than polarity in determining the structure of the international system, it certainly contains information that polarity lacks. As Snyder and Diesing (1977: 419) argue, "the 'structure' of an international system is defined by the *number* of major actors and the *distribution of power and potential among them.*" So concentration may not replace polarity but it undoubtedly supplements it. That being said, some have argued (Mansfield 1994: 16) that "concentration is a fundamentally important aspect of the distribution of power from both a conceptual and an empirical standpoint. Further, for the purposes of explaining the onset of war, patterns of international trade, and structural change, polarity is a considerably less salient feature of the concentration of power than is commonly asserted."

Mansfield (1994) uses the concentration measure to test an argument not easily analyzed with measures of polarity. In particular, Mansfield argues that war is less likely when power is concentrated *and* when it is diffused. According to Mansfield (1994: 81), when the balance of power is diffused, "states have an incentive to block the aggressor in order to avert the possibility that victory on its part will undermine their respective positions." In addition, when the power is concentrated, "each of the smaller states is expected to be deterred from attacking the preponderant states, and the dominant state is likely to try to manage and limit conflict, rather than participate in (or encourage) it, because it can achieve its own objectives through coercion, intimidation, and other measures short of war" (Mansfield 1994: 82). The implication of these arguments is that systems of moderate power concentration (perhaps similar to Wilkenfeld and Brecher's (2003) polycentrism) are most at risk of experiencing major power wars, something Mansfield (1994) confirms in his statistical models.

Mansfield's use of concentration was based on previous work that tested more simple relationships with the concentration measure. For instance, Singer, Bremer, and Stuckey (1972, 1979) found that power concentration was associated with war in the nineteenth century but peace in the twentieth century. Using similar data, Cannizzo (1978) found a similar pattern, but Bueno de Mesquita (1981) showed that power concentration was unrelated to war. Stoll and Champion (1985) found that, in the hands of revisionist states, power concentration increases the risk of war. Rasler and Thompson (1994) discovered that as the gap between global and regional concentration narrows, the risk of war increases as a regional challenger rises to challenge the global powers.

To understand the relationship between the systemic distribution of power and international conflict, two periods will be examined. The first is a multipolar system that ended in the outbreak of the First World War. The second is the bipolar system of the Cold War, which has also been known as "the long peace." While at first glance it looks like the multipolar system led to war and the bipolar system peace, the question is how the distribution of capabilities influenced the onset of war and/or the durability of peace.

The First World War

In many ways, the First World War is the ultimate cautionary tale of the risk of multipolar systems. The entangling alliances forced states into a conflict that they would have preferred to avoid. These alliance ties were part of the intricate balancing act forced on states by the multipolar system. Prince Bernhard von Bulow described the "inadvertent" nature of the war when relating his meeting with German Chancellor Bethmann Hollweg shortly after the war began:

> Bethmann stood in the center of the room; shall I ever forget his face, the look in his eyes? There is a picture by some celebrated English painter, which shows the wretched scapegoat with a look of ineffable anguish in its eyes, such a pain I now saw in Bethmann's. For an instant we neither of us spoke. At last I said to him, "Well, tell me, at least, how it all happened." He raised his long, thin arms to heaven and answered in a dull exhausted voice: "Oh, if only I knew." In many later

polemics on war guilt I have often wished it had been possible to produce a snapshot of Bethmann Hollweg standing there at the moment he said those words. Such a photograph would have been the best proof that this wretched man had never wanted war. (As quoted in Nye 2005: 68)

This conventional wisdom, however, generates more questions than it answers. For instance, if the major powers in Europe wanted to avoid the conflict so badly, then what stopped them from simply breaking their alliance commitments? What about the situation that led the states to maintain their alliance commitments in the face of an "unwanted" war? Perhaps most important for our purposes, what effect, if any, did the multipolar structure of the international system have on the decision-making processes of the major powers?

In the run up to the First World War, Europe essentially became divided into two main camps: the Triple Entente (formed in 1907) between the United Kingdom, France, and Russia, and the Triple Alliance of Germany, Italy, and the Austro-Hungarian Empire, which was signed in 1882, well before the Triple Entente. At the heart of the dispute between these opposing alliances rested the rapid rise of Germany in the late nineteenth century and the challenge that it posed to the British. The British were especially concerned about the German plans to expand its navy, which was a direct challenge not only to British hegemony but also to its fundamental security.

The German rise in power in the years preceding the First World War was truly astounding. In the 1890s, the German industrial production passed the British and by the beginning of the twentieth century the German gross national product (GNP) was growing twice as fast as that of the British. In 1860, Britain possessed 25 percent of the world's industrial production, which fell to 10 percent by 1913 just as Germany's share rose to 15 percent. As noted above, the German attempt to translate this economic wealth into military (especially naval) power sent shudders through British policy-makers. The "Tirpitz Plan" of 1911 set Germany on course to have the world's second largest navy, which "alarmed Britain's First Lord of the Admiralty, Winston Churchill, [who] worried about how [Britain] would defend its far-flung empire" (Nye 2005: 70).

The British government essentially decided that they needed to respond to the rise of Germany. In 1907, Sir Eyre Crowe, permanent secretary of the British Foreign Office, wrote a memorandum arguing that Britain could not allow a single state to dominate continental Europe. In particular, Crowe argued:

History shows that the danger threatening the independence of this or that nation has generally arisen, at least in part, out of the momentary predominance of a neighboring State at once militarily powerful, economically efficient, and ambitious to extend its frontiers or spread its influence, the danger being directly proportionate to the degree of its power and efficiency, and to the spontaneity or "inevitableness" of its ambitions. The only check on the abuse of political predominance derived from such a position has always consisted in the opposition of an equally formidable rival, or of a combination of several countries forming leagues of defense. The equilibrium established by such a grouping of forces is technically known as the balance of power, and it has become almost an historical truism to identify England's secular policy with the maintenance of this balance by throwing her weight now in this scale and now in that, but ever on the side opposed to the political dictatorship of the strongest single, State or group at a given time.

If this view of British policy is correct, the opposition into which England must inevitably be driven to any country aspiring to such a dictatorship assumes almost the form of a law of nature, as has indeed been theoretically demonstrated, and illustrated historically, by an eminent writer on English national policy. (Crowe 1907)

Crowe interpreted German actions in the context of the balance of power, where the only way to stop aggression was with a balancing coalition. Not only was Britain's imperative to balance Germany, but it was practically a "law of nature." From this perspective, the multipolar system of Europe moved states in the same way gravity moves objects.

While it is easy to understand the British desire to balance against a rising German threat, this does not explain why the balancing led to war. In fact, the actions by the British reinforce the arguments of the balance of power theorists. In particular, Britain responded to a threat by balancing against it. In addition, the multipolarity of the system gave Britain a number of potential allies to choose from in its attempt to balance. Eventually the Triple Entente was formed to balance the rising Germany and its Triple Alliance. So up until the outbreak of hostilities, the European multipolar system seemed to be acting in ways predicted by the theories. What failed?

One of the most common explanations for the failure of the multipolar system to stop the war was the increasing rigidity of the alliance system. Once the Triple Alliance and Triple Entente were set, the states became increasingly wrapped in what was essentially a bipolar system. Lacking the ability to alter alliances to mitigate the risk of conflict, the major powers of Europe would slowly descend into conflict. While there was certainly a bit of tightening of the alliances, it is questionable as a root cause of the failure. If the alliances were so tight, then why did Italy switch sides in 1915? While this occurred after the onset of the war, one would expect such a "rigid" system to take more than a year of war to crack.

Liddell Hart (1930) felt that the new alliance system mattered, but not because it was too rigid. Liddell Hart (1930: 17–18) argued that "the new grouping of Europe was not the old balance of power but merely a barrier between powers. That barrier, moreover, was charged with explosives [and the] fear of a sudden detonation led the autocratic powers to at least give the military custodians of these armaments a dangerously free hand in disposing them." So for Liddell Hart the new alliances were not really alliances in the old sense but merely recognitions of the divisions that everyone already knew existed.

The fear of war eventually turned into a fatalism about the impending conflict. The president of France (Poincaré) noted in 1913 that "France did not want war, but did not fear it" (as quoted in Liddell Hart 1930: 22). This sort of fatalistic view of the impending conflict in conjunction with the increased influence of the military across Europe created a fruitful environment for the hounds of war to grow. The momentum for action (and war) "multiplied on all sides – bellicose speeches, articles, rumors, frontier incidents. President Wilson's confidant, Colonel House, left Berlin with the conviction that the military party was determined on war, at the earliest opportunity, and would force the Kaiser to abdicate if he opposed their desire" (Liddell Hart 1930: 21).

The closer the states of Europe moved toward the abyss of the war, the stronger, and more irresistible, the voices of violence became. The approach of conflict changed what could have been a game of absolute gains into one of relative gains. The only way to make one's state more secure was to decrease the security of other states. After the assassination of Archduke Franz Ferdinand, the momentum toward war became irresistible. In fact, Tuchman argues that:

War pressed against every frontier. Suddenly dismayed, governments struggled and twisted to fend it off. It was no use. Agents at frontiers were reporting every cavalry patrol as a deployment to beat the mobilization gun. General staffs, goaded by their relentless timetables, were pounding the table for the signal to move lest their opponents gain an hour's head start. Appalled upon the brink, the chiefs of state who would be ultimately responsible for their country's fate attempted to back away but the pull of the military schedules dragged them forward. (Tuchman 1962: 72)

This theme is echoed in Liddell Hart (1930: 29) when he noted that "the one thought of generals during these critical days was to start their machines. Desire for war, and fear of being caught at a disadvantage, reacted on each other." In other words, the states of Europe were playing a dangerous game of brinkmanship in the years leading up to the First World War. The problem was that the closer to the edge you get, the greater the risk that you might fall. Once that descent begins, there comes a point at which return is impossible, no matter how much you scramble to recover. After the assassination of the archduke, the statesmen of Europe quickly learned the perils of brinkmanship.

In some ways this leads to the argument that the First World War resulted from the conviction, especially among the military, that offense was predominant. This led to the fundamental belief, held across Europe, that conquest was easy (in many ways the exact opposite of Angell's view in *The Great Illusion*). Van Evera (1999: 236–7) argued, for example, that "German expansion stemmed from German security fears and from German faith in the feasibility of a quick victory in a war of conquest . . . The European arms races of 1898–1914 stemmed from security competition fueled by the cult of the offensive . . . [but these issues] would have abated or disappeared had the actual power of the defense been recognized." Yet even if the cult of the offensive existed, one would still expect that the balance of power of the multipolar system would continue to act as a deterrent.

Another explanation deals with the ineptitude of German policies in the years leading up to the conflict. Crowe, in his 1907 memorandum, noted the less than adroit foreign policies of the Germans, although he still considered Germany a threat. Perhaps more problematic than the lack of skill of the German diplomats was the continual way in which the Kaiser provoked, most likely unintentionally, the other major powers. The increase in naval power directly challenged the core of British power. This challenge was a fundamental error in German policy as "Bismarck had warned Germany to be content with land power, but his successors were neither separately or collectively Bismarcks" (Tuchman 1962: 5). The Germans additionally antagonized the Russians with their policies in Turkey and the Balkans and the French were challenged over a protectorate in Morocco. In many ways, the Kaiser felt he could "shock Britain into a friendship, believing that if he scared Britain enough, it would realize how important Germany was and the need for good relations with Germany" (Nye 2005: 71). Clearly, the British did not react as the Germans expected (or hoped).

The poor policy choices of Germany and the reactions that they created in some ways challenge the heart of the multipolar stability theory. As Gaddis noted earlier (1987: 222), "the great multipolar systems of the nineteenth century collapsed in large part because of their intricacy: they required a Metternich or Bismarck to hold them together, and when statesmen of that caliber were no longer available, they tended to come apart." In other words, multipolar systems are great at maintaining peace when everyone understands the game, the rules of the game, and plays within the context of the game. In many ways, Germany, either purposely or because of the inexperience of its leaders, did not play by the rules and this led to the collapse of the multipolar peace of late nineteenth-century Europe.

Finding the "ultimate" cause of the First World War and the failure of the multipolar system is, in many ways, a chicken-and-egg question. So many factors were overlapping and pushing the states to war it is difficult to isolate one as *the* cause. Note, however, that many of the explanations for the failure of multipolarity to produce peace rest at the state and dyadic level of analyses: German rise in power and inept foreign policy, hostility between the states, the lack of capable diplomats, and so on. Does this mean that systemic factors did not matter? No, but it highlights a point made earlier by Liska about the conditionality of the systemic effect. In other words, multipolarity produces peace in some systems because the component states fit its assumptions but, when this is not the case, the balance of power fails, as in the First World War.

Cold War aka The Long Peace

With the defeat of Hitler and fascism in 1945, the long-term prospects for peace in Europe seemed the highest in generations. Unfortunately, the confrontation between the United States and the Soviet Union had already begun and had been simmering under the surface as the Second World War drew to a close. As a consequence of the utter carnage of the Second World War, continental Europe was a wasteland and its major powers severely weakened. This meant that the evolving distribution of power rested on two pillars: the United States and the Soviet Union. Despite repeated crises between the superpowers, a Third World War never developed from their rivalry, which led many to label it "the long peace." So what effect did the bipolar distribution of power play in the stability of the post-war system?

The Second World War, in particular the attack on Pearl Harbor, left the Americans feeling vulnerable and led to a fundamental change in how they perceived their security. According to Gaddis (1987: 22), in the United States "there arose a new 'globalist' consensus among opinion-shapers both within and outside the government: that the primary American postwar interest now lay, not just in securing the Western hemisphere, but in keeping its Eastern counterpart as well free from control by a single potentially hostile power." In addition, the German invasion of the Soviet Union left their policy-makers with a new sense of vulnerability. According to Kennan (quoted in Gaddis 1987: 39fn), "security is their basic motivation . . . but they are so anxious and suspicious about it that the objective results are much the same as if the motive were aggression, indefinite expansion. They evidently seek to weaken all centers of power they cannot dominate, in order to reduce danger from any possible rival." So underlying the Cold War was a security dilemma based on perceived vulnerabilities.

The Cold War saw any number of conflicts between the Soviets and Americans that failed to start a general war. These conflicts occurred in Europe (Berlin blockade crisis of 1948–9, Berlin crisis of 1958–9, Berlin crisis of 1961), the western hemisphere (Bay of Pigs invasion of 1961, Cuban Missile Crisis of 1962), Asia (Korean War of 1950–3, Taiwan Straits crisis of 1954–5, Korean airliner incident of 1983), and Middle East (Yom Kippur War of 1973). The two sides continually fought proxy wars from Nicaragua to Angola to Afghanistan. Yet despite the inherent animosity of their relationship and the deep sense of insecurity that appeared to drive both states, peace (defined as a lack of a major war) was maintained between the Soviets and Americans.

In some ways, the development of the Cold War and the division of the world into two blocs minimized the need for the Soviets and Americans to seek a revision of the status quo. While relative gains certainly mattered to the superpowers, the risks associated with a conflict (i.e., the loss of superpower status and the benefits accrued by it) meant that both sides were relatively satisfied. Kegley and Raymond (1994: 56) note that "both superpowers found their interests served by promoting norms that circumscribed the use of force, prohibited the desertion of an ally from its bloc commitments, and supported clear lines of demarcation around spheres of influence." This status quo bias of the superpowers meant that they sought only limited gains, which bounded the crises in terms of the amount of violence a state was willing to use (would you really want to start a nuclear war to stop the Soviet invasion of Afghanistan?).

Aside from the limited nature of the revisions that each side wanted to make to the international system, the United States and the Soviets, it can be argued, actually had very little to fight over. Gaddis makes this point in his analysis of the long peace:

> The Russian–American relationship, to a remarkable degree for two nations so extensively involved with the rest of the world, has been one of mutual *in*dependence. The simple fact that they occupy opposite sides of the earth has something to do with this: geographical remoteness from one another has provided little opportunity for the emergence of irredentist grievances comparable in importance to historic disputes over, say, Alsace-Lorraine, or the Polish Corridor, or the West Bank, the Gaza Strip and Jerusalem. In the few areas where Soviet and American forces – or their proxies – have come into direct contact, they have erected artificial barriers like the Korean demilitarized zone, or the Berlin Wall, perhaps in unconscious recognition of an American poet's rather chilly precept that "good fences make good neighbors." (Gaddis 1987: 225)

So, from this perspective, the peace of the Cold War resulted from the lack of an underlying grievance that was salient enough to both sides to cause a war. If two states had nothing to fight over, it should not be surprising that they did not fight.

In some ways, these arguments are similar to the case of the First World War where the factors below the systemic level affect the nature of the system (peace or war). Yet, the question must be asked: are bipolar systems more likely to create status quo major powers, or are multipolar systems more likely to create revisionist major powers? By sheer chance alone, one would expect multipolarity to be more at risk of spawning revisionist states. This may not be problematic for the multipolar system because it would offer more avenues for balancing the rising, revisionist power. In a bipolar system, however, the options to counteract a revisionist state would be severely limited. That being noted, the limited number of options decreases the risk of miscalculation.

One of the advantages of the bipolar system of the Cold War was that both sides knew the game and had a clear understanding of the power of their opponent.[1] In fact, all states in the international system understood the balance of power between the Soviets and Americans. This clarity had a number of effects (Gaddis 1987: 221–2). First, it did not require a Bismarck to successfully manage it. Second, allied patterns tended to last longer (NATO has lasted much longer than the most durable nineteenth-century alliance). Third, even when changes in the alliances occurred, the effect on the stability of the system was minimal. So bipolarity seemed to act in a way that Waltz (1979) hypothesized, although the Cold War was also more than a bipolar system: it was a bipolar system with nuclear armed superpowers.

The development of nuclear weapons has often been used to explain the peace during the Cold War. In fact, mutually assured destruction (which occurs when both sides have secured second-strike capabilities) creates many of the same "benefits" of bipolarity. First, with the explosive increase of nuclear stockpiles in the superpowers, there was both a clarity of the enemy and a balance of power. Second, the importance of the balance of terror made changes in alliances fairly inconsequential to the Soviets and Americans. Third, mutually assured destruction (MAD) made the costs of major revisions to the status quo so prohibitive that the sides remained fairly satisfied. As a consequence of these factors, it is argued, nuclear weapons (and not bipolarity) maintained the peace between the superpowers.

Nuclear weapons acted as an emergency brake during crises between the Americans and the Soviets: the closer to the brink, the more real the risk of annihilation, the stronger the incentive to pull back from the edge. In addition, Gaddis (1987: 231) notes that this "same pessimism has provided the super-powers with powerful inducements to control crises resulting from the risk-taking of third parties. It is worth recalling that World War I grew out of the unsuccessful management of a situation neither created nor desired by any of the major actors in the international system." So not only did nuclear weapons deter the Soviets and Americans but they also forced the superpowers into proactive roles in minimizing the risky behavior of third parties.

The effect of nuclear weapons leads to a natural question: was bipolarity or nuclear deterrence the cause of the peace between the Soviets and Americans? Given that both factors occurred at basically the same time and both (theoretically) predict the same outcome, it is impossible to conclusively show one factor right and the other wrong. In some ways, it does not matter because, regardless of the effect of nuclear weapons, it appears that the Soviets and Americans acted in ways predicted by bipolar stability theory. Did other factors (lack of issues to dispute, nuclear weapons, and so on) intervene to make the relationship look stronger than it was in reality? Most likely, but, despite the alternatives, it seems that the Cold War ("long peace") was, to some extent, the result of bipolarity.

Conclusion

This chapter should have shed light on two separate questions. First, do changes in the structure of the international system affect the amount of conflict? Second, assuming an affirmative to the first question, what distribution of power in the international system leads to the greatest amount of stability (peace)? In general, it appears that the structure of the system does alter the cost and benefit calculations of states, which implies that system structure certainly matters. In terms of the second question, the answer is less clear. Perhaps the easiest answer is that all distributions of power have the potential to be stable, but the context matters in terms of both the interaction of states and the nature of the individual states. As such, to truly understand the role of polarity requires researchers to incorporate both dyadic- and state-level factors.[2]

In terms of multipolar stability, scholars have traditionally viewed the outbreak of the First World War as an indictment against the balance of power. Yet for a long time, the multiple avenues of interactions allowed for a relatively smooth balancing act between the states. As these interactions continued, the flexibility of states waned as sub-system-level effects began to alter the calculations of the major powers. For instance, Germany's ignorant belligerence pushed the British into the Triple Entente (an outcome the British did not originally want). In addition, the growing fear of war led the leadership of Europe to delegate to their militaries, which severely curtailed the time European diplomats had to secure a peaceful resolution to their crises. Eventually, the sub-system effects became large enough to overwhelm the stability effects of the multipolar system. The foreign policies of the Europeans went from flexible to brittle and the shock of the assassination of the archduke simply shattered the system.

The peace of the Cold War seems to offer substantially more evidence for bipolar stability, but questions remain. Perhaps the most difficult question revolves around the role of nuclear weapons. In particular, would the Cold War have remained cold if nuclear weapons did not exist? While this question can never be definitively answered, it certainly appears that nuclear deterrence added a layer of stability to the Soviet–American relations, especially when the risk of war was heightened during crises. Outside of the effect of nuclear weapons, however, the bipolarity still created a clear balance of power that accurately reflected the underlying distribution of power. As such, alliances were stable and, even when defections occurred, they had little impact on the overall relationship between the Americans and Soviets.

In general, two points need to be made clear in terms of the effect of system structure. First, the distribution of capabilities does affect the cost–benefit calculations of the individual states in the system, which ultimately alters how they interact. Second, how the system structure changes the behavior of states is, in many ways, determined by the nature of the states that compose the system. For instance, for a system of aggressive, unsatisfied major powers, the flexibility of multipolarity would offer the best chance of containing their bellicose nature. The ability of a multipolar system to provide various methods of balancing would be critical to maintaining peace in this situation. A bipolar system, however, would generate fewer balancing opportunities which means the system could devolve into war. So if one wants to understand the role of system structure, understanding the states becomes critical. Jervis (1997: 48) places a similar observation in the context of cause and effect when he argues that "initial behaviors and outcomes often influence later ones, producing powerful dynamics that explain change over time and that cannot be captured by labeling one set of elements 'causes' and the other 'effects.'"

7 THE RISE AND FALL OF STATES

The real cause [of the Peloponnesian War] I consider to be the one which was formally most kept out of sight. The growth of power of Athens, and the alarm which this inspired in Lacedaemon [Sparta], made war inevitable.

Thucydides, *The Peloponnesian War* (I, 23)

It is generally admitted that the present rivalry in armaments in Europe – notably such as that now in progress between Great Britain and Germany – cannot go on in its present form indefinitely . . . There are two current solutions which are offered as a means of egress from this impasse. There is that of the smaller party, regarded in both countries for the most part as dreamers and doctrinaires, who hope to solve the problem by a resort to general disarmament, or at least a limitation of armament by agreement. And there is that of the larger, commonly deemed the more practical party, who are persuaded that the present state of rivalry and recurrent irritation is bound to culminate in an armed conflict, which, by definitely reducing one or other of the parties to a position of manifest inferiority, will settle the thing for at least some time, until after a longer or shorter period a state of relatively equilibrium is established, and the whole process will be recommenced da capo.

Normal Angell, *The Great Illusion* ([1909]2007)

The previous chapters have essentially examined the onset of war from a static perspective. Whether it was the level of democracy, the ratio of power, or the systemic distribution of capabilities, the causes of war were essentially fixed. Clearly these factors change across time but analyses generally only look at the level and not how they change. This chapter remedies this myopic view by taking into account change over time. While this analysis is couched at the systemic level of analysis, it will draw heavily on the state and dyadic levels in terms of both theory and evidence. In some ways, investigating how changes in power affect international war integrates the three levels of analysis.

This chapter looks at two main ways in which changes in power in the international system affect the amount of war. First, power transition theory examines how a confrontation to the hegemon by a dissatisfied challenger leads to hegemonic war (world wars, so to speak). While this theory was originally cast to explain the major power system, further work has extended its reach in minor power (regional) hierarchies. In many ways, the classic example of power transition theory rests in the rise and fall of Germany and its challenge to British hegemony.

Changes in the distribution of power in the international system can have broader effects. It could be argued that the history of recurring global wars results from a cycle of power concentration, deconcentration, and reconcentration. These long-term global cycles affect the entire system as the major powers fight to either maintain or remake the international system. While the wars sparked by this long-term cycle are exceedingly rare, they account for about 79 per cent of casualties associated with major power conflict over the past 500 years (Thompson 1988b: 5). As such, it is critically important to understand these unlikely, but devastating, conflicts.

To garner a better understanding of how changes in power affect the risk of conflict, this chapter looks at two intriguing cases. First, the rise of Germany and its challenge to British hegemony demonstrates, on the surface, the empirical accuracy of power transition theory. The second case offers a cautionary tale in that the rise of the United States in the late nineteenth century, where it surpassed Britain in power, led to rapprochement not war. So why did a power transition lead to peace in one case and war in another? How would the long-term cycles of power shed light on these cases? What role did factors at the state and dyadic levels of analysis play?

Power transition theory

Power transition theory was developed to address the competition between a hegemon and a rising, dissatisfied challenger. While addressing only a small number of cases and states, these were arguably the most important wars to understand. Since its original explication, power transition theory has been expanded to cover regional hierarchies and changes in their power structures. In addition, the conception of satisfaction that was developed in power transition theory has been touted as an explanation of, among other things, the democratic peace.

In many ways, power transition theory centers on changes in power as opposed to the level (or balance) of power. Organski and Kugler (1980: 8) note a fairly intuitive, but previously ignored, fact that "the sources of strength and power just mentioned are not constants. They vary in slow, intricate, and, in the long run, largely predictable ways." States rise and fall in their power as populations and economies boom and bust, and changes in military technologies quickly alter the effectiveness of various militaries. Where previous research examined how the outcome of these changes affected the onset of war, power transition theory explicitly concentrates on the variation in power.

At the core of power transition theory rests the conception that a change in the balance of power between states is the ultimate source of war, i.e., similar to Thucydides' argument about the onset of the Peloponnesian War. Organski and Kugler summarize power transition when they note that

> if one nation gains significantly in power, its improved position relative to that of other nations frightens them and induces them to try to reverse this gain by war. Or, vice versa, a nation gaining on an adversary will try to make its advantage permanent by reducing its opponent by force of arms. Either way, changes in power are considered *casae belli* [sic]. (Organski and Kugler 1980: 13)

So once again the self-help anarchy of the international system forces states into a zero-sum security dilemma where changes in the balance of power spark enough fear to ignite a war.

Yet even with the anarchy of the international system, a hierarchy exists among the great powers with the hegemon at the apex. The hegemon shapes the international system to maximize its security and utility. Under the hegemon, in terms of power, rests a set of major powers that have a certain level of satisfaction with the status quo. The amount of satisfaction directly relates to their position in the hierarchy and the amount of utility that the current system provides. The set of major powers that receive benefits from the status quo that are in line with (or better) their position in the hierarchy will remain satisfied. In contrast, there exists a set of the major powers that feel aggrieved in that their benefits from the status quo are less than they expect (given their power). Eventually, a state from the set of dissatisfied, major powers will rise to challenge the hegemon for control of the international system.

So for power transition theory, the threat to the hegemon comes from a dissatisfied, rising power. Dissatisfaction and rise in power, however, are not necessarily independent events. In other words, major powers that are quickly gaining in their relative power will want more benefits from the status quo (as would be due to a more powerful state). Despite the demands of the rising power, the hegemon would be hard pressed to alter the system to transfer benefits away from the satisfied major powers to the rising power. As such, a quick and significant change in the relative power between a major power and the hegemon leads to dissatisfaction. The combination of dissatisfaction and rising challenger then generates the conditions necessary for a global war that challenges the hegemon's position. In general, power transition theory argues that "the source of war is to be found in the differences in size and rates of growth of the members of the international system" (Organski and Kugler 1980: 20).

Power transition theorists have failed, however, to arrive at a consensus as to when the war between the hegemon and challenger will occur. Organski (1958) originally argued that the challenger would initiate the war before the transition occurred (how else would one explain the two losses of Germany?). This view has been supported in Thompson's (1983) test of power transition theory. In contrast, Organski and Kugler (1980) find evidence that the challenger initiated the war after the transition occurred. To add to the confusion, Levy (1987) argues that the dominant power has the incentive to pre-empt the challenger, knowing that its position is weakening. Kugler and Zagare (1990: 263) dispute Levy's (1987) claim when they argue that power transition theory "postulates that the nature of the status quo is negative for the challenger, [and] that the challenger alone is willing to take risks." Despite the questions surrounding the exact timing of the war, all power transition theorists agree that the risk of war peaks in the period around the transition.

The power transition has a number of implications about the maintenance of peace in the international system. First, the international system is more stable when a strong hegemon can preserve order and keep states satisfied. In fact, Organski and Kugler (1980: 27) argue that "to preserve peace and security, the power distribution must be lopsided in favor of the defenders of the system and against the nations that wish to attack it." Second, the international system will be more stable when changes in the relative power are minimized, although this would be hard to sustain indefinitely. Without changes in the relative power, a dissatisfied challenger has no chance to arise and push for changes to the status quo. Finally, power transition theory argues that the challenger will attack before it surpasses the hegemon because "it is an attempt to hasten this passage [and] at the same time it is a desperate attempt on the part of the still-dominant nation to intercept the challenger's progress" (Organski and Kugler 1980: 28).

Power transition theory rests on a number of assumptions about international politics and the international system. First, and perhaps most importantly, power transition theory argues that the international system is a hierarchy as opposed to anarchy. Powerful nations are able to "create, impose and maintain a hierarchy over the weak" (Lemke and Kugler 1996: 8). This stands in stark contrast to the anarchy assumed by realists. Second, unlike the flexible alliances in the balance of power theories, power transition assumes that alliances are fairly stable across time, where the satisfied powers align with the hegemon and the dissatisfied powers coalesce around the challenger. Finally, Lemke and Kugler (1996: 9–10) note that "power transition theory identifies domestic power changes as the sources of the greatest disturbance in the international system." Often these domestic changes have resulted from the industrialization of a state, such as Germany's rise in the late nineteenth and early twentieth centuries.

Power transition theory also implies that wars occur when power is balanced (when the challenger catches up to the hegemon). This has an implication for dyadic theories in that power balances between states in a dyad should be more conflict-prone than dyads where an asymmetry exists. While power transition is not the only theory to make this claim, there certainly exists consistent empirical evidence that power preponderance in a dyad leads to fewer conflicts. Doran and Parsons (1980) found evidence in their analysis of major powers back to 1816, which was confirmed in Houweling and Siccama (1988). In addition, Kim (1989, 1992) found similar evidence even when he accounted for the possibility of third-party interventions in dyadic conflicts.[1]

While power transition theory was certainly influential, it remained essentially a theory about a small, but important, sub-set of the international system. Lemke (2002: 5) makes this point when he argues that "hopefully, those who write books about great power politics understand that they are restricting themselves." To break free from this restriction, Lemke (2002) extended the logic of power transition to minor power and regional hierarchies. Lemke (2002: 49) essentially takes "the same diagrammatic depiction of the international system, but nests smaller pyramids of power within the overall international power pyramid." So, just as there is an international hierarchy of power, there exist regional power hierarchies that experience the same dynamics as the major power hierarchy. In his tests of the multiple hierarchy model, Lemke (2002: 197) found "meaningful and empirically substantiated expectations about when both great powers and minor powers will and will not make war on one another."

Despite the empirical success of power transition theory, questions still remain as to its validity (both empirical and theoretical). First, even though Germany's rise and the subsequent world wars appear to confirm power transition, the fact remains that in neither case did Germany initiate the world wars by attacking the hegemon (United Kingdom). Second, in the late nineteenth century, the United States surpassed the British and, rather than a war, the two sides essentially made a lasting peace. Third, it remains unclear as to when the wars occur in the transition process and who actually will initiate the conflict. Finally, scholars have argued that the dominant power should become satisfied as it catches the hegemon (de Soysa, Oneal, and Park 1997) because rising in power implies success. Why would a state want to risk its accomplishments with a costly conflict? Before delving further into these issues, it is important to examine other theories that relate changes in the distribution of power to international war.

Cycles and war

Power transition theory appears to implicitly argue that periods of major wars occur in some cycle. This does not mean that regular intervals separate the peaks and valleys in international conflict; rather, the risk of war waxes and wanes in a fairly predictable manner (it correlates with the hegemon's relative power). Where power transition theory only hints at the cycles of war, a number of theories make more explicit claims about long-term patterns in international war.

The structural interpretation of major power conflicts breaks with some of the traditional assumptions about the international system. Perhaps the biggest difference is the assumption that world politics "is not characterized by the persistent randomness of anarchy assumed by classical analysts of international relations. Structures, order, rules, and some degree of regulative capability influence foreign policy behavior. To the extent that a structural set of rules affects who gets what, when, and how, systemic orders are inherently biased. Some actors win (lose) more than others" (Thompson 1988b: 14). Moving from a conceptualization of the international system as anarchic to one which is hierarchic alters how states would interact. Waltz (1979) argues that only the distribution of capabilities changes across time, which means it is able to explain changes in the amount of conflict since the other aspects of the system are constant. If the level of anarchy, or hierarchy, changes across time, then not only will the level of hierarchy affect the amount of conflict but the explanatory power of the distribution of capabilities has been exaggerated.

Similar to power transition theory, Gilpin (1981) argues that the risk of war peaks when changes in the distribution of power undermine the foundation of the current international system. Where power transition theory emphasizes the hegemon (or at most regional powers), Gilpin's analysis broadens to include virtually all of the international system (although he is clearly most concerned with the major powers). When the structure that maintains the international system becomes fragile enough, states will engage in territorial, political, and/or economic expansion until the marginal costs exceed the marginal benefits. Ultimately this process could develop a state with both the interest and capability to remake the international system for their benefit.

Gilpin (1981) clearly places his argument within the context of classic realist beliefs about the international system. Gilpin (1981: 7) assumes that "the fundamental nature of international relations has not changed over the millennia. International relations continue to be a recurring struggle for wealth and power among independent actors in a state of anarchy." Despite such congruence in the underlying beliefs, Gilpin explicitly accounts for changes in the international system, whereas most realists concentrate on the static aspects of the system structure. This does not mean that Gilpin argues that the system is in a constant state of flux. In fact, the first assumption of Gilpin's theory describes when the system will be stable: "an international system is stable (i.e., in a state of equilibrium) if no state believes it profitable to attempt to change the system" (Gilpin 1981: 10).

While international systems may remain stable for long periods of time, it is almost inevitable that change will occur. Gilpin (1981: 50) provides the motivation for change in his second assumption: "a state will attempt to change the international system if the expected benefits exceed the expected costs (i.e., if there is an expected net gain)." Thus, states continually search for ways to improve their position in the international system. When the costs associated with an attempt to change the system exceed the expected benefits, states would rationally accept the status quo. The high cost/low benefit scenario explains the stability of systems in equilibrium without having to assume that states stop competing in these systems.

The international system moves out of equilibrium when states begin to believe that the benefits of change exceed the costs. This change can derive from two sources: the state may expect an increase in future benefits or a decrease in future costs. It is also important to understand that the expected benefits and costs from change (or no change) derive from the beliefs of the state and "the notion that a state will seek to change the system if the expected benefits exceed the expected costs does not mean that the benefits will in fact exceed the costs" (Gilpin 1981: 52). In other words, states act on their beliefs, which may or may not accurately reflect reality.

Once the balance shifts and states have positive and expected net benefits from change, the process will not continue indefinitely. Gilpin (1981: 106) argues that "a state will seek to change the international system through territorial, political, and economic expansion until the marginal costs of further change are equal to or greater than the marginal benefits." Gilpin is essentially arguing both that states continue to make rational calculations and that each change to the international system alters the costs and benefits associated with future change. In many ways, Gilpin argues that states experience decreasing marginal returns to changes in the international system, i.e., each successive alteration of the system provides fewer benefits than previous changes. Ultimately, the benefits from additional change equal, or fall below, the costs of the change and the system once again reaches equilibrium.

Once the costs and benefits of change reach equilibrium, it does not guarantee stability. Gilpin's (1981: 156) fourth assumption argues that "once an equilibrium between the costs and benefits of further change and expansion is reached, the tendency is for the economic costs of maintaining the status quo to rise faster than the economic capacity to support the status quo." In other words, states that wish to maintain the status quo have to pay a cost which tends to rise faster than their capacity to pay the cost. In many ways, this is similar to power transition where a challenger has arisen and altered some aspects of the status quo. In such a scenario, the satisfied power, and the hegemon in particular, are required to pay ever increasing costs to maintain the current structure of the international system.

While the hegemon and satisfied major powers may be able to maintain the status quo in the face of a rising challenger, this situation is inherently untenable. Gilpin's (1981: 186) fifth and final assumption addresses this situation: "if the disequilibrium in the international system is not resolved, then the system will be changed, and a new equilibrium reflecting the redistribution of power will be established." So the status quo powers either have to find a way to maintain the system or face a war against the challenger(s), although it would be quite difficult as "the power base on which the governance of the system ultimately rests has eroded because of differential growth and development among states" (Gilpin 1981: 186). The challenge to the system will either reinforce the old equilibrium by defeating the challenger(s), or instigate a reordering of the system and the establishment of a new order.

Whereas Gilpin explicitly breaks with the assumption of anarchy, Modelski (1970, 1972) argues that the world is basically anarchic with no state capable of ruling the international system. This does not mean that anarchy is always the same in that "Modelski is quick to point out that the absence of a world state or empire does not preclude the existence of some form of political organization or order. That is to say, one may still have a political system whether or not one has a specific and concrete legal framework of centralized authority or sovereignty" (Thompson 1988b: 45). In addition, Modelski breaks with classical realists in that he argues that the international system has three separate structures: the global political system, the world economy, and the world cultural sub-system.

The international system fluctuates in terms of the amount of control that a state (or group of states) can exert. It can range from control by "a single powerful state [to a control] shared among several units or simply not attempted in a situation bordering on anarchy" (Thompson 1988b: 46). According to Modelski, it is the movement between these degrees of management that affect the amount of conflict. In broad terms, the system begins with a global war that sets the structure of the international system, which is managed by a single, dominant state. The position of the dominant power deteriorates over time, which gives rise to multipolarity. Eventually the system drifts toward anarchy at which point a new global war occurs after which a new global order is established. Modelski labels these stages as (1) global war, (2) world power, (3) delegitimation, and (4) deconcentration.

In many ways, Modelski sees global war (and its associated long cycles) as creative destruction in the international system. In particular, global war is a decision point for the international system.

> It is noteworthy, however, that its function is not that of global war as such, but rather a more generalized one of systemic decision-making – an opportunity for a political system to make a decisive choice, one that

> commits the global system on two crucial points: (1) the character of its political leadership and the occupancy of its chief offices, and (2) the priority program of public policy for global problems to which the global system (although not really the world as a whole) will be committed for the next two or three generations. (Modelski 1987: 125–6)

Just as competition in capitalism destroys inefficient companies by more efficient ones (creative destruction), the competition of the international system uses global war to replace inefficient global orders with ones that better reflect the underlying distribution of power.

Underlying all of the above theories is the importance of change across time. In particular, change in the distribution of capabilities is, in many ways, the inexorable, underlying cause of war. In power transition theory, the rise of the dissatisfied, major power sparks a hegemonic war. For Gilpin, the inevitable inability of the dominant power to maintain control of the system sparks international conflict. Finally, global war for Modelski acts to rebalance the management of the system when the old system no longer reflects reality. Given the importance of change, what are its fundamental causes?

The inevitability of changes in the distribution of power

In all of the previous theories, changes in the power of states act as the critical catalyst that alters the international system. The rising power of a dissatisfied challenger sparks hegemonic war in power transition theory. The slow deterioration of the hegemon's relative power alters the cost–benefit analyses of states according to Gilpin and/or delegitimizes the international order according to Modelski. While the ebb or flow of relative power appears quite natural and inevitable, what are the underlying factors that lead to the fluctuations?

According to Organski and Kugler (1980), state power remains rooted in the demographic resources available to a state modified by its level of development. So the most powerful states would be populous, resource rich, and economically developed, and the least powerful states would be small, resource sparse, and economically undeveloped. At the heart of the differences in power between states, when one factors out the sheer size of populations and resource endowments, is the level of development. As Organski and Kugler (1980: 20) note, "most important are economic productivity and the efficiency of the political system in extracting and aggregating human and material resources into pools available for national purposes."

In the long run, state power will be virtually identical to its demographic characteristics such as population and resource endowment. The long run, however, assumes that all states have identical levels of development and capacities to pool resources for national purposes. In reality, the long run may never occur but in the short run two facts remain.[2] First, development has a limit that states move toward asymptotically. Those states that have reached the plateau in development have gone through a "power transition" and are at "power maturity." Second, the level of development is negatively correlated with the rate of development (the more developed the state, the slower the rate of change). The implication is that states have spurts in the development process that cause rapid changes in relative power. In addition, the dominant states will be those that have already developed and are less likely to experience rapid growth. The challenging states, however, are generally in the process of growing rapidly.

It seems evident from Organski and Kugler's (1980) argument that only a sub-set of states have the innate capacity to become major powers or challengers to the status quo. In fact, "it is obvious that capacity to disturb the equilibrium of the system is largely dependent on the base from which the country begins. The full development of Guatemala, Costa Rica, or Albania will pass unnoticed, for these countries are small; but if India or Indonesia begins to modernize in earnest, the effects of such events will inevitably shake up the international power distributions" (Organski and Kugler 1980: 20–1). In addition, the speed of the transition matters in that faster transitions allow less time for the system to adjust and thus create a greater risk of conflict.

Gilpin (1981) has a similar view as to why power changes across time. Where Organski and Kugler (1980) focus mainly on the role of economic development, Gilpin's (1981) explanation is a little broader. Gilpin (1981: 13) argues that there "is a tendency in an international system for the powers of member states to change at different rates because of political, economic, and technological developments." This view of power growth offers a little more agency in the process as states can purposely work on technology that will increase their rate of growth. In addition, exogenous (random) shocks may also cause dramatic shifts in power. For example, before the use of oil in engines, the oil reserves of Saudi Arabia gave it little power. If a new source of power were discovered tomorrow that made the "oil economy" obsolete, then it would gravely affect the relative power of Saudi Arabia (among other states).

Modelski's view of power differs slightly from the previous theories, although they are not mutually exclusive. The problem for the dominant power is that maintaining the international system requires resources. These resources could have been used in more productive areas that would generate long-term growth but instead are spent on maintaining the international order. All other states can reap the benefits from the international order without having to dedicate resources to its maintenance. As such, they can dedicate more of their resources to more productive endeavors. In the long run, this means that "order tends to deteriorate over time" (Thompson 1988b: 49).

The rise of Germany and the fall of the United Kingdom

The second half of the nineteenth century saw the rise of two powers that challenged British dominance of the international system: the United States and Germany. These power transitions, and the subsequent diffusion of power, led the British into conflict with the Germans but peace with the United States. How does power transition theory account for the divergent outcomes? Are the conflicts, and peace, associated with these power transitions better explained by hegemonic stability theory or long cycles? To answer these questions, it is useful to start with the dog that barked: the United Kingdom–Germany power transition.

As Organski and Kugler (1980) argue, the rise of British hegemony was entwined with its industrialization just as the German challenge coincided with its industrialization in the late nineteenth century. By the time Germany began its move, the British had already reached a relative plateau. As such, the second half of the nineteenth century saw the balance of power between the British and Germans move toward equality and then ultimately in favor of the Germans. Perhaps most frightening to the British was how the Germans translated their growing economic clout into military power. In particular, the United Kingdom felt acutely worried about the rising power of the German navy.

The Germans, however, never felt that their naval program directly threatened the British (at least not in the same way as the British). Professor von Schulze-Gaevernitz argued that:

We want our [i.e., Germany's] navy in order to confine the commercial rivalry of England within innocuous limits, and deter the sober sense of the English people from the extremely threatening thought of attack upon us . . . The German navy is a condition of our bare existence and independence, like the daily bread on which we depend, not only for ourselves, but for our children. (As quoted in Angell [1909]2007: 120)

So from the German perspective, the navy was defensive in nature and needed as an instrument to secure German sovereignty from British threats. The British, however, perceived the growing German navy in a completely different manner. According to Frederic Harrison, previously a pro-peace British philosopher, a surpassing by the Germans would lead to:

famine, social anarchy, [and] incalculable chaos in the industrial and financial world . . . Britain may live on . . . but before she began to live freely again she would have to lose half her population, which she could not feed, and all her overseas Empire, which she could not defend . . . How idle are fine words about retrenchment, peace and brotherhood, whilst we lie open to the risk of unutterable ruin, to a deadly fight for national existence, to war in its most destructive and cruel form. (As quoted in Angell [1909]2007: 120)

So, like the Germans, the British felt that their sovereignty depended on the outcome of the German naval program. Unlike the Germans, however, British survival depended upon the failure of German expansion.

It is important to note that the change in relative power in this case was certainly driven by the rapid economic development of Germany, which supports the argument of power transition theory. Yet the expansion of the German economy in and of itself was not the root cause of the growing hostility of the British. What seems most problematic from the British perspective was the way in which the Germans translated their economic power into military power: naval expansion. Writing the year before the outbreak of the First World War, Hurd and Castle (1913: vii) argued that

to many political prophets we appear to have reached the opening phase of a long struggle which will decide whether British or German civilization is to dominate the world in the future. This Anglo-German antagonism finds its most acute expression in naval policy, and it is believed in many quarters that the struggle will eventually be decided by naval combat.

While the Germans claimed that their naval expansion was defensive in nature, it still struck at the heart of Britain's last line of defense. Without absolute control of the seas, the island nation had a starkly different sense of security.

The expansion of the German navy did not lead it to necessarily surpass the British but the relative balance of forces was slipping away from the British. For instance, from the years 1897 to 1906, the British averaged the production of 3 battleships and 6 destroyers a year compared to German production of 2 battleships and 5 destroyers. From 1905 to 1913 (known as the Dreadnought period), British production was increased to 5 battleships and 16 destroyers a year as Germany boosted its production to 3.5 battleships and 12 destroyers a year. While these numbers seem to indicate continued British dominance, it must be noted that the United Kingdom needed to spread its forces across the globe but the Germans could focus their navy on the seas around Britain. Perhaps more striking than the number of ships is the expenditure on naval production. British naval expenditure went from £34,872,299 in 1901 to £47,021,636 in 1913 (a 35 percent increase). German production, however, shot from £9,530,000 in 1901 to £22,876,675 in 1913 (a 140 percent increase).[3]

While the build-up of German arms stoked fears in the United Kingdom, it remains unclear as to why the Germans insisted on forcing the issue to the point of alienating the British. In many ways, the military culture in the rising Germany limited its ability to understand its effect on opposing states. Unlike most armed forces that are tasked to defend the state from outside enemies, "the (Prussian) army's most important task after 1815 was [the] defense of the monarchy against its internal political enemies, and later national consolidation and definition" (Hull 2005: 103). This meant that domestic political authority flowed through the military, which helps explain the German monarchy's obsession with their image as military men. According to Hull (2005: 104), "both Kaiser Wilhelm I and his grandson, Wilhelm II, conceived of themselves as military men, appearing in public exclusively in uniform. They cultivated strong personal relations with the members of the officer corps, and Wilhelm II (ruled 1888–1918) surrounded himself with military advisers."

The militarism of Germany expanded significantly in the 1880s and 1890s as it coalesced around colonial politics. The late nineteenth century saw the development of both the Pan-Germanic League and the Navy League, which, along with the Army League, pushed for the expansion and consolidation of German power and influence. The Navy League, in particular, would push German foreign policies into direct conflict with the British. Hull (2005: 105) noted that the Navy League, "the largest and best founded group, was founded surreptitiously by the government to whip up popular support for the new instrument of *Weltpolitik*, the navy." Ultimately, the militarism of the government even turned its opponents in the Reichstag into supporters as a result of the revolts in Southwest Africa in 1904–5. This transformation of the Center Party and Left Liberals "was a profound political transformation, for it brought a much larger spectrum of liberal, bourgeois opinion into the government camp than had ever before been possible" (Hull 2005: 106).

So the industrialization of Germany led to a massive increase in its economic capabilities that it then translated into military capabilities to unify and expand the state. Part and parcel of the expansion of the German military was a rise in militarism among the population that increasingly saw the development of the navy as the next logical step. As the Germans expanded their naval capabilities, they never really surpassed the British but managed to instigate an almost impossible security dilemma. Unlike the German navy, which Churchill referred to as a "luxury fleet" in 1912, the British navy was absolutely vital to the defense of the United Kingdom. Tuchman noted the set of incredible responsibilities of the British navy:

> The British Empire could not survive naval defeat or even loss of naval supremacy through individual ship losses. Its tasks were enormous. It had to prevent invasion of the British Isles; it had to escort the BEF safely to the Continent; it had to bring home troops from India to add to the Regular Army and replace them with Territorials; above all, it had to safeguard seaborne commerce over all the oceans of the world. (Tuchman 1962: 325)

Given the enormity of its duties, the British navy had little room for error and its supremacy of the seas was *the* most salient issue for the British. As such, the development of a significant naval force, such as the German "luxury fleet," that could limit British naval supremacy was an issue about which Britain could not, and would never, compromise.

So as one would expect, power transition theory generally comports with the rise of Germany and its challenge to the dominance of Great Britain. In addition, as power transition predicts, the growth of Germany related to its industrialization, which was then used to increase its military capabilities. What remains difficult for power transition theory to explain is the source of the "dissatisfaction" of

Germany. According to the theory, Germany's quick rise would lead to dissatisfaction as it felt it deserved more benefits from the status quo. While Germany certainly acted to alter the status quo, it seemed more driven by internal domestic factors as opposed to an inherent dissatisfaction with the international status quo.

Perhaps most problematic for power transition theory was the role that the naval arms race played in generating the conflict between the British and the Germans. In many ways, power transition theory would predict that the Germans would build their navy to directly challenge the British, although it seems clear that domestic politics played a large role in the decision to expand the navy. It just so happened that the navy was the straw that would break the camel's back. If the Germans had refrained from expanding their navy and used those resources for the army, would the rise of Germany have generated the same response from the British? Would a compromise have been possible? While we can never definitively answer that counterfactual, the power transition between the United States and the United Kingdom may shed some light on the issue.

The American power transition

The nineteenth century saw dramatic changes in the relations between the United States and Great Britain. The century began essentially as the revolutionary war ended and the war of 1812 began. By the end of the century, however, the belligerents managed to bury the hatchet, so to speak, with a far-ranging rapprochement. For instance, during the Spanish–American War, the Germans wanted the Americans to relinquish either Hawaii or Samoa but this was resisted by the British who went as far as to applaud American annexation of the Philippines. Beisner summarizes the new relations when he quotes an exchange between two government officials:

> Britain's colonial secretary Joseph Chamberlain wrote John Hay in 1898: "I should rejoice in an occasion which we could fight side by side. The good effect of it would last generations." And Hay, by then secretary of state, remarked a year later: "As long as I stay here, no action shall be taken contrary to my conviction that the indispensable feature of our foreign policy should be a friendly understanding with England." (Beisner 1986: 142)

While states make peace fairly often, the rapprochement between the United States and United Kingdom is astounding in that it occurred as the United States surpassed the British in terms of power. Rather than sparking a hegemonic war, it instigated over 100 years of peace (and counting).

The growth of American power, like the growth of Germany, was based on the economic transition from an agrarian to an industrialized economy (although the United States maintained a larger agricultural base than Germany). From 1869 to 1901, a period of 32 years, the American economy quadrupled from $9.11 billion to $37.1 billion. Included in this expansion was a tripling of the gross farm product from $1.484 billion in 1860 to $3.799 billion in 1900. Accompanying the economic growth was a concomitant spread of industrial infrastructure. For instance, in 1865 the United States had 35,085 miles of railway and this exploded into 250,143 miles in 1899. Finally, the manufacturing production index started at 17 in 1865 and rose to 100 by 1900.[4]

The economic expansion naturally led to a growth in American exports. In 1865, total American exports were about $281 million, which grew to $1.394 billion in 1900. Most of the expansion in trade was with states across the Atlantic. For instance, from 1865 to 1900, exports to the United Kingdom went from $103 million to $534 million. In addition, exports to Germany and France grew from $20 million and $11 million to $187 million and $83 million, respectively. As a result of such astounding expansion, Campbell (1976: 86) notes that "commercial expansion in the New World, in Europe, and even in darkest Africa and little known areas in Asia was an important objective of United States foreign policy."

Given such an expansion in exports, it would make sense that American foreign policies would alter to reflect the increased importance of trade. In the case of Germany, Angell ([1909]2007: 120) notes that the increasing importance of trade meant the development of a large navy. It makes perfect sense that a state would increase its navy to protect its international trading interests. One would expect the incentive for the Americans to increase their navy would be stronger, given that most of their trading partners were an ocean away. Yet even by 1884, 11 other nations had more naval vessels than the United States, which sparked the later Secretary of the Navy John D. Long to remark in 1885 that the American navy was "an alphabet of floating wash-tubs" (as quoted in Beisner 1986: 8).

The United States did, however, begin a modest refurbishment program in the 1880s, which quickened its pace in the 1890s. While the "new" American navy had notable success against the Spanish at the naval battles in Manila Bay and off Cuba, it remained sub-par.

For instance, Beisner (1986: 8) noted that in "1884 a ship ordered to Nicaragua during the Corinto Affair . . . had sunk ignominiously en route, and on the eve of war in 1898 the navy possessed only eight heavily armored ships, none of which met the European standard for 'battleship.'" The 1890s, however, still marked a turning point in the history of the American navy. In 1889, the secretary of the navy (Benjamin F. Tracy) wrote in his annual report that "to carry on even a defensive war with any hope of success we must have armored battleships . . . We must have the force to raise blockades . . . we must be able to divert an enemy's force from our coast by threatening his own, for a war, though defensive in principle, may be conducted most efficiently by being offensive in its operations" (as quoted in Campbell 1976: 158). This report, among other factors, led Congress in 1890 to authorize the construction of three coastline battleships.

The growth of the United States and its power transition occurred in a context in which it did not directly challenge the heart of British hegemony (its navy). This obviously stands in stark contrast to the Germans who seemed to go out of their way to transform economic power into naval power. In many ways, the rise of the United States was the rise of a commercial power (perhaps what Rosecrance (1986) would call a trading state) and not a military power, although the United States clearly saw its role in the world as having changed and acted in ways to make itself into a military power. Beisner (1986: 89) quotes Assistant Secretary of State John Bassett Moore who wrote in 1899 that the United States had moved "from a position of comparative freedom from entanglements into the position of what is commonly called a world power . . . Where formerly we had only commercial interests, we now have territorial and political interests as well." Fortunately for the British and Americans, this transformation occurred slowly and in a manner that did not directly conflict with British interests.

Despite the lack of a "luxury fleet" of German strength, the growth of American commercial power did coincide with a more aggressive foreign policy. Beisner (1986: 95) notes that (by the end of the nineteenth century) "once wedded to noninterventionism, Americans now put their oar in waters everywhere – in Samoa, Chile, Hawaii, Brazil, Nicaragua, Venezuela, Cuba, Puerto Rico, the Philippines, and China." This stands in stark contrast to the America of Washington's Farewell Address, who wanted the United States to act as a beacon on a hill. This expansive view of American interests also coincided with a growing sense of American territorial expansion. As Commodore Dewey rested in Manila Bay after defeating the Spanish in 1898,

Senator Henry Cabot Lodge argued that "we hold the other side of the Pacific and the value to this country is almost beyond imagination" (as quoted in Campbell 1976: 282).

American views on territorial expansion appeared based not simply on cost–benefit calculations, but also on a new sense of entitlement. Campbell (1976: 286) provides quotes from a number of American senators that reflect the growing view of America's right place in the international community. Senator Marcus A. Hanna argued that "the time has come when we must take our place in the Orient . . . We are bound to share in the commerce of the Far East, and it is better to strike for it while the iron is hot." These views were reflected by the Chairman of the Senate Foreign Relations Committee, Cushman K. Davis, who argued that "providence has stepped in to point the future course for us. We must police the Pacific Ocean!" These statements actually appear more bellicose than many of the arguments of the Germans, who felt almost on the defensive versus Great Britain.

Despite the rhetoric of American politicians, the actions of the American military, and the continuing rise of American power, the British remained calm. In fact, an editorial in the *Spectator* (a British paper) noted that "the United States is the one Power with which we could enter into an arbitration treaty with perfect confidence. She is neither aggressive or acquisitive . . . The United States may be described as a satisfied nation" (as quoted in Perkins 1968: 241). Clearly this perspective explains the ability of the Americans and British to achieve a rapprochement. In addition, it seems to comport with power transition theory that a *dissatisfied* rising power provoked a hostile British response while the (as perceived by the British) satisfied rising power reached a negotiated solution. In fact, Lewis Einstein, an American diplomat, noted that "in every region of the world we find similarity in our political interests . . . and the reason is unquestionably because England, with the greatest colonial empire the world has yet witnessed, can seek only to preserve her birthright and not expand it further" (as quoted in Perkins 1968: 242).

This perception that the British and Americans shared an interest in the status quo did not extend to the American perception of the Germans. Like the British, the Americans feared the expansion of Germany. For instance, Professor Roland G. Usher wrote *Pan Germanism* in 1913, where he argued that "the Germans aim at nothing less than the domination of Europe and the world" (as quoted in Perkins 1968: 242). So quite ironically, as the Americans expanded their reach across the globe and surpassed the British, it was Germany that became labeled as the revisionist challenger on both sides of the

Atlantic. This shared view of the Germans probably reinforced the perception that American and British interests coincided.

In many ways, at the time of the rapprochement with the United States, the British position had weakened considerably (perhaps the deconcentration phase of Modelski). With her power waning and threats multiplying, Britain could not fight everywhere and everyone. As such, it made sense to reach an accommodation with some of the challengers so as to concentrate on the larger perceived threats. As Campbell (1957: 26) notes, the British precarious position related to "her anxieties as to the Chinese market, her involvement with France, her concern about Russia, her fear of Germany. Amidst such perils she could not afford to alienate America."

Conclusions

This chapter attempts to answer a fundamental question about the role of power in international politics: how do changes in the distribution of power affect the likelihood of war? In general, the theoretical arguments all point to power changes (or transitions) as being periods of heightened risk. For power transition theory, the key remains the transition between the dominant power (global or regional) and a rising dissatisfied challenger. Both Gilpin and Modelski offer similar, but more general, views. For their models, the movement from a system characterized by power concentration toward one with a more equitable distribution alters the incentives of states, which leads to challenges to the status quo and war.

The nineteenth century saw the rise of two critical challenges to British dominance and most likely reflects the deconcentration of power. As expected, the rapid growth of Germany and the United States resulted from economic transitions as these states moved from agrarian to industrial economies. Germany and the United States diverged, however, in how the British viewed the challengers. The Germans were clearly seen as being dissatisfied and a direct (and mortal) threat to British security. The United States, in contrast, both shared the English view of the Germans and was perceived by the British as being generally satisfied with the status quo. As a result, the predicted hegemonic war occurred between the United Kingdom and Germany, i.e., the hegemon and the rising, dissatisfied challenger.

The cases show both the limits and strength of power transition theory. Perhaps one of the biggest weaknesses rests on the assumption that the hegemon faces only one challenger at a time. Yet given that the source of the changing distribution of power is domestic economic transitions, why would we expect this to occur sequentially? In fact, economic transitions are probably linked in that they occur in clusters across time and are then followed by periods of relative calm. In this case, we would expect that the hegemon would almost always face multiple challengers. We certainly see this with the case of the British who had to contend with both the United States and Germany. The United States may face a similar situation in the twenty-first century as it may have to contend with the European Union, India, China, and perhaps a resurgent Russia or rapidly developing Brazil. In these cases, a rational hegemon would reach accommodation with some challengers to better fend off others.

While power transition theory seemed correct in arguing that dissatisfied powers are most dangerous for international peace, the cases of the United States and Germany indicate that much of the "dissatisfaction" comes from domestic politics. It was mainly for domestic political reasons and not out of a sense of insecurity that the Germans pushed their naval expansion, although both clearly mattered. In terms of the United States, the growing sense of entitlement among the population made expansionist policies both more feasible and likely. These examples do, however, confirm the argument of power transition theory that the power transition itself alters the level of satisfaction within a state. It seems highly unlikely, for instance, that the United States would not have had a growing sense of entitlement if it had remained weak and undeveloped.

Finally, the cases demonstrate that how the rising power translates economic power into military power matters more than power transition theory originally argued. The German naval expansion appears to have caused more consternation in the United Kingdom than any American military expansion. This obviously occurred because the German program more directly threatened the heart of British security. In addition, it may be the case that, despite its global empire, the United Kingdom was still a regional (European) hegemon. As such, a growing challenger at the heart of its region was more important than the rise of a regional power an ocean away.

PART IV CHANGES AND CONCLUSION

8 CONFLICT WITH NON-STATE ACTORS

In guerilla warfare, select the tactic of seeming to come from the east and attacking from the west; avoid the solid, attack the hollow; withdraw; deliver a lightning blow, seek a lightning decision. When guerillas engage a stronger enemy, they withdraw when he advances; harass him when he stops; strike him when he is weary; pursue him when he withdraws. In guerilla strategy, the enemy's rear, flanks, and other vulnerable spots are his vital points, and there he must be harassed, attacked, dispersed, exhausted, and annihilated.

Mao Tse-tung, *On Guerrilla Warfare*

The world knows the full evil and capability of international terrorism which menaces the whole of the democratic world. The terrorists responsible have no sense of humanity, of mercy, or of justice. To commit acts of this nature requires a fanaticism and wickedness that is beyond our normal contemplation.

Prime Minister Tony Blair, September 12, 2001

It is very strange for Americans and other educated people to talk about the killing of innocent civilians. I mean, who said that our children and civilians are not innocents, and that the shedding of their blood is permissible? Whenever we kill their civilians, the whole world yells at us from east to west, and America starts putting pressure on its allies and puppets. Who said that our blood isn't blood and that their blood is blood? What about the people that have been killed in our lands for decades?

Osama bin Laden, October 21, 2001

The previous chapters paint a state-centric view of war but states often have violent engagements with non-state actors. The non-state actors can be broadly grouped into purely domestic in nature or transnational. When domestic groups fight the state, it is often characterized as a civil war. Recently, however, we have seen states having conflicts with transnational groups, i.e., Israel versus Hezbollah or United States versus al-Qaeda. These wars, while similar to the interstate conflicts described above, have many divergent characteristics. This chapter highlights these similarities and differences.

The international system contains more than states and rebels and recent events continue to highlight the growing role of non-state actors. In fact, the "war on terror" and Israel's recent engagements with Hezbollah highlight the renewed importance of transnational groups. While the effect of transnational actors is not unique (see the *Condotierri* of Renaissance Italy, the Ismaili Assassins, or Thuggee Cult of Kali for historic examples), they seem to have taken on additional importance in the twenty-first century. For instance, the *Condotierri* of Renaissance Italy were mercenary bands of warriors that sold their services to the highest bidders. The Assassins were a well-trained religious sect in the Middle East that both fought states to take control of territory and sold their services to the highest bidder. Finally, the Thuggee were a religious sect in India that would abduct and sacrifice travelers to Kali and ended up killing over one million individuals over a couple of centuries.

Conflicts with these transnational organizations differ from interstate wars in two main ways. First, transnational organizations often require either the support of a state, or a region outside the control of a state, to establish a central base of operation. For instance, al-Qaeda first used Afghanistan, with the explicit support of the Taliban, as a safe haven. When the Taliban were removed from power, al-Qaeda was forced to seek a new center of operations and have apparently settled on the lightly governed tribal regions of Pakistan. Second, transnational organizations have fairly diffuse (cellular) organizational structures, especially as their geographic reach increases. This makes decisive defeats difficult as the elimination of one cell has a minimal impact on the rest of the organization. In fact, even a successful strike at the leadership would still leave the cells unscathed, although they would clearly have a diminished capacity to coordinate. As with civil wars, these differences make wars against transnational actors different from interstate conflicts. In particular, these conflicts tend to be drawn out, often involve the use of terrorism, and are targeted against regional (Israel) or global (United States) powers.

Understanding civil wars

Recent scholarship has discerned two main causes of civil wars: greed and grievance. The argument for grievance is perhaps the most intuitive, where a group within a state develops a certain level of dissatisfaction with the government and then uses violence to effect change. The exact nature of the grievance matters less than its ability to mobilize the population and the government's inability (or unwillingness) to adequately alleviate the perceived injustice. Collier and Hoeffler (1998, 2002, 2004) dispute this stylized depiction of civil war onset. According to Collier and Hoeffler, all states at all times have some portion of the population that has a grievance with the government. Despite the ubiquity of grievances, civil wars are relatively rare. So what explains why some grievances lead to civil wars and other grievances are peacefully addressed? Greed.

According to Collier and Hoeffler (1998, 2002, 2004), greed simply represents the opportunity to rebel. For instance, a group could have tremendous grievances, but if they do not have the weapons, money, or time to fight, then one would not expect a civil war to occur. At its most basic level, the greed argument stipulates that rebellions only occur where (and when) it is profitable. Without the possibility of profit, rebel movements would not have the resources that they require to adequately fight the government. According to Collier and Hoeffler (1998, 2002, 2004), the best gauge of the possible profitability of a civil war is the presence of natural resources.

The natural resource wealth of a state provides rebel groups with the capacity to make rebellion profitable through looting. While most natural resources can be looted to some extent, the ones most often tied to rebellion are oil, diamonds, and mineral wealth (although agriculture may additionally provide rebels with looting possibilities). What makes natural resources lootable is the ability of the rebels to take physical possession of the territory that contains the resources. Once they obtain the physical possession of the resource, they can sell it for the money needed to recruit and supply their soldiers.

While theoretically the greed and grievance explanations appear fairly distinct, measuring the two aspects is more problematic. For instance, Collier and Hoeffler (2004) use economic growth as a measure of greed, but negative economic growth could also act as a source of grievance. Because it is not always obvious whether a resource is lootable, tests of the greed argument need to rely on proxies. As noted above, these proxies may also represent grievances, which limits the conclusions that one can draw from the statistical analyses. Even the theoretical arguments about the role of greed straddle the line. For instance, Ross (2003: 19) argues that "resource dependence tends to make countries more susceptible to civil war through two economic effects: a reduction in growth and increase in poverty." Both of these paths to civil war could easily be argued as sources of grievances and not an indication of the greed effect.

Despite the problems with measuring aspects of the greed argument, there certainly appears to be a relationship between lootable resources (in the form of natural resources) and civil war. For instance, Bannon and Collier (2003: 5) show that the states with double the average natural resource endowment have a 3 percent risk (a year) of an ideology-based civil war but a whopping 8 percent risk of a secessionist war. When a state does not have oil, the odds that its civil war is secessionist are 68 percent, but this jumps to 100 percent if a state contains oil resources. Why would natural resources make secessionist civil wars so much more likely? As Bannon and Collier note:

> in most societies, wherever a valuable resource is discovered, some particular ethnic group is living on top of it and has an incentive to assert its rights to secede. All ethnically differentiated societies have a few romantics who dream of creating an ethnically "pure" political entity, but the discovery of resources has the potential to transform such movements from the romantic fringe into an effective and violent secessionist movement. (Bannon and Collier 2003: 5–6)

In many ways, the greed argument has little to do with greed and more to do with the capacity of the rebels to sustain relevance. In particular, financing a rebel movement, especially one meant to challenge the state, is costly and requires a recurring source of income. So for Collier and Hoeffler (1998, 2002, 2004), natural resources represent aspects of a state's wealth that are readily lootable, which means that they could be used to maintain an armed resistance. Ross points out that

> there are hundreds, perhaps thousands, of rebel organizations around the world at any given time. Yet only a handful grow large enough to challenge the armed forces of a sovereign government. Why are these groups successful, while most other groups fail?
>
> There is good evidence that rebel financing is a large part of the answer. To assemble and sustain a fighting force of hundreds or thousands of soldiers, a rebel group needs a regular source of income. Before

the end of the cold war, successful rebel groups in the developing world typically were financed by one of the great powers. Since the cold war ended, insurgent groups have been forced to find other ways to bankroll themselves; many have turned to the natural resource sector. (Ross 2003: 30)

So while Collier and Hoeffler (1998, 2002, 2004) label this as greed, it is more about rebel groups that have access to regular finances which grant them a greater capacity to resist the state and so they are more likely to begin (and sustain) a civil war.

Regardless of the ultimate theoretical reason, recent history has demonstrated a propensity of rebel groups to use natural resources to fund their activities (see Ross (2003) for a more detailed review). In Angola, UNITA sold hundreds of millions of dollars (at least) of diamonds (Le Billion 1999). The Northern Alliance in Afghanistan funded itself through selling $40 to $60 million a year of lapis lazuli (Rubin 2000). In the 1970s and 1980s, groups in Myanmar maintained themselves through selling jadeite, opium, rubies, sapphires, and timber (Lintner 1999). The Khmer Rouge in Cambodia sold $120 million to $240 million a year of rubies and timber (Brown and Zasloff 1998; Le Billion 2000). Rebels in the Democratic Republic of Congo have sold coffee, coltan, diamonds, gold, and timber to generate funds (UN Panel of Experts 2001). Charles Taylor's National Patriotic Front of Liberia made about $75 million a year in sales of cannabis, diamonds, iron ore, rubber, and timber. In the 1990s, the Revolutionary United Front in Sierra Leone sold $25 to $125 million a year of diamonds.

Despite this plethora of examples, many still challenge the greed argument. For instance, Humphreys (2005) argues that rebellion simply stems from utility-maximizing behavior of individuals in poor countries. According to Humphreys (2005), civil wars are more likely in weak states and states with agricultural dependence, although natural resources still have an independent effect. Along the same lines, Dunning (2005: 475) finds that "understanding the political incentives posed by resource wealth can help contribute to more nuanced, conditional theories of the resource curse." Finally, Fearon (2005: 486) attacks the statistical analyses that support the greed argument and argues that "better rebel funding opportunities probably do imply a greater risk of civil war, other things equal. But there is little reason to expect that primary commodity exports as a percentage of GDP are a good measure of rebel financing potential."

The argument that civil wars result from grievances has a relatively long lineage. For instance, industrialization of an economy fundamentally alters the balance of power within a state. This can lead to a revolt from the newly strengthened bourgeoisie (Moore 1966) or the previously deprived proletariat (Skocpol 1979). Grievances do not have to result from economic dislocations, as Olson (1963) argues that those who gain from economic transformations may develop resentment. In addition, economic growth can lead to unrealistic expectations which will generate grievance when growth moderates (Parvin 1973; Rodrik 1999).

At the center of most grievance explanations for civil war onset rest the concepts of deprivation and dislocation. The deprivation experienced by an individual can be either absolute or relative. Absolute deprivation occurs when an individual falls below some objective measure, i.e., poverty line. Theoretically it is possible for all members of a society to suffer from absolute deprivation. Relative deprivation, however, occurs when an individual is worse off relative to other members of society. In any given society, a portion of the population will suffer from relative deprivation but it is not possible for all members to be relatively deprived. This implies that a state can have a population that is absolutely deprived (all below poverty level) but not suffer from relative deprivation because they are *all* poor. In contrast, a state could have no one below the poverty line (no absolute deprivation) but relative deprivation could exist if income was not equally distributed.

Ted Gurr (1970) finds that rebellion occurs as a result of economic deprivation, which would typically be associated with industrialization or rapid societal changes (Kuznets 1955, 1968; Sorokin 1957; Olson 1963; Huntington 1968). Economic deprivation alone cannot explain all civil wars because many of the poorest states in the world remain relatively stable (Huntington 1968). For Huntington, the attempt to achieve modernity "increases economic inequality at the same time that social mobilization decreases the legitimacy of the inequality" (Huntington 1968: 59). In addition, these transitioning states may not have the capacity to address the recently mobilized groups within the society. This implies that states at the intermediate stages of economic development are most at risk of civil war (Russett 1964; Hibbs 1973; Hegre et al. 2001). In addition, Homer-Dixon (1999) notes that environment scarcity can increase the risk of civil war as it generates gaps between demands (for resources) and supplies (North 1977). More recently, Diamond (2005) argues that resource depletion and environmental pollution can lead to the collapse of a civilization. Finally, research has shown that both famines (Dirks 1980; Brass 1986) and simply low levels of food supply (Sobek and Boehmer 2008) increase the risk of civil war onset.

While it is theoretically easy to differentiate greed from grievance, it is quite difficult to differentiate them in empirical tests. When measuring the aspects of greed, Collier and Hoeffler (1998, 2002, 2004) have generally focused on economic growth, development, and the role of commodities in an economy. Their analyses have consistently found that dependence on lootable resources increases the risk of civil war. Additional work by de Soysa (2002) discovered more evidence for the role of greed (especially reliance on oil), although creed, need, and poor governance had important effects as well. Ross (2004a), in his analysis of 13 recent civil wars, discovered strong links between oil, narcotics, and non-fuel minerals and civil war. Many researchers have begun to focus on oil as a key lootable resource (Fearon and Laitin 2003; Ross 2004a, 2004b; Fearon 2005).

Perhaps underlying a lot of the research on civil war onset is the role of state capacity, or the lack thereof (Sobek 2008). The capacity of a state to handle demands can arise from competent leadership, effective institutional designs, social capital, and so on. When the capacity of the state is low, it is unable to address even minor grievances. In fact, Herbst (2000: 3) notes "the failure of many African states to consolidate their authority has resulted in civil wars in many countries." While the actual ability to address demands certainly matters, the perception of state capacity may matter even more. So when the citizens feel that the state is able to resolve grievances as they arise, the risk of civil war is low. If, however, the population has little confidence in the government, it seems intuitive that they would be more willing to take matters into their own hands.

The Democratic Republic of Congo

If ever a people had grievances enough to overthrow their government, it would certainly be the population of the Democratic Republic of Congo. Ever since their first contact with Europeans, the Congolese have been killed, maimed, raped, and pillaged. For instance, its Belgian colonial legacy decimated the population. It has been estimated that, between 1880 and 1920, about 50 percent of the population was killed: "this would mean, according to the estimates, that during the Leopold period and its immediate aftermath the population of the territory dropped by approximately ten million people" (Hochschild 1999: 233). This essentially is a 2 percent population decline per year for 40 years.

Even after the colonization period, the population had to suffer years of misrule and corruption. Independence started off with high hopes as Patrice Lumumba was elected prime minister in 1960 in the state's first-ever democratic election. Unfortunately, Lumumba immediately alienated the West as he argued against the economic colonization of Africa. Less than two months after the election, he was assassinated. As CIA chief Allen Dulles noted: "the President [Dwight D. Eisenhower] would have vastly preferred to have him taken care of some way other than by assassination, but he regarded Lumumba as I did and a lot of other people did: as a mad dog . . . and he wanted the problem dealt with" (as quoted in Hochschild 1999: 302). The nationalist Lumumba was eventually replaced by a crook, Joseph Desire Mobutu, who ran one of the most kleptocratic regimes until his removal from power in 1997. Despite ruling over one of the poorest nations in the world, Mobutu became exceptionally wealthy. Hochschild (1999: 303) notes that "his thirty-two years in power had made him one of the world's richest men; his personal wealth at its peak was estimated at \$4 billion."

In the years leading up to the civil war in the Democratic Republic of Congo, the country was falling apart at the seams. For instance, at independence the state had roughly 90,000 miles of road, but by 1997 only several thousand remained intact (Robinson 1997). In the three years before the start of the civil war, GDP growth averaged −5.56 percent a year (Ross 2003: 20). This performance was, unfortunately, neither the exception nor unrelated to years of government abuse. Dunning argues that

> post-independence Zaire has provided social scientists with an archetype of the "predatory state," [in addition] Mobutu's reign of power . . . offers an example of a leader taking steps to concentrate economic production in easily exploitable resource sectors while discouraging the growth of economic sectors from which a future challenge to his political power might stem . . . Indeed, poor economic performance and political stability were, in a sense, jointly determined by Mobutu's effort to de-diversify the economy. (Dunning 2005: 466)

While successful for over thirty years, Mobutu only delayed the inevitable implosion of Zaire.[1]

While the inept, predatory government of Zaire (Democratic Republic of Congo) provided the population with any number of grievances, Mobutu's concentration on natural resources supplied prospective rebels with a ready source of funding. During Mobutu's reign, the economic reliance on commodities increased. In 1961, the top three exports (all minerals) were about 52 percent of total exports, but this grew to 91 percent by 1978 (Shafer 1983: 95). This reliance on natural resources provided the rebels with ample wealth. For instance, the coltan (a mixture of columbium and tantalum used in the electronics industry) resources of the Democratic Republic of Congo were used to fund both the rebels and the Rwandan army. In fact, it was estimated that the Rwandan army was mining $20 million worth of coltan a month in 2000 (Ware 2001).

In many ways, rebels and foreigners simply continued to pillage the natural resources of the Democratic Republic of Congo. Winer and Role note the pervasiveness of looting:

> In addition to coltan, illicit trade in cobalt, coffee, diamonds, gold, and timber contributed to what is sometimes referred to as Africa's "first world war," in which the death toll approached 4 million in three years; of these, coltan is the most lucrative. Rebel forces and armies from neighboring states funded their operations through full-fledged commercial operations in coltan, thus helping prolong the conflict. (Winer and Role 2003: 201)

Clearly, this supports the arguments of Collier and Hoeffler (1998, 2002, 2004) in that everyone involved in the civil war (which became internationalized) used the resource wealth to fund their activities. Without the abundance of lootable resources, it becomes questionable whether the rebels would have been able to fund their operations.

Despite the presence of grievances, natural resource dependence, and the outbreak of a civil war, it remains unclear as to why the civil war started in 1997 and not earlier or later. In other words, Zaire was in dire straits for a long period of time before 1997. In addition, in the years before the civil war the economy was still reliant on natural resources. So why did these factors fail to produce a civil war in the decades of poverty before 1997? In many ways, it comes down to state strength in that, despite all of the country's problems, Mobutu's hold on the reins of power was quite strong. Dunning comes to a similar conclusion when he notes that

> Mobutu's failure to invest in the diversification of the economy and, indeed, his de-diversification of the economy, limited the development of sources of autonomous societal power that could threaten his rule. Regime change, when it finally came, was prompted substantially by

changes in the international environment and, particularly, by support that Rwanda and Uganda provided to the rebel army of Laurent Kabila. (Dunning 2005: 472)

In fact, the United States sponsored and supported the regime of Mobutu during the Cold War, which certainly helped minimize the risk of civil war. The United States played quite an active role in defending the Mobutu regime:

> U.S. military aid helped Mobutu repel several attempts to overthrow him. Some of his political enemies he ordered tortured and killed; some he co-opted into his ruling circles; others he forced into exile. The United States gave him well over a billion dollars in civilian and military aid during his three-decade rule; European powers – especially France – contributed more. For its heavy investment, the United States and its allies got a regime that was reliably anti-Communist and a secure staging area for CIA and French military operations, but Mobutu brought his country little except a change of name, in 1971, to Zaire. (Hochschild 1999: 302–3)

When the Cold War ended, the need to aid Mobutu ceased. Without subsidies from western powers, Mobutu's grip on power slowly ebbed. By the mid- to late-1990s, Zaire's neighbors capitalized on Mobutu's weakness and supported the armed uprising of Laurent Kabila.

The case of Zaire (Democratic Republic of Congo) seems to reinforce the argument of Dunning (2005) that the onset of civil war derives from an integration of the theories and an emphasis on conditionality. Clearly, the precondition for civil strife existed in Zaire as the population was exceptionally aggrieved and Mobutu designed the economy to easily loot. Despite such a primed situation, Mobutu survived for over thirty years on the back of bipolarity, which created incentives for the major powers to prop up weak states that otherwise would have collapsed. The end of the Cold War simply uncorked the pressure that had been building. By 1997, Zaire's neighbor saw advantage in supporting Kabila which was the last little push that was needed to spiral the country into civil war.

International terrorism

The events of September 11, 2001 brought home to America, and the world, the threat that transnational terrorism poses to states. While many had thought terrorism an annoyance, the attacks appeared to mark the beginning of a new era. In fact, Bush noted in his prime-time speech to the nation that "this is a day when all Americans from every walk of life unite in our resolve for justice and peace . . . None of us will forget this day." Despite such rhetoric, however, transnational actors have been a force in the international system as long as there have been states. The Cold War minimized their role for a time but, just as its ending uncorked Zaire, it appears to have let the genie out of the bottle in terms of transnational actors.

Before we can understand the causes of terrorism, it first becomes critical to define it. Unfortunately, no single definition for terrorism exists upon which everyone agrees. In fact, Schmid (1984) spent over 100 pages examining more than 100 different definitions of terrorism. Laqueur (1977, 1987) argued that developing a proper definition was not worth the effort. Schmid and, Jongman (1998: 5–6) analyzed 109 definitions of terrorism and found that 22 elements appeared in at least 4 percent of the definitions. The most common element was violence or force, although 16.5 percent of the definitions even excluded this element. In addition, only 17.5 percent contained an element that related terrorism to civilians (non-combatants) and a measly 6 percent mentioned criminality. Given these monumental efforts to define terrorism, how does one even develop any sort of theoretical argument about its nature and patterns?

The key is to settle on a definition that captures the critical aspects that one wants to analyze and to understand how one's definition limits the investigation. For the purposes of understanding international/ transnational terrorism, Hoffman (1998: 43) offers a good definition in that terrorism is:

- ineluctably political in aims and motives;
- violent or, equally important, threatens violence;
- designed to have far-reaching psychological repercussions beyond the immediate victim or target;
- conducted by an organization with an identifiable chain of command or conspiratorial cell structure (whose members wear no uniform or identifying insignia); and
- perpetrated by a subnational group or non-state entity.

Hoffman's definition essentially argues that international terrorism is an attempt by an organized, non-state group to achieve some set of political aims through violence that intimidates a larger audience than those immediately attacked.

Perhaps the most critical aspect of the definition is its emphasis on the political nature of terrorism. While the media and politicians like to portray terrorists as crazed killers, it is almost universally incorrect. The Irish Republican Army had political grievances against the United Kingdom, the ETA has issues with Spain, al-Qaeda wants the West out of the Middle East, and so on. So while the means of these groups may be repulsive, it does not alter the fact that the ends of these attacks are political in nature. In addition, the definition points out that the real target of the attacks is not those immediately harmed by the violence. When al-Qaeda's attacks on September 11, 2001 killed many in New York, Pennsylvania, and Washington DC, they were really targeting the Americans that survived. By sparking fear in the survivors, terrorists hope to achieve political change.

In some ways, the debate over the definition of terrorism leads into another unresolved issue: are terrorists rational? Obviously, researchers fall into two broad camps. The first, such as Hoffman (1998), believes that terrorism is simply another tactic used by rational political actors seeking to achieve political aims in a competitive international system. Others, such as Reich (1998a) and Post (1998), see the source of terrorism lying in the psychology of terrorists. In other words, terrorists commit acts of terrorism because they are psychologically predisposed to engage in violence. Depending upon one's underlying assumption about the rationality of terrorism, the theories about the causes, consequences, and responses to terrorism vary dramatically. Reich (1998a: 3), however, warns that "neither of these approaches offers an adequate explanation of all terrorist behaviors and motivations."

Given that most view the killing of innocent victims as morally repulsive, scholars often turn to psychology to understand why. Reich (1998b: 261) argues that "the aspect of terrorism that seems most susceptible of all to [psychological] inquiry – that, for better or worse, almost begs for it – is the psychology of the terrorists themselves: their developments, motivations, personalities, decision-making patterns, behaviors in groups, and, some would argue, psychopathologies." While it is impossible to survey all of the ways that psychology matters, perhaps most important is how individuals argue that the choice to engage in terrorism is not a rational, cost–benefit analysis. Post (1998: 25) argues that "*political terrorists are driven to commit acts of violence as a consequence of psychological forces*, and that their special psychologic is constructed to rationalize *acts they are compelled to commit.*"

The psycho-logic is essentially used to justify acts of violence that an individual is predisposed to commit. Post (1998) argues that terrorists tend to rely on externalization and splitting. An individual is apt to split when they suffer a narcissistic wound in early life (termed the "injured self") which causes them to split the good and bad parts of the self. The ultimate result of splitting is that an individual "idealizes his grandiose self and *splits out* and *projects* onto others all the hatred and devalued weakness within" (Post 1998: 27). This complements the externalization seen in terrorists in which they blame the external environment for their situation. In the 1980s, a consortium of West German social scientists studied the life course of 250 West German terrorists (227 left-wing and 23 right-wing). The study found a prevalence of fragmented families and severe conflict within their families. In general, Post (1998: 28) notes that the study showed that the "terrorists whose lives they had studied demonstrated a pattern of failure both educationally and vocationally."

Regardless of the psychological disorders associated with terrorists, it remains clear that they develop a moral code that justifies their actions. For instance, Commander Pirabakaran (2004: 455) of the Tamil Tigers argued that his organization actually helps civilians whom they target with violence: "but now, after an attack, we give protection to the people. The Sri Lankan government attacks the people because we are close to the people and also it does it to create a gap between the people and us." Karl Heinzen (2004: 57) justified his actions by highlighting the "hypocrisy" of individuals: "no clear-thinking, rational person can accept the hair-splitting distinctions by which certain methods of obliterating the enemy are justified and others [condemned]." Ayman al Zawahiri argues that Islamic fundamentalism is

a growing power that is rallying under the banner of jihad for the sake of God and operating outside the scope of the new world order . . . It is anxious to seek retribution for the blood of martyrs, the grief of mothers, the deprivation of the orphans, the suffering of detainees, and the sores of the tortured people throughout the land of Islam, from eastern Turkestan to Andalusia. (Ayman al Zawahiri 2004: 428)

While each of the previous quotes highlights the rationalization of certain terrorists, it also points to the fact that these actions are inherently political in nature. Terrorism is not wanton violence but coercive force meant to push a government to change its policies. From this perspective, terrorism is simply a tactic used by a group that is attempting to alter the status quo. For instance, Nikolai Morozov (2004: 79) couched his actions in broad (perhaps historical) terms: "the goal of the terrorist movement in our country should not become concentrated only on disarraying contemporary Russian despotism. The movement should make the struggle popular, historical, and grandiose." Even Osama bin Laden has expressed clear political goals in October 2002 when he wrote to the American public to answer two questions: why are we fighting you and what are we calling for you to do? Among a long list of claims, bin Laden wrote:

> Why are we fighting and opposing you? The answer is very simple: (1) Because you attacked us and continued to attack us . . . What are we calling you to do, and what do we want from you? . . . (4) We also advise you to stop supporting Israel, and to end your support of the Indians in Kashmir, the Russians against the Chechens, and also to cease supporting the Manila Government against the Muslims in the Southern Philippines . . . (6) Sixthly, we call upon you to end your support of the corrupt leaders in our countries. Do not interfere in our politics and method of education. Leave us alone, or else expect us in New York and Washington. (Lawrence 2005: 162–71)

While one may or may not believe bin Laden's words, it remains clear that he has a set of political demands and threatens to use force to achieve them. In many ways, this is exactly the sort of interaction we would expect between rational states that want to achieve their goals in the international system.

So if terrorists are goal-oriented individuals using coercion to effect political change, why do they attack civilians as opposed to military targets? Hoffman succinctly summarizes the rational actions of terrorists:

> The wrath of the terrorist is rarely uncontrolled. Contrary to both popular belief and media depiction, most terrorism is neither crazed nor capricious. Rather, terrorist attacks are generally both premeditated and carefully planned . . . the terrorist act is specifically designed to communicate a message. But, equally important, it is also conceived and executed in a manner that simultaneously reflects the terrorist group's particular aims and motivations, fits its resources and capabilities and takes into account the "target audience" at which the act is directed. (Hoffman 1998: 157)

Terrorism is targeted at civilians because it sends the message that the group wants but, if attacks against military units were more effective (as we see in Iraq), then terrorist organizations are more than willing to attack non-civilians. What matters is the effect that the attack has on the target audience, generally those civilians of a state who survive a terrorist attack. It is the target audience that will pressure the government for change. So the challenge for the terrorists is to pick the method and target that maximizes the pressure the target audience will place on their government. A recent example of this was the 2004 Madrid train bombings which swayed the Spanish elections and led to the withdrawal of Spanish forces from Iraq.

As such it is hard to argue that terrorism is simply gratuitous violence. Sederberg (1989: 77) echoes this sentiment when he argues that "terrorist events are seldom, if ever, *radically* senseless or absurd. If they were, then no *answerable* questions could be asked." In other words, if terrorism was truly random, or driven by no consistent understandable cost–benefit analysis, then it would be impossible to develop theories about the source of terrorist violence. Defending against terrorism would be the equivalent of trying to predict random numbers. While it may be the case that terrorists are not rational, it seems highly unlikely that terrorist organizations have no goals except to kill in a random manner.

Perhaps the best way to demonstrate the rationality of terrorism is to look at what appears most irrational: suicide terrorism. Pape (2006: 4) argues that suicide terrorism, despite appearing crazy, is designed with "a specific secular and strategic goal: to compel modern democracies to withdraw military forces from territory that the terrorists consider to be their homeland." To test this argument, Pape (2006) compiles a list of all suicide terrorist attacks between 1980 and 2003 (a total of 315) to find patterns in the attacks. Of the 315 attacks, Pape (2006) found that 301 have connections to a larger political and military campaign, i.e., they were not random acts of violence. Second, democratic states were exceptionally at risk of suicide terrorism. Finally, and perhaps most important, the pattern of attacks demonstrates that "suicide terrorist campaigns are directed toward a strategic objective. From Lebanon to Israel to Sri Lanka to Kashmir to Chechnya, the sponsors of every campaign have been terrorist groups trying to establish or maintain political self-determination by compelling a democratic power to withdraw from the territories they claim" (Pape 2006: 4).

Broader patterns of terrorism seem to indicate that these groups respond to changes in the international system. For instance, Enders and Sandler (2002) show that changes in state security policies affect the number of transnational terrorist attacks. Huber and Powell (1994), Reynol-Querol (2002), and Li (2005) all argue that democratic structures allow for multiple avenues of contention and thus decrease the amount of terrorism. Mousseau (2003) sees the rise in terrorism as a response to globalization and the concomitant economic and social dislocations. Finally, Sobek and Braithwaite (2005) argue that American dominance of the international system has closed off conventional methods of contention. In particular, Sobek and Braithwaite find that:

> overwhelming success in the realm of international politics appears to act as a sword of Damocles hanging over the United States. The more dominant America becomes, the thinner the thread that holds it at bay. This situation creates an unpleasant trade-off in the realm of foreign policy, where increasing American security against other states in fact decreases its security against terrorist actors. (Sobek and Braithwaite 2005: 147)

In other words, as attacking a state in a conventional manner becomes more difficult, groups are more likely to eschew that tactic for another where the conventional dominance matters less (such as terrorism).

The recent conflict between Israel and Hezbollah offers a chance to better understand the dynamics behind international terrorism and the groups that use it. In many ways, this conflict is a combination of terrorism, civil conflict, and international war and thus demonstrates the blurring of the lines between these seemingly distinct forms of violence. What is quite clear from the conflict is that Hezbollah uses different types of attacks (ranging from rocket attacks against civilians to kidnapping soldiers to attack Israeli military units) in an attempt to achieve its objects.

Israel, Hezbollah, and war

Hezbollah has a clear history of using terrorism (including suicide bombings) to achieve its political goals. Formed among militant Shia groups in Lebanon in the early 1980s, Hezbollah's first spectacular attack was in 1983 against the United States marine barracks in Beirut, killing 241 soldiers. Between 1982 and 1986, Pape (2006: 129) counts 36 suicide attacks (involving 41 attackers) against American, French, and Israeli political and military targets in Lebanon. While many argue that the rise of Hezbollah was associated with the rise of Islamic fundamentalism in Iran, Pape (2006) finds that only 8 out of 41 Hezbollah suicide bombers were associated with Islamic fundamentalism. According to Pape, the rise of Hezbollah and large popular support for the movement were directly caused by a clear external event, Israel's massive occupation of southern Lebanon in 1982. Further, although religion was a recruiting tool . . . Hezbollah and other Lebanese political leaders overwhelmingly justified suicide terrorist acts . . . as an extreme measure necessary to end foreign occupation of the homeland, while explicitly ruling out such acts as an end in themselves or for other, even religious, goals." (Pape 2006: 130)

While the exact development of Hezbollah is unclear, it appears to have formed in the aftermath of the Israeli invasion of June 1982 when Hussain Mussawi broke away from Amal and was reinforced with about 800 Revolutionary Guards from Iran. Establishing its head-quarters in the Bekaa Valley, the new group went about developing active resistance to the Israeli occupation. Over time, the popular support for Hezbollah grew as "any Shia euphoria soon developed into resentment and militancy following the realization that Israel would continue to occupy southern Lebanon" (Ranstrop 1997: 30). With growing support, Hezbollah continued to expand its reach "into an umbrella organization coordinating the resistance operations of a loose collection of groups with a variety of religious and secular aims" (Pape 2006: 132). So while aspects of Hezbollah had religious (non-political) motivations, the core grievance was the Israeli occupation of southern Lebanon (clearly political in nature).

Even the motivation of individual suicide bombers indicates a pre-eminence of political motivations. For instance, Sanaa Muhaidly, a 17-year-old Sunni female, recorded a statement of her motivations for becoming a suicide bomber: "I have witnessed the calamity of my people under occupation. With total calmness I shall carry out an attack of my choice hoping to kill the largest number of the Israeli army . . . I am now planted in the earth of the South [of Lebanon] irrigating and quenching her with my blood and my love for her" (as quoted in Pape 2006: 135). These words do not reflect the ranting of a crazed religious radical but a political activist willing to sacrifice her life for her "land." In many ways, these suicide bombers have more in common with *kamikaze* pilots than with lunatics. In general, Hezbollah was able to "exploit the growing mood of alienation and anger felt by Lebanese Shi'ites against what they saw as the betrayal and weakness shown by Lebanese and other Arab regimes [who failed] to protect their people adequately in the Israeli invasion of 1982" (Wilkinson 2001: 35).

This emphasis on the political motivations of Hezbollah does not mean that religion played no role in the conflict. In fact, the Jewish–

Muslim divide allowed Hezbollah to portray the Israeli occupation as part of the larger threat to the Shia community. In their "open letter" released in February of 1985, Hezbollah made this explicit when they argued that Israel "poses a great danger to our future generations and to the destiny of our nation . . . [W]e view the recently voiced Jewish call for settlement in south Lebanon . . . as part of the expansionist scheme" (as quoted in Pape 2006: 136). In many ways, the fact that Israel was a Jewish state made the aggression all the more damning in the eyes of Hezbollah.

The leaders of Hezbollah also used religion to locate suicide terrorism under a blanket of martyrdom. In fact, Hezbollah needed some justification because Islam is quite clear in its prohibition of suicide, where the person who commits suicide is doomed to continually repeat the action that killed them. Sayyid Muhammad Husayn Fadlallah delineated the circumstances in which suicide bombings were justified (and coincidentally Hezbollah's actions were defensible). The first condition was "if an oppressed people does not have the means to confront the United States and Israel with weapons in which they are superior, then they possess unfamiliar weapons . . . [and] they must fight with special means of their own" (as quoted in Kramer 1998: 144–5). In addition, the context matters in that, if the action "is to have a political impact on an enemy whom it is impossible to fight by conventional means, then his sacrifice can be part of a jihad, a religious war. Such an undertaking differs little from that of a soldier who fights and knows that in the end he will be killed" (as quoted in Kramer 1998: 145).

It is interesting to note that, as the Israeli army redeployed further south and Hezbollah received more Iranian training in conventional warfare, the tactics of Hezbollah changed. By 1985, Fadlallah noted that

> we believe that suicide operations should only be carried out if they can bring about a political or military change in proportion to the passions that incite a person to make of his body an explosive bomb . . . the present circumstances do not favor such operations any more, and attacks that only inflict limited casualties (on the enemy) and destroy one building should not be encouraged, if the price is the death of the person who carries them out." (As quoted in Kramer 1998: 148)

In other words, the suicide bombing attacks were only one tool of Hezbollah, justified in the most extreme circumstances and only when their effect would be equally extreme.

The role that religion plays in cases such as Hezbollah is difficult to determine decisively. Religion clearly matters, although many of Hezbollah's core demands are political in nature. Perhaps Wilkinson (2001: 7) best captures this mix: "This trend towards waging armed struggle in the name of religion is, however rarely ever manifested in pure form. In almost every case these groups' fanatical adherence to doctrines of religious fundamentalism is wedded to a political agenda which is implicitly nationalistic in character. Hence Hezbollah wants to establish an Islamic republic in Lebanon." Despite clearly having a mix of political and religious motives, the preeminent goal remains unclear. Given that the group was originally formed in response to the Israeli invasion of southern Lebanon, one might reasonably infer the primacy of politics. In addition, Hezbollah has a history of altering its tactics in response to the changing political environment.

In general, Hezbollah seems to reinforce the view that terrorist organizations are simply other actors in the international system that balances costs and benefits. In other words, Sobek and Braithwaite were correct (2005: 136) when they argued that "terrorism is the choice of the powerless. In general, terrorists do not have the capacity to alter the status quo through conventional military or diplomatic channels. The tactic of terrorism both mitigates and circumscribes the strengths of the terrorist's target, while hiding the organization's weakness." So when Hezbollah was weakest and most threatened, it turned to suicide bombings, but when its position improved it resorted to more conventional tactics.

Conclusion

Trying to examine both civil wars and wars against transnational actors (terrorism) is a daunting task for a single chapter. Attempting to summarize the research in a couple of paragraphs is nearly impossible but I will of course do it anyway. Rather than emphasize the differences between these wars and interstate war, I want to concentrate on two similarities. First, the actions of both rebels and terrorists seem to indicate the rationality of their choices. This means that many of the same assumptions we make about states may also apply to these non-state actors. Second, there is a clear relationship between international politics and civil war/terrorism. In particular, the international environment affects the cost–benefit calculations of non-state actors, making civil war/terrorism more, or less, likely.

Despite the conventional wisdom that rebels and terrorists are crazy, the evidence indicates the opposite: they have political goals and choose the method that has the best chance of achieving those goals at the lowest cost. For instance, rebellions occur in states where financing is more readily available (through looting). Hezbollah altered their use of suicide terrorism in their conflict with Israel in response to changes in the political environment. Theoretically this makes perfect sense in that truly crazy individuals/groups will have a hard time competing in the international system (think about how long an irrational state would survive). This does not mean that every non-state actor is completely rational; rather, it is only the rational ones that succeed and thus have a sustained impact on the international system.

Domestic and international politics are definitely linked and the behavior of the non-state actors reinforces this view. For instance, Mobutu was kept in power for over thirty years on the back of United States support, which was only possible because of the Cold War and its bipolar distribution of power. When the Soviet Union collapsed and altered the international system, then western support for Mobutu collapsed and this altered the calculations of sub-state actors both within Zaire and in the states willing to support a rebellion. In addition, the collapse of the Soviet Union and the rising influence of the United States has pushed actors toward non-conventional attacks as conventional military operations against American interests are almost guaranteed to fail (Sobek and Braithwaite 2005). In general, non-state actors make their decisions based on their domestic environment but the costs and benefits associated with various actions are certainly influenced by the international system.

9 CONCLUSION

Thucydides, an Athenian, wrote the history of the war between the Peloponnesians and Athenians, beginning at the moment that it broke out, believing that it would be a great war, and more worthy of relation than any that had preceded it.

> Thucydides, *The Peloponnesian War* (I, 1)

For it is my belief that the Greeks' stark way of battle left us with what is now a burdensome legacy in the West: a presumption that battle under any guise other than a no-nonsense, head-to-head confrontation between sober enemies is or should be unpalatable.

> Victor Davis Hanson (1989: XV), *The Western Way of War: Infantry Battle in Classical Greece*

Nobody knows how tired we are,
Tired we are, Tired we are,
Nobody knows how tired we are,
And Nobody seems to care.

> World War I marching song

War hath no fury like a noncombatant.

> C. E. Montague

War has been part of the human condition for basically as long as there has been a human condition. Generation upon generation has sent their young men and women off to fight someone they have, in all likelihood, never met or seen before. The costs of these conflicts range from the minor to the catastrophic, yet neither side escapes unscathed. Two immutable facts of war, however, remain: wars are always costly and wars always end. So this leaves the most logical of questions. If wars always end, then why do we need such death and destruction? Can we not just skip the carnage? Unfortunately, history has clearly answered the second question with a resounding "no." Even in the earliest history of humanity, Gat (2005: 35) finds "across a very large variety of native peoples living in their original settings that hunter-gatherers, from the very simple to the more complex, fought among themselves. Deadly conflict, if not endemic, was ever to be expected." Despite the pessimistic answer to the second question, the first question, in many ways, is the subject of this book (and many books and articles that preceded it).

In attempting to understand the motivations behind war, it seems both logical and satisfying to focus on finding the *single cause* of war. Despite thousands of years of research that has combed through thousands of conflicts, scholars have failed to uncover this universal "cause." This does not mean, however, that research was unproductive or that all of the conclusions were incorrect. Previous research failed because much of it rested on a flawed assumption: war can be explained with a single theory. In reality, wars result from a number of factors interacting to increase or decrease the risk of violence. By focusing on single causes, researchers have been trying to place round pegs in square holes, although occasionally they do find the round hole, in which case they argue all holes are round.

To understand the onset of war and why the human condition is stuck in these cycles of violence requires that we develop two tools. First, we need to know the underlying risk factors that affect the likelihood of war. In many ways, this is similar to figuring out the shape of the pegs. Most of the previous research has done an admirable job in discovering the factors that impact the risk of war but they often stop at this point. The second tool requires researchers to figure out the effect of context and how it alters the effect of the risk factors. This would essentially be the equivalent of figuring out the shape of the holes. So a true, deeper theory of war requires the analysis of both the risk factors and the context. Once both of these influences are taken into account, scholars will be able to place all of their shapes into the proper holes.

So what are the theories that matter most and under which conditions do they matter? As noted above, the previous research has done a good job in highlighting a plethora of factors that affect the risk of international war. The factors exist at the state, dyadic, and system levels of analysis, which means that a proper understanding of war requires an investigation across the various levels. That being said, each of the theories discussed in chapters 1 through 8 are limited in that they do not equally apply to all contexts across time. As such, the cases were used to delve into various historic events to develop a deeper understanding of the theories. Throughout the analysis, a number of factors appeared to be quite important in terms of the context that they generated. In particular, state capacity played a vital role in the effect of regime type on war onset. In addition, domestic politics matters more than even the democratic peace implies.

State capacity

Throughout the book, state capacity continually appears as an important context for how various risk factors affect the likelihood of war. In many ways, it makes perfect sense that the ability of a state to develop and implement policies would affect how it interacts in the international system. In addition, many have looked at the role of state capacity in relation to the political development of the state but few have examined the impact of state capacity on how a state acts in the international system. Weak states tend to have fewer options and are more constrained by their domestic environment. This can dramatically affect the importance of some of the most consistent correlates of war, such as the democratic peace.

While a number of researchers have provided compelling evidence that regime type affects the prospects of peace (democratic peace), it appears that these results are contingent on the capacity of states. This makes sense in that many of the causal pathways described in the democratic peace literature assume that the central government is able to make, and enforce, authoritative decisions. Yet as was seen with Hamas, some governments are weak and need to account for the interest of other groups within the state that may or may not want peace. As such, even if Hamas wanted to moderate its official policy goals associated with Israel, it was handcuffed by the more militant wing of Hamas that was headquartered in Syria.

Democratic institutions have a much stronger (pacifying) effect in the case of more capable states, such as the democracies in Europe. With regard to the European Union, not only were the states highly capable but the populations were generally war-weary. As such, the pacific impulses of the population were conveyed through democratic institutions which had the capability of enacting these policies, even in the face of opposition. The result was peace across Europe (between the democracies), although other factors surely contributed to the lack of conflict. Regardless, it seems quite clear that in a situation where there are strong states with a generally dovish population, democratic pacifism (and the democratic peace for that matter) exerts a strong influence on foreign policy choices.

In some ways, the strength of the democratic regimes in France and England during the Fashoda Crisis additionally highlights the role of state strength. On both sides of the Channel, governments wanted peace but were besieged on all fronts by those pushing for war. Hawkish advisers that sought to instigate further conflict existed in both governments. In addition, the populations were each being stoked by a jingoistic press. Despite these influences, the governments of France and Britain decided upon diplomacy and were able to enforce this decision over the objections of a significant portion of the respective governments and citizenry. Contrast this scenario with the 1971 war between India and Pakistan which resulted from the inability of a democratic Pakistan (a relatively new state) to incorporate the Bengali population of East Pakistan.

This finding does not dispute the democratic peace per se because the bulk of democracies tend to be quite capable. In many ways, detailing the role of state capacity makes the democratic peace more important because we now understand why it may fail. Huntington offers quite a compelling case for the importance of studying state capacity:

> The United States, Great Britain, and the Soviet Union have different forms of government, but in all three systems the government governs. Each country is a political community with an overwhelming consensus among the people on the legitimacy of the political system. . . . All three countries have strong, adaptable, coherent political institutions: effective bureaucracies, well-organized political parties, a high degree of popular participation in public affairs, working systems of civilian control over the military, extensive activity by the government in the economy, and reasonably effective procedures for regulating succession and controlling political conflict. . . . If the Politburo, the Cabinet, or the President makes a decision, the probability is high that it will be implemented through the government machinery. (Huntington 1968: 1)

In states that lack such control over the political system, the effect of variables such as regime type becomes problematic. For instance, if the government says peace, but cannot control all factions within the state, then does it matter (as much) that the central government said peace?

While it is important to understand that state capacity contextualizes many of the theories in international politics, it is equally critical to have the ability to identify those cases where state capacity is low. Empirically, one could simply design a measure of state capacity, which has been done in the past, and integrate this measure into one's models. These cases could also be identified theoretically. For instance, the scholars interested in dangers-of-democratization literature (Mansfield and Snyder 2002, for instance) have repeatedly argued that new democracies do not have the norms (or institutional strength) to generate the democratic peace effect. While this may be the case, one could broaden this insight and argue that new regimes/governments/states (such as we see with Hamas) have a weakened capacity. As such, we should be wary of blindly applying our theories to these cases.

Domestic politics matters

While the literature on the democratic peace clearly demonstrates that domestic politics matters, the cases often show a larger role of domestic politics. In particular, in their rise to power, the Japanese leadership dedicated a tremendous amount of resources to shaping domestic opinion. Without changing the social make-up of Japanese society, it seems unlikely that their rise to major power status would have occurred as quickly (if at all). Perhaps the best way to conceptualize the effect of domestic politics is to allow that it has the potential to reinforce or hinder the policies of government so states act in ways to ensure that it reinforces their choices.

Even the authoritarian states examined in this book paid close attention to the domestic political environment. The Japanese leadership acted to break the samurai monopoly on military service and to expand support for both the military and nationalistic policies. The Kaiser in nineteenth-century Germany attempted to cement his support by appealing to the innate respect that the Germans had for the military. Even Hitler hesitated in his plan to attack France during the Second World War when the military leadership resisted. Finally, in the kleptocratic regime of Zaire, Mobuto Sese Seko restructured the economy to emphasize the natural resource sector which minimized the rise of alternative centers of power. In all of these cases, leaders in authoritarian states were acting in response to domestic politics.

The importance of domestic politics challenges one of the core assumptions of realism, i.e., that domestic politics does not matter. Scholars have often touted the democratic peace as evidence that the realists are incorrect. While the democratic peace offers compelling support for the contention of the liberals, the fact that leaders in non-democratic states also are affected by domestic politics is even more problematic for realists. These are leaders that supposedly should not have to care about domestic support but it seems quite clear that they do. Domestic support is obviously more important in democracies but one should not then conclude that domestic support does not matter in autocracies.

In many ways, this dovetails with Bueno de Mesquita, Smith, Siverson, and Morrow (2003), who argue that all leaders want to maintain control of their domestic political system and design policies with this end in mind. The difference between democracies and autocracies is not that one cares about domestic politics and one does not but that in democracies the leadership is required to maintain support in a much broader coalition. As such, democratic leaders push policies that provide public goods, where leaders in autocracies generate private good for members of their winning coalition. So when autocratic leaders pay attention to the domestic politics of their states, they are doing so in ways that benefit a smaller portion of their society. In particular, these policies benefit those whose support is critical for the leadership to maintain control.

Rationality and international politics

While the purpose of this book was not to determine the rationality of political actors, it seems apparent that the assumption of rationality is more often correct than it is wrong. In general, one could characterize the interactions between states as rational, although this may occasionally be violated. In addition, even the actions of non-state actors imply a degree of rational calculation. Often the behavior of non-state actors is characterized as crazy, but the cases of Hamas and Hezbollah show that both have clear political objectives and they vary their use of violence (even suicide terrorism) in an attempt to achieve their goals. In other words, they use coercive violence as a means to an end and not simply as an end in and of itself.

In addition, the apparent importance of context hints at the rational calculations of the actors. In order for changes in context to alter the behavior of states (and non-state actors), they have to be cognizant both of their environment and of how the context affects the costs and benefits of various policies. For instance, if an irrational actor chose policy A, then it does not matter if the context changes because they did not choose policy A for its fit to the context. If a rational actor enacted policy A and then noticed a change in the context, it would make sense for them to re-evaluate their choice given the new environment. This may or may not lead to a change in all cases but the fact that states vary their behaviors in response to the environment implies a rational process is at work.

The German invasion of Denmark during the Second World War shows a clear change in policy given a change in the international environment. In the lead up to the war and in its early days, Germany was quite content to maintain its latent military control over Denmark. For its part, Denmark understood its situation and acted in every way to minimize the risk of a German invasion. The Soviet invasion of Finland, however, changed the strategic calculations of the Germans. An area that was essentially open to passive German control was now threatened by the Soviet Union and soon to be in the crosshairs of the British. Given the alteration of the strategic situation, the Germans modified their plans and launched an invasion of Denmark.

Rationality may also matter in terms of the effect of interdependence. As states become increasingly tied to one another, policy changes in one state will causes ripples around the system. Often these ripples may have unintended consequences but, given that states recognize the interconnectedness of policies, it hints at rational calculation. In other words, to operate in a world of interdependent states, a policy-maker needs to engage in strategic thought to fully appreciate the outcome of a given policy. This is at the heart of rationality, where an actor weighs the costs and benefits on a menu of options and chooses the one that creates the most benefits with the fewest costs. As policies become more entwined, the calculations become more difficult and require a deeper analysis, which again implies a rational analysis (and ultimately a more rational policy).

Understanding conflict in the world today and tomorrow

Perhaps one of the most important questions yet to be answered deals with the prospect of peace in the world. Keeping in mind that the outbreak of war is a probabilistic event, the findings of the book certainly help us in understanding where wars are most likely to occur in the near future. First, it seems clear that Africa, the Middle East, and the Asian sub-continent are most at risk. In particular, many of the states are less than democratic but, even if this were not the case, the lack of state capacity would mitigate the peace-generating effect of joint democracy. In addition, these regions of the world are experiencing a more rapid economic growth than Europe, North America, and Latin America, which means regional power transitions are likely to occur. Finally, the end of the bipolar structure has decreased the incentive of the major powers to mitigate conflict in these regions.

It seems less likely that Europe, North America, or Latin America will experience a lot of interstate violence. In general, these states are democratic, developed, and are relatively strong. As such, many of the war-risk factors will be mitigated. In addition, these regions of the world are highly interdependent, which makes wars both costly and less profitable. Finally, states in these regions of the world have the most to gain from the current status quo. As long as the United States remains the hegemon, North America, Latin America, and Europe all stand to gain, which makes these states less likely to challenge the status quo (of course, Hugo Chavez in Venezuela may have something to say about this).

It is important to note that these broad predictions are not going to be universally accurate. In fact, most of the states in the war-prone regions will be at peace but the odds that a war will occur are higher in those regions than in North America, Latin America, and Europe. In addition, an exogenous shock may occur that drastically alters the international system in ways that can change the war-prone areas into regions of peace and stability. However, barring any unforeseen event, it appears that the near future will continue to see the bulk of interstate wars occurring in Africa, the Middle East, and the Asian subcontinent. Unfortunately, those same areas are most at risk of civil war as well. Again, the relatively low state capacity combined, in this case, with a general reliance on natural resources creates an environment ripe for civil conflict. In addition, the poverty in these regions generates any number of grievances that can be used by political entrepreneurs to stoke civil disturbance. In terms of terrorism, however, the near future presents more risks for Europe and North America. Not only are most of these states democratic but they are generally seen as being part of the American hegemonic system that a lot of transnational terrorism targets.

Given that one can point to regions of the world that are at risk of war, can states implement policies that can mitigate this risk? Clearly, states have the option of pushing for democracy (for example) which in the long run would lead to fewer conflicts. Yet the American experience in Iraq highlights an important caveat: some aspects of the international system are quite difficult to change and actions to alter the international system may have unintended consequences. In fact, some of the most powerful correlates of war are quite difficult to change, such as contiguity, regime type, and preferences. That being said, state capacity can be supplemented through either direct aid or international organizations. In addition, states, either individually or collectively, can push for more trade.

Perhaps the next step for researchers is to look at factors that both impact the amount of conflict and are relatively easy for states to alter. For instance, Sobek, Abouharb, and Ingram's (2006) work on the democratic peace shows that states that mutually respect the human rights of their citizens are less likely to have conflicts. Concentrating on the human rights' practices of a state (instead of its regime type) is important in two ways. First, it represents a policy that a state has decided to implement, so it should convey more information about the state. For instance, a state may pass a law protecting minorities but what really matters is if they actually follow through in practice. Second, policies of states (such as respect for human rights) are much easier to change (at least when compared to contiguity, regime type, and preferences) and, as such, offer more room for states to directly affect the risk of conflict.

In addition, future research needs to account for how the risks of war are affected across the levels of analysis. While the bulk of research focuses on a single level (for instance, the democratic peace research concentrates naturally on the dyad), it seems clear that factors at one level affect other levels. Some work has already moved toward a more holistic analysis (Bennett and Stam 2004) but more is required. So where Bennett and Stam (2004) provide a head-to-head comparison of the theories across the levels, they do not account for how factors at one level may condition the effect of other factors at other levels. For example, it could be the case that the democratic peace is more effective in systems with a bipolar distribution of power. It is these sorts of relationships that future scholarship needs to address.

NOTES

Chapter 1 The Power of States

1 In this case, realism is a traditional view of international politics that emphasizes the role of power politics and minimizes the effect of both economic factors and domestic politics.

2 This argument implies that the first priority of states is security and that they seek power as a means toward that end. This logic is more a characteristic of neo-realism as exemplified by Waltz (1979). Realist thought, exemplified by Morgenthau (1948), generally argued that power was the end and not a means used to gain security.

3 When delineating preferences, it is important that actors can distinguish between the outcomes. For instance, I cannot distinguish between no sugar in my coffee and a single grain. In addition, I cannot distinguish between one and two grains and so on. If one assumes transitive preferences, then this becomes problematic because if no sugar = one grain = two grains = . . . = one hundred million grains, then I should not have a preference between no sugar and one hundred million grains. To address this paradox, the actor needs to be able to distinguish between the outcomes.

4 The player could rationally bluff in this situation if they believed that their opponent would fold.

Chapter 2 Liberal Pacifism

1 To be fair to Rummel, his specific argument was not that democracies would be more peaceful in terms of the frequency of disputes; rather, they would be more peaceful in terms of the severity of violence. (See Ray 1995, chapter 1, for a discussion of Rummel and his critics.)

2 The report can be downloaded at: http://www.accessdemocracy.org/
   library/2068_ps_elect_012506.pdf.
3 Fattah 2006, Section A; Column 1; Foreign Desk Palestinian Landslide:
   The Neighbors, p. 11.
4 Fattah 2006, Section A; Column 1; Foreign Desk Palestinian Landslide:
   The Neighbors, p. 11.
5 Fotini and Mitter 2006, Section A; Column 2; Editorial Desk, p. 23.
6 Fisher 2006, Section A; Column 4; Foreign Desk, p. 8.
7 Erlanger 2006a, Section A; Column 1; Foreign Desk, p. 1.
8 Erlanger and Myre 2006, Section A; Column 5; Foreign Desk, p. 1.
9 Smith 2006, Section A; Column 1; Foreign Desk; Turmoil in the Mideast:
   Gaza, p. 10.
10 Smith 2006, Section A; Column 1; Foreign Desk; Turmoil in the Mideast:
   Gaza, p. 10.
11 Feldman 2006, Section 6; Column 3; Magazine; The Way We Live Now,
   p. 9.
12 Atran 2006, Section A; Column 1; Editorial Desk, p. 25.
13 Atran 2006, Section A; Column 1; Editorial Desk, p. 25.
14 Erlanger 2006b, Section 4; Column 1; Week in Review Desk; The World,
   p. 4.
15 Erlanger 2006b, Section 4; Column 1; Week in Review Desk; The World,
   p. 4.
16 The council originally had 10 members: Belgium, Netherlands, Luxembourg, Denmark, France, Britain, Ireland, Italy, Norway, and Sweden.
   Eventually membership expanded to include Greece, Turkey, the Federal
   Republic of Germany, Austria, Cyprus, Switzerland, Malta, Spain, and
   Portugal.
17 The EEC originally contained the six members of the ECSC (France,
   West Germany, Italy, Belgium, the Netherlands, and Luxembourg).

Chapter 4   The Democratic Peace

1 While France and Britain are generally referred to as being democracies
   during this period of time, it should be noted that neither state allowed
   universal suffrage. In particular, women were excluded from the democratic process. While this is certainly an indictment on the democratic
   nature of these states, it would not necessarily make this case less important for the democratic peace. In particular, even though women could not
   vote, the governments still were forced to compete in elections and were
   thus answerable to the "citizens" (and by citizens I mean men in this case).
   Second, both states had a separation of power, which should have an effect
   independent of who is allowed to vote. So while France and Britain were
   not paragons of democracy at this time, they still had the democratic
   structures that should generate a democratic peace.

2 Delcasse's response is roughly translated as "You do not understand the honor of France."
3 Fattah 2006, Section A; Column 1; Foreign Desk; Palestinian Landslide: The Neighbors, p. 11.
4 Fattah 2006, Section A; Column 1; Foreign Desk; Palestinian Landslide: The Neighbors, p. 11.
5 Fotini and Mitter 2006, Section A; Column 2; Editorial Desk, p. 23.
6 Fisher 2006, Section A; Column 4; Foreign Desk, p. 8.

Chapter 5 Trade and Peace

1 Hegre (2000) examines the conditions that lead a state from the military-political to the trading world and finds that the peace-enhancing effects of trade are contingent on the states being wealthy.

Chapter 6 The Systemic Distribution of Power

1 Of course, this clarity did not extend to understanding the actions of one another. Gaddis (1987) notes "that Soviet foreign policy was the product of internal influences not susceptible to persuasion, manipulation, or even comprehension from the outside. Without pushing the point too far, the same might be said of American foreign policy."
2 Huth, Bennett, and Gelpi (1992) found that the risk aversion/acceptance of states altered the effect of the systemic distribution of power.

Chapter 7 The Rise and Fall of States

1 Evidence for the relationship between power preponderance and peace continues to accumulate, even in studies that are not explicitly testing power transition (see Russett and Oneal 2001, for example).
2 Organski and Kugler (1980: 20) argue that "even today, only one-third of the earth's nations are developed and at the stage of power maturity. Roughly one-third are still developing and are at some lower point of power transition. The remainder have barely begun the long trek toward wealth and power."
3 The production data is from Hurd and Castle (1913: 374–7).
4 This data comes from Campbell (1976: 84).

Chapter 8 Conflict with Non-State Actors

1 By the 1990s, the situation reached critical as Hochschild (1999: 303) describes:

> When [Mobutu] ran out of money to pay the army and other state workers in 1993, he printed up a new kind of currency. Because shopkeepers would not

accept it, soldiers rioted, looting shops, government buildings, and private homes . . . For years, garbage piled up in heaps, uncollected. A few foreign airlines continued to stop in the country, but they avoided leaving the planes overnight; insurance would not cover it . . . The US embassy advised staff in the capital not to unlock car doors or roll down windows when stopped by police at roadblocks: they should show their papers through the window only, lest their wallets be taken.

REFERENCES

Angell, Norman. [1909] 2007. *The Great Illusion*. New York: Cosimo.

Atran, Scott. 2006. "Is Hamas Ready to Deal?" *New York Times*, August 17.

Axelrod, Robert M. 1984. *The Evolution of Cooperation*. New York: Basic Books.

Bannon, Ian and Collier, Paul (eds.). 2003. *Natural Resources and Violent Conflict: Options and Actions*. Washington DC: World Bank.

Barbieri, Katherine. 1996. "Economic Interdependence: A Path to Peace or a Source of Interstate Conflict?" *Journal of Peace Research* 33: 29–49.

——. 2002. *The Liberal Illusion: Does Trade Promote Peace?* Ann Arbor: University of Michigan Press.

Beisner, Robert L. 1986. *From the Old Diplomacy to the New, 1865–1900*, 2nd edn. The American History Series. Arlington Heights, IL: Harlan Davidson.

Bennett, D. Scott and Stam, Allan C. 2004. *The Behavioral Origins of War*. Ann Arbor: University of Michigan Press.

Benoit, Kenneth. 1996. "Democracies Really Are More Pacific (In General): Reexamining Regime Type and War Involvement." *Journal of Conflict Resolution* 40: 636–58.

bin Laden, Osama. 2001. As quoted in Osama bin Laden and Bruce B. Lawrence. 2005. *Message to the World: The Statements of Osama bin Laden*. London: Verso.

Bismarck, Otto von. 1898. As quoted in Richard C. Hall (2000). *Balkan Wars 1912–1913: Prelude to the First World War*. New York: Routledge.

Blainey, Geoffrey. 1988. *The Causes of War*, 3rd edn. New York: The Free Press.

Blair, Tony. 2001. As quoted in Sandra Silberstein (2004). *Language, Politics, and 9/11: War of Words*. New York: Routledge.

Boehmer, Charles R. and Sobek, David. 2005. "Violent Adolescence: State Development and the Propensity for Militarized Interstate Conflict." *Journal of Peace Research* 42: 5–26.

Brass, Paul R. 1986. "The Political Uses of Crisis: The Bihar Famine of 1966–1967." *Journal of Asian Studies* 45: 245–67.

Bremer, Stuart. 1980. "National Capabilities and War Proneness," in J. David Singer, ed., *The Correlates of War: II. Testing Some Realpolitik Models.* New York: Free Press.

——. 1992. "Dangerous Dyads: Conditions Affecting the Likelihood of Interstate War, 1816–1965." *Journal of Conflict Resolution* 36: 309–41.

Brown, MacAlister and Zasloff, Joseph J. 1998. *Cambodia Confounds the Peacemakers.* Ithaca: Cornell University Press.

Bueno de Mesquita, Bruce. 1980. "Theories of International Conflict: An Analysis and an Appraisal," in Ted R. Gurr, ed., *Handbook of Political Conflict.* New York: Free Press.

——. 1981. *The War Trap.* New Haven: Yale University Press.

Bueno de Mesquita, Bruce, Morrow, James D., Siverson, Randolph M. and Smith, Alastair. 1999. "An Institutional Explanation of the Democratic Peace." *American Political Science Review* 93: 791–807.

Bueno de Mesquita, Bruce, Smith, Alastair, Siverson, Randolph M. and Morrow, James D. 2003. *The Logic of Political Survival.* Cambridge, MA: MIT Press.

Campbell, Charles S. 1957. *Anglo-American Understanding, 1898–1903.* Baltimore: The Johns Hopkins University Press.

——. 1976. *The Transformation of American Foreign Relations, 1865–1900.* New York: Harper & Rowe.

Cannizzo, Cynthia. 1978. "Capability Distribution and Major-Power War Experience, 1816–1965." *Orbis – A Journal of World Affairs* 21: 947–57.

Carr, Edward Hallett. 1939a. *Twenty Years' Crisis, 1919–39.* New York: Harper Torchbook.

——. 1939b. *Britain: A Study of Foreign Policy from the Versailles Treaty to the Outbreak of War.* London: Longmans, Green.

Carter Center. 2006a. "National Democratic Institute. Final Report on the Palestinian Legislative Council Elections." http://www.accessdemocracy. org/library/2068_ps_elect_012506.pdf.

Cederman, Lars-Erik and Rao, Mohan P. 2001. "Exploring the Dynamics of the Democratic Peace." *Journal of Conflict Resolution* 45: 818–33.

Chan, Steve. 1984. "Mirror, Mirror on the War . . . Are Democratic States More Pacific?" *Journal of Conflict Resolution* 28: 617–48.

Cioffi-Revilla, Claudio A. 1998. *Politics and Uncertainty: Theory, Models, and Applications.* Cambridge: Cambridge University Press.

Claude, Inis L. 1962. *Power and International Relations.* New York: Random House.

Collier, Paul and Hoeffler, Anke. 1998. "On Economic Causes of Civil War." *Oxford Economic Paper – New Series* 50: 563–73.

——. 2002. "On the Incidence of Civil War in Africa." *Journal of Conflict Resolution* 46: 13–28.

——. 2004. "Greed and Grievance in Civil War." *Oxford Economic Papers* 56: 563–96.

Copeland, Dale. 2000. *The Origins of Major War.* Ithaca: Cornell University Press.

Crowe, 1907. "Memorandum on the Present State of British Relations with France and Germany." http://tmh.floonet.net/pdf/eyre_crowe_memo. pdf.

Dahl, Robert. 1971. *Polyarchy: Participation and Opposition.* New Haven: Yale University Press.

Deighton, Len. 1981. *Blitzkrieg: From the Rise of Hitler to the Fall of Dunkirk.* St Albans: Triad.

Deist, Wilhelm. 1981. *The Wehrmacht and German Rearmament.* Toronto and Buffalo: University of Toronto Press.

de Soysa, Indra. 2002. "Paradise is a Bazaar? Greed, Creed, and Governance in Civil War, 1989–99." *Journal of Peace Research* 39(4): 395–416.

de Soysa, Indra, Oneal, John R. and Park, Yong-Hee. 1997. "Testing Power-Transition Theory Using Alternative Measures of National Capabilities." *Journal of Conflict Resolution* 41: 509–28.

Deutsch, Karl W. and Singer, J. David. 1964. "Multipolar Power Systems and International Stability." *World Politics* 16: 390–406.

Diamond, Jared. 2005. *Collapse: How Societies Choose to Fail or Succeed.* New York: Viking.

Dirks, Robert. 1980. "Social Responses during Severe Food Shortages and Famine." *Current Anthropology* 21: 21–44.

Dixon, William J. 1994. "Democracy and the Peaceful Settlement of International Conflict." *American Political Science Review* 88: 14–32.

Doran, Charles F. and Parsons, Wesley. 1980. "War and the Cycle of Relative Power." *American Political Science Review* 74: 947–65.

Downs, Anthony. 1957. "An Economic Theory of Political Action in Democracy." *Journal of Political Economy* 65: 135–50.

Doyle, Michael. 1997. *Ways of War and Peace: Realism, Liberalism, and Socialism.* New York: Norton.

Dunning, Thad. 2005. "Resource Dependence, Economic Performance, and Political Stability." *Journal of Conflict Resolution* 49: 451–82.

Eberwein, Wolf-Dieter. 1982. "The Seduction of Power: Serious International Disputes and the Power Status of Nations, 1900–1976." *International Interactions* 9: 55–74.

Enders, Todd and Sandler, Walter. 2002. "Patterns of Transnational Terrorism, 1970–1999: Alternative Time-Series Estimates." *International Studies Quarterly* 46: 145–65.

Erlanger, Steven. 2006a. "Seizures Show New Israel Line Against Hamas." *New York Times*, June 30.

——. 2006b. "Hamas: Rivalry Breeds Extremes." *New York Times*, July 2.

Erlanger, Steven and Myre, Greg. 2006. "Fighting Surges and Deaths Rise as Israel Drives Deeper in Gaza." *New York Times*, July 7.

Fattah, Hassan M. 2006. "Joyful Arabs Voice Concern at How Hamas Will Swim in the Mainstream." *New York Times*, January 27.

Fearon, James D. 1994. "Domestic Political Audiences and the Escalation of International Disputes." *American Political Science Review* 88: 577–92.

—. 1995. "Rationalist Explanations for War." *International Organization* 49: 379–414.

—. 2005. "Primary Commodity Exports and Civil War." *Journal of Conflict Resolution* 49: 483–507.

Fearon, James D. and Laitin, David. 2003. "Ethnicity, Insurgency, and Civil War." *American Political Science Review* 97: 75–90.

Feldman, Noah. 2006. "Ballots and Bullets." *New York Times*, July 30.

Ferejohn, Michael T. 1991. *The Origins of Aristotelian Science*. New Haven: Yale University Press.

Fisher, Ian. 2006. "In Gaza, Defiantly Awaiting Israeli Retaliation." *New York Times*, June 26.

Fotini, Christia and Mitter, Sreemati. 2006. "Hamas at the Helm." *New York Times*, January 27.

Gaddis, John Lewis. 1987. *The Long Peace: Inquiries into the History of the Cold War*. New York: Oxford University Press.

Gandhi, Mahatma. www.saidwhat.co.uk/members/viewbook.php?id=201.

Gartzke, Erik. 2007. "The Capitalist Peace." *American Journal of Political Science* 51: 166–91.

Gartzke, Erik, Li, Quan and Boehmer, Charles. 2001. "Investing in the Peace: Economic Interdependence and International Conflict." *International Organization* 55: 391–438.

Gat, Azar. 2005. *War in Human Civilization*. Oxford: Oxford University Press.

Geller, Daniel S. 1985. *Domestic Factors in Foreign Policy: A Cross-National Statistical Analysis*. Cambridge, MA: Schenkman Publishing Company.

—. 1988. Power System Membership and Patterns of War. *International Political Science Review* 9: 365–79.

Gerring, John. 2004. "What is a Case Study and What is it Good For?" *American Political Science Review* 98: 341–54.

Geyer, Michael. 1985. "The Dynamics of Military Revisionism in the Interwar Years: Military Politics between Rearmament and Diplomacy," in Wilhelm Deist, ed., *The German Military in the Age of Total War*. Warwickshire, UK: Berg Publishers.

Gilpin, Robert. 1981. *War and Change in World Politics*. Cambridge: Cambridge University Press.

Goering, Reichmarshal Hermann. 1936. Radio broadcast. As quoted in William L. Safire (1968), *The New Language of Polities: An Anecdotal Dictionary of Catchwords, Slogans, and Political Usage*. p. 178.

Green, Donald P. and Shapiro, Ian. 1994. *Pathologies in Rational Choice Theory: A Critique of Applications in Political Science.* New Haven: Yale University Press.

Gurr, Ted R. 1970. *Why Men Rebel.* Princeton, NJ: Published for the Center of International Studies, Princeton University [by] Princeton University Press.

Haas, Ernst. [1953] 1961. "The Balance of Power: Prescription, Concept, or Propaganda?" in James Rosenau, ed., *International Politics and Foreign Policy.* New York: Free Press.

Haikio, Martti. 1983. "The Race for Northern Europe, September 1939–June 1940," in Henrik S. Nissen, ed., *Scandinavia During the Second World War.* Minneapolis: University of Minnesota Press.

Hanson, Victor Davis. 1989. *The Western Way of War: Infantry Battle in Classical Greece.* New York: Knopf.

Harrison, Ewan. 2002. "Waltz, Kant and Systemic Approaches to International Relations." *Review of International Studies* 28: 143–62.

Hart, Liddell. 1930. *The Real War, 1914–1918.* Boston: Little, Brown, and Co.

Hegre, Håvard. 2000. "Development and the Liberal Peace: What Does it take to be a Trading State?" *Journal of Peace Research* 37: 5–30.

——. 2002. "Trade Decreases Conflict More in Multi-Actor Systems: A Comment on Dorussen." *Journal of Peace Research* 39(1): 109–14.

Hegre, Håvard, Ellingsen, Tanja, Gates, Scott and Gleditsch, Nils Petter. 2001. "Toward a Democratic Civil Peace? Democracy, Political Change, and Civil War 1816–1992." *American Political Science Review* 95: 33–48.

Heinzen, Karl. 2004. "Murder," in Walter Laqueur, ed., *Voices of Terror: Manifestos, Writings, and Manuals of Al Qaeda, Hama, and Other Terrorists from Around the World and Throughout the Ages.* New York: Reed Press.

Herbst, Jeffrey I. 2000. *States and Power in Africa: Comparative Lessons in Authority and Control.* Princeton Studies in International History and Politics. Princeton, NJ: Princeton University Press.

Hewitt, J. Joseph and Young, Garry. 2001. "Assessing the Statistical Rarity of Wars Between Democracies." *International Interactions* 27: 327–51.

Hibbs Jr., Douglas A. 1973. *Mass Political Violence: A Cross-National Causal Analysis.* New York: John Wiley.

Hiden, John. 1992. "Introduction: Baltic Security Problems Between the Two World Wars," in John Hiden and Thomas Lane, eds., *The Baltic and the Outbreak of the Second World War.* Cambridge: Cambridge University Press.

Hobbes, Thomas. [1651] 1985. *Leviathan.* London: Penguin Books.

Hochschild, Adam. 1999. *King Leopold's Ghost: A Story of Greed, Terror, and Heroism in Colonial Africa.* Boston: Houghton Mifflin.

Hoffman, Bruce. 1998. *Inside Terrorism.* New York: Columbia University Press.

Holland, John H. 1999. *Emergence: From Chaos to Order*. New York: Helix Books.

Homer-Dixon, Thomas F. 1999. *Environment, Scarcity, and Violence*. Princeton, NJ: Princeton University Press.

Houweling, Henk and Siccama, Jan. 1988. "Power Transitions as a Cause of War." *Journal of Conflict Resolution* 32: 87–102.

Howe, Anthony. 1997. *Free Trade and Liberal England, 1846–1946*. Oxford: Clarendon Press.

Huber, John D. and Powell Jr, G. Bingham. 1994. "Congruence between Citizens and Policymakers in Two Visions of Liberal Democracy." *World Politics* 46: 291–326.

Hull, Isabel V. 2005. *Absolute Destruction: Military Culture and the Practices of War in Imperial Germany*. Ithaca: Cornell University Press.

Humphreys, Macartan. 2005. "Natural Resources, Conflict, and Conflict Resolution: Uncovering the Mechanisms." *Journal of Conflict Resolution* 49: 508–37.

Huntington, Samuel. 1968. *Political Order in Changing Societies*. New Haven, CT: Yale University Press.

Hurd, Archibald S. and Castle, Henry. 1913. *German Sea-Power, Its Rise, Progress, and Economic Base*. London: J. Murray.

Huth, Paul, Bennett, D. Scott and Gelpi, Christopher. 1992. "System Uncertainty, Risk Propensity, and International Conflict Among the Great Powers." *Journal of Conflict Resolution* 36: 478–517.

Huth, Paul and Russett, Bruce. 1993. "General Deterrence Between Enduring Rivals – Testing 3 Competing Models." *American Political Science Review* 87: 61–73.

Jackson, Robert. 1975. *South Asian Crisis: India, Pakistan and Bangla Desh: A Political and Historical Analysis of the 1971 War*. New York: Praeger Publishers.

James, Patrick. 2002. *International Relations and Scientific Progress: Structural Realism Reconsidered*. Columbus, OH: Ohio State University Press.

Jervis, Robert. 1968. "Hypotheses on Misperception." *World Politics* (April) 20: 454–79.

—. 1976. *Perception and Misperception in International Politics*. Princeton, NJ: Princeton University Press.

—. 1997. *System Effects: Complexity in Political and Social Life*. Princeton, NJ: Princeton University Press.

—. 1999. "Realism, Neoliberalism, and Cooperation: Understanding the Debate." *International Security* 24: 42–63.

Kegley, Charles W. and Raymond, Gregory A. 1994. *A Multipolar Peace? Great-Power Politics in the Twenty-First Century*. New York: St Martin's.

Keohane, Robert O. and Nye, Joseph S. 1989. *Power and Interdependence*. Glenview, IL: Scott, Foresman.

Keshk, Omar M. G., Pollins, Brian M. and Reuveny, Rafael. 2004. "Trade Still Follows the Flag: The Primacy of Politics in a Simultaneous Model of Interdependence and Armed Conflict." *Journal of Politics* 66: 1155–79.

Kim, Woosang. 1989. "Power, Alliance, and Major Wars, 1816–1975." *Journal of Conflict Resolution* 33: 255–73.

—. 1992. "Power Transitions and Great Power War from Westphalia to Waterloo." *World Politics* 45: 153–72.

Kishlansky, Mark A. 1986. *Parliamentary Selection: Social and Political Choice in Early Modern England.* Cambridge: Cambridge University Press.

Kohler, Gernot. 1975. "Imperialism as a Level of Analysis in Correlates-of-War Research." *Journal of Conflict Resolution* 19: 48–62.

Kramer, Martin. 1998. "The Moral Logic of Hizballah," in Walter Reich, ed., *Origins of Terrorism: Psychologies, Ideologies, Theologies, States of Mind.* Washington, DC: Woodrow Wilson Center Press.

Kugler, Jacek and Zagare, Frank. 1990. "The Long-Term Stability of Deterrence." *International Interactions* 15: 266–78.

Kuznets, Simon. 1955. "Economic Growth and Income Inequality." *American Economic Review* 45: 1–28.

—. 1968. *Toward a Theory of Economic Growth.* New York: Norton.

Laqueur, Walter. 1977. *Terrorism.* Boston: Little, Brown.

—. 1987. *The Age of Terrorism.* Boston: Little, Brown.

Lawrence, Bruce (ed.) 2005. *Messages to the World: The Statements of Osama Bin Laden.* London: Verso.

Layne, Christopher. 1994. "Kant or Cant: The Myth of the Democratic Peace." *International Security* 19(2): 5–49.

Le Billion, Philippe. 1999. *A Land Cursed by its Wealth? Angola's War Economy 1975–1999.* Helsinki: World Institution of Development Economics Research.

—. 2000. "The Political Economy of Transition in Cambodia 1989–1999: War, Peace, and Forest Exploitation." *Development and Change* 31: 785–805.

Leckie, Gould Francis. 1817. "An Historical Research into the Nature of the Balance of Power in Europe." London: Printed for Taylor and Hessey.

Lemke, Douglas. 2002. *Regions of War and Peace.* Cambridge Studies in International Relations 80. Cambridge: Cambridge University Press.

Lemke, Douglas and Kugler, Jacek. 1996. "The Evolution of the Power Transition Perspective," in J. Kugler and D. Lemke, eds., *Parity and War.* Ann Arbor: University of Michigan Press.

Lenin, Vladimir I. 1939. *Imperialism, the Highest Stage of Capitalism: A Popular Outline.* New York: International Publishers.

Levy, Jack. 1987. "Declining Power and the Preventive Motivation for War." *World Politics* 40: 82–107.

Li, Quan. 2005. "Does Democracy Promote or Reduce Transnational Terrorist Incidents?" *Journal of Conflict Resolution* 49: 278–97.

Liddell Hart, Basil Henry. 1930. *The Real War, 1914–1918*. Boston: Little, Brown and Co.

Lintner, Bertil. 1999. *Burma in Revolt: Opium and Insurgency Since 1948*, 2nd edn. Chiang Mai: Silkworm.

Linz, Juan J. 1978. *The Breakdown of Democratic Regimes: Crisis, Breakdown and Reequilibration*. Baltimore: Johns Hopkins University Press.

Liska, George. 1962. *Nations in Alliance*. Baltimore: Johns Hopkins University Press.

Locke, John and Peardon, T. P. [1689]1952. *The Second Treatise of Government*. New York: Liberal Arts Press.

Luebbert, Gregory M. 1991. *Liberalism, Fascism, or Social Democracy: Social Classes and the Political Origins of Regimes in Interwar Europe*. New York: Oxford University Press.

MacCunn, John. 1910. *Six Radical Thinkers: Bentham, J. S. Mill, Cobden, Carlyle, Mazzini, T. H. Green*. London: E. Arnold.

Machiavelli, Niccolo. [1513]1984. *The Prince*. Daniel Donno, ed. and trans. New York: Bantam Dell.

Mainzer, Klaus. 1997. *Thinking in Complexity: the Complex Dynamics of Matter, Mind and Mankind*, 3rd edn. Berlin, Heidelberg: Springer-Verlag.

Mansfield, Edward D. 1994. *Power, Trade, and War*. Princeton, NJ: Princeton University Press.

Mansfield, Edward D. and Snyder, Jack. 1995. "Democratization and the Danger of War." *International Security* 19(2): 5–38.

——. 1997. "A Tale of Two Democratic Peace Critiques – Reply." *Journal of Conflict Resolution* 41(3): 457–61.

——. 2002. "Incomplete Democratization and the Outbreak of Military Disputes." *International Studies Quarterly* 46: 529–49.

Maoz, Zeev and Abdolali, Nasrin. 1989. "Regime Types and International Conflict, 1816–1976." *Journal of Conflict Resolution* 33: 3–35.

Maoz, Zeev and Russett, Bruce. 1992. "Alliances, Contiguity, Wealth, and Political Stability: Is the Lack of Conflict Among Democracies a Political Artifact?" *International Interactions* 17: 245–67.

——. 1993. "Normative and Structural Causes of Democratic Peace, 1946–1986." *American Political Science Review* 87: 624–38.

Mearsheimer, John J. 1983. *Conventional Deterrence*. Cornell Studies in Security Affairs. Ithaca: Cornell University Press.

——. 2001. *The Tragedy of Great Power Politics*. New York: Norton.

Metternich, Prince Klemens Wenzel von. December 2, 1822. Letter.

Mill, John Stuart. [1863] 2002. *Utilitarianism*.

Modelski, George. 1970. "The Promise of Geopolitics." *World Politics* 22 (July): 617–35.

——. 1972. *Principles of World Politics*. New York: Free Press.

——. 1987. *Exploring Long Cycles*. Boulder, CO: Lynne Reinner.

Montague, Charles Edward. 1922. *Disenchantment*. London: Chatto & Windus.

Moore, Barrington. 1966. *Social Origins of Dictatorship and Democracy: Lord and Peasant in the Making of the Modern World*. Boston: Beacon Press.

Morgan, T. Clifton and Schwebach, Valerie. 1992. "Take Two Democracies and Call Me in the Morning: A Prescription for Peace." *International Interactions* 17: 305–20.

Morgenthau, Hans. 1948. *Politics Among Nations: The Struggle for Power and Peace*. New York: A. A. Knopf.

Morozov, Nikolai. 2004. "The Terrorist Struggle," in Walter Laqueur, ed., *Voices of Terror: Manifestos, Writings, and Manuals of Al Qaeda, Hama, and Other Terrorists from Around the World and Throughout the Ages*. New York: Reed Press.

Morrow, James. 1994. *Game Theory for Political Scientists*. Princeton, NJ: Princeton University Press.

——. 1999. "How Could Trade Affect Conflict?" *Journal of Peace Research* 36(4): 481–9.

Most, Benjamin and Starr, Harvey. 1989. *Inquiry, Logic and International Politics*. Columbia, SC: University of South Carolina Press.

Mousseau, Michael. 2003. "The Nexus of Market Society, Liberal Preferences, and Democratic Peace: Interdisciplinary Theory and Evidence." *International Studies Quarterly* 47(4): 438–510.

Mowat, R. B. 1923. *The European States System: A Study of International Relations*. London: Oxford University Press.

Niou, Emerson M. S. and Ordeshook, Peter C. 1986. "A Theory of the Balance of Power in International Systems." *Journal of Conflict Resolution* 30: 685–715.

Niou, Emerson M. S., Ordeshook, Peter C. and Rose, Gregory F. 1989. *The Balance of Power: Stability in International Systems*. Cambridge: Cambridge University Press.

Nissen, Henrik S. 1983. "The Nordic Society," in Henrik S. Nissen, ed., *Scandinavia During the Second World War*. Minneapolis: University of Minnesota Press.

North, Robert C. 1977. "Toward a Framework for the Analysis of Scarcity and Conflict." *International Studies Quarterly* 21: 569–91.

Nurek, Mieczyslaw. 1992. "Great Britain and the Baltic in the Last Months of Peace, March–August 1939," in John Hiden and Thomas Lane, eds., *The Baltic and the Outbreak of the Second World War*. Cambridge: Cambridge University Press.

Nye, 2005. *Understanding International Conflicts*, 5th edn. New York: Longman Publishers.

Olson, Mancur. 1963. "Rapid Growth as a Destabilizing Force." *Journal of Economic History* 23: 529–52.

Oneal, John and Russett, Bruce. 1997. "The Classical Liberals Were Right: Democracy, Interdependence and Conflict, 1950–1985." *International Studies Quarterly* 41: 267–94.

——. 2001. "Clear and Clean: The Fixed Effects of the Liberal Peace." *International Organization* 55: 469–85.

Organski, A. F. K. 1958. *World Politics*. New York: Alfred A. Knopf.

Organski, A. F. K. and Kugler, Jacek. 1980. *The War Ledger*. Chicago: The University of Chicago Press.

Overy, R. J. 1989. *Air Power, Armies, and the War in the West, 1940*. Boulder: US Air Force Academy.

Pakenham, Thomas. 1991. *The Boer War*. London: Cardinal.

Pape, Robert A. 2006. *Dying to Win: The Strategic Logic of Suicide Terrorism*. New York: Random House Trade Paperbacks.

Parvin, Manoucher. 1973. "Economic Determinants of Political Unrest." *Journal of Conflict Resolution* 17: 271–96.

Pecquet, Antoine. 1757. *Spirit of Political Maxims*. Paris: Chez Prault Pere.

Perkins, Bradford. 1968. *The Great Rapprochement: England and the United States, 1895–1914*. New York: Atheneum.

Pevehouse, John. 2004. "Interdependence Theory and the Measurement of International Conflict." *Journal of Politics* 66: 247–66.

Pirabakaran, Vellupillai. 2004. "The Tamil Tigers: An Interview with Commander Pirabakaran," http://www.eelamonline.com, in Walter Laqueur, ed., *Voices of Terror: Manifestos, Writings, and Manuals of Al Qaeda, Hama, and Other Terrorists from Around the World and Throughout the Ages*. New York: Reed Press.

Poggi, Gianfranco. 1990. *The State: Its Nature, Development, and Prospects*. Stanford, CA: Stanford University Press.

Post, Jerrold N. 1998. "Terrorist Psycho-logic: Terrorist Behavior as a Product of Psychological Forces," in Walter Reich, ed., *Origins of Terrorism: Psychologies, Ideologies, Theologies, States of Mind*. Washington, DC: Woodrow Wilson Center Press.

Przeworski, Adam. 1991. *Democracy and the Market: Political and Economic Reforms in Eastern Europe and Latin America*. Studies in Rationality and Change. Cambridge: Cambridge University Press.

Putin, Vladimir. 2007. "Russia: Putin Delivers Annual State-of-the-Nation Address." Radio Free Europe Radio Liberty, April 26, 2007. Accessed at http://www.rferl.org/featuresarticle/2007/04/55cb4bdf-a5cf-4d24-9145-6c99258a72d1.html.

Ranstrop, Magnus. 1997. *Hizb'allah in Lebanon*. New York: St Martin's Press.

Rasler, Karen A. and Thompson, William R. 1994. *The Great Powers and Global Struggle 1490–1990*. Lexington, KY: University Press of Kentucky.

Ray, James Lee. 1995. *Democracy and International Conflict: An Evaluation of the Democratic Peace Proposition*. Columbia, SC: University of South Carolina Press.

Reed, William. 2003. "Information and Economic Interdependence." *Journal of Conflict Resolution* 47: 54–71.

Reed, William and Clark, David. 2002. "Toward a Multiprocess Model of Rivalry and the Democratic Peace." *International Interactions* 28: 77–92.

Reich, Bernard. 1995. *Arab–Israeli Conflict and Conciliation: A Documentary History*. Westport, CT: Greenwood Press.

Reich, Walter (ed.) 1998a. *Origins of Terrorism: Psychologies, Ideologies, Theologies, States of Mind*. Washington, DC: Woodrow Wilson Center Press.

Reich, Walter. 1998b. "Understanding Terrorist Behavior: The Limits and Opportunities of Psychological Inquiry," in Walter Reich, ed., *Origins of Terrorism: Psychologies, Ideologies, Theologies, States of Mind*. Washington, DC: Woodrow Wilson Center Press.

Reiter, Dan and Stam, Allan C. 2002. *Democracies at War*. Princeton, NJ: Princeton University Press.

Reynol-Querol, Marta. 2002. "Political Systems, Stability and Civil Wars." *Defense and Peace Economics* 13: 465–83.

Rice, Condoleezza. 2005. "Opening Remarks by Secretary-of-State-Designate Dr Condoleezza Rice." Delivered to the Senate Foreign Relations Committee, Washington DC. January 18.

Richardson, Lewis F. 1960. *Arms and Insecurity*. Pittsburgh: Boxwood Press.

Robinson, James. 1997. "When is a State Predatory?" Manuscript, Department of Government, Harvard University, Cambridge, MA.

Rodrik, Dani. 1999. "Where Did all the Growth Go? External Shocks, Social Conflict, and Growth Collapses." *Journal of Economic Growth* 4: 385–412.

Rosecrance, Richard N. 1986. *The Rise of the Trading State: Commerce and Conquest in the Modern World*. New York: Basic Books.

Ross, Michael. 2003. "The Natural Resource Curse: How Wealth Can Make You Poor," in Ian Bannon and Paul Collier, eds., *Natural Resources and Violence Conflict: Options and Actions*. Washington DC: World Bank.

——. 2004a. "Paradigm in Distress? Primary Commodities and Civil War." *Journal of Conflict Resolution* 49: 443–50.

——. 2004b. "What Do we Know about Natural Resources and Civil War?" *Journal of Peace Research* 41: 443–50.

Rowe, Vivian. 1959. *The Great Wall of France: The Triumph of the Maginot Line*. London: Putnam.

Rubin, Barnett R. 2000. "The Political Economy of War and Peace in Afghanistan." *World Development* 28: 1789–1803.

Rummel, Rudolph J. 1979. *Understanding Conflict and War: Volume 4, War, Power, Peace*. Beverly Hills, CA: Sage.

——. 1983. "Libertarianism and International Violence." *Journal of Conflict Resolution* 27: 27–71.

Russett, Bruce. 1964. *World Handbook of Political and Social Indicators*. New Haven: Yale University Press.

——. 1993. *Grasping the Democratic Peace: Principles for a Post-Cold War World*. Princeton, NJ: Princeton University Press.

Russett, Bruce and Oneal, John. 2001. *Triangulating Peace: Democracy, Interdependence, and International Organizations*. New York: Norton.

Russett, Bruce, Oneal, John and Davis, David R. 1998. "The Third Leg of the Kantian Tripod for Peace: International Organizations and Military Disputes, 1950–1985." *International Organization* 52: 441–67.

Samuels, Richard J. 1994. *Rich Nation, Strong Army: National Security and the Technological Transformation of Japan*. Ithaca, NY: Cornell University Press.

Schmid, Alex P. 1984. *Political Terrorism: A Research Guide to Concepts, Theories, Data Bases, and Literature*. New Brunswick, NJ: Transaction Books.

Schmid, Alex P. and Jongman, Albert J. 1998. *Political Terrorism: A New Guide to Actors, Authors, Concepts, Data Bases, Theories and Literature*. New Brunswick, NJ: Transaction Books.

Schmitter, Philippe C. and Karl, Terry Lynn. 1991. "What Democracy Is . . . and Is Not." *Journal of Democracy*: 75–88.

Schultz, Kenneth A. 1998. "Domestic Opposition and Signaling in International Crises." *American Political Science Review* 92: 829–44.

——. 1999. "Do Democratic Institutions Constrain or Inform? Contrasting Two Institutional Perspectives on Democracy and War." *International Organization* 53: 233–66.

Schumpeter, Joseph. 1950. *Capitalism, Socialism, and Democracy*. New York: Harper.

——. 1951. *Imperialism and Social Classes*. New York: A. M. Kelly.

Sederberg, Peter C. 1989. *Terrorist Myths: Illusion, Rhetoric, and Reality*. Englewood Cliffs, NJ: Prentice Hall.

Shafer, Michael. 1983. "Capturing the Mineral Multinationals – Advantage or Disadvantage." *International Organization* 37(1): 93–119.

Singer, J. David, Bremer, Stuart A. and Stuckey, John. 1972. "Capability Distribution, Uncertainty, and Major Power War, 1820–1965," in Bruce Russett, ed., *Peace, War and Numbers*. Beverly Hills: Sage.

——. 1979. "Capability Distribution, Uncertainty, and Major War," in J. D. Singer, ed., *Explaining War*. Beverly Hills: Sage.

Siverson, Randolph M. and Tennefoss, Michael R. 1984. "Power, Alliance, and the Escalation of International Conflict, 1815–1965." *American Political Science Review* 78: 1057–69.

Skocpol, Theda. 1979. *States and Social Revolutions: A Comparative Analysis of France, Russia and China*. Cambridge: Cambridge University Press.

Small, Melvin and Singer, J. David. 1970. "Patterns in International Warfare: 1816–1965." *Annals of the American Academy of Political and Social Science* 391: 145–55.

——. 1976. "The War Proneness of Democratic Regimes, 1816–1965." *Jerusalem Journal of International Relations* 1: 50–69.

——. 1982. *Resort to Arms: International and Civil Wars, 1816–1980*. Beverly Hills: Sage Publications.

Smethurst, Richard J. 1974. *A Social Basis for Prewar Japanese Militarism: The Army and the Rural Community*. Berkeley and Los Angeles: University of California Press.

Smith, Craig S. 2006. "Despite Ties to Hamas, Militants Aren't Following Political Leaders." *New York Times*, July 20.

Snyder, Glenn H. and Diesing, Paul. 1977. *Conflict Among Nations: Bargaining, Decision Making, and System Structure in International Crises*. Princeton, NJ: Princeton University Press.

Sobek, David. 2003. "Regime Type, Preferences, and War in Renaissance Italy." *Journal of Conflict Resolution* 47: 204–25.

——. 2008. *State Capacity and the Opportunity for Civil War: Perceptions of Property Rights Protection and the Onset of Civil War, 1960–1999*. Typescript.

Sobek, David, Abouharb, M. Rodwan and Ingram, Christopher G. 2006. "The Human Rights Peace: How the Respect for Human Rights at Home Leads to Peace Abroad." *Journal of Politics* 68: 519–29.

Sobek, David and Boehmer, Charles. 2008. *If They Only Had Cake: The Effect of Food Supply on Civil War Onset, 1960–1999*. Typescript.

Sobek, David and Braithwaite, Alex. 2005. "Victims of Success: American Dominance and Terrorism." *Conflict Management and Peace Science* 22: 135–48.

Sorokin, Pitrim A. 1957. *Social and Cultural Dynamics*. Boston: Horizon Books.

Starr, Harvey. 1999. *Anarchy, Order, and Integration: How to Manage Interdependence*. Ann Arbor: University of Michigan Press.

Stiglitz, Joseph E. 2002. *Globalization and its Discontents*. New York: W. W. Norton.

——. 2003. *The Roaring Nineties: A New History of the World's Most Prosperous Decade*. New York: W. W. Norton.

Stoll, Richard J. and Champion, M. 1985. "Capability Concentration, Alliance Building, and Conflict Among the Major Powers," in A. N. Sabrosky, ed., *Polarity and War*. Boulder, CO: Westview.

Tannenwald, Nina. 2005. "Stigmatizing the Bomb: Origins of the Nuclear Taboo." *International Security* 29: 5–49.

Thompson, William R. 1988a. "Succession Crises in the Global Political System," in A. Bergesen, ed., *Crises in the World-System*. Beverly Hills: Sage.

——. 1988b. *On Global War: Historical-Structural Approaches to World Politics*. Columbia, SC: University of South Carolina Press.

Thompson, William R. and Tucker, Richard. 1997. "A Tale of Two Democratic Peace Critiques." *Journal of Conflict Resolution* 41(3): 426–54.

Thucydides. 1982. *History of the Peloponnesian War*. T. E. Wick, ed. New York: McGraw Hill Publishers.

Tocqueville, Alexis de. [1835/1840] 1956. *Democracy in America.* New York: New American Library. (Original work published in 1840.)

Tse-tung, Mao. 1961. *On Guerrilla Warfare.* Samuel B. Griffith II, trans. Urbana and Chicago: University of Illinois Press.

Tuchman, Barbara W. 1962. *The Guns of August.* New York: Macmillan.

United Nations. 2001. Report of the Panel of Experts on the Illegal Exploitation of Natural Resources and Other Forms of Wealth of the Democratic Republic of the Congo, April 12, http://www.un.org/news/dh/latest/drcongo.htm.

Urwin, Derek W. 1995. *The Community of Europe: A History of European Integration Since 1945.* London: Longman.

Van Evera, Stephen. 1999. *Causes of War: Power and the Roots of Conflict.* Cornell Studies in Security Affairs. Ithaca, NY: Cornell University Press.

Vasquez, John A. 1993. *The War Puzzle.* Cambridge Studies in International Relations. Cambridge: Cambridge University Press.

Waltz, Kenneth. 1979. *Theory of International Politics.* Reading, MA: Addison-Wesley.

Ward, Michael D. and Gleditsch, Kristian S. 1998. "Democratizing for Peace." *American Political Science Review* 92(1): 51–61.

Weede, Erich. 1984. "Democracy and War Involvement." *Journal of Conflict Resolution* 28: 649–64.

Wendt, Alexander. 1999. *Social Theory of International Politics.* Cambridge Studies in International Relations. Cambridge: Cambridge University Press.

Wilkenfeld, Jonathan and Brecher, Michael. 2003. "Interstate Crises and Violence: Twentieth-Century Findings," in Manus Midlarski, ed., *Handbook of War Studies II.* Ann Arbor, MI: University of Michigan Press.

Wilkinson, Paul. 2001. *Terrorism versus Democracy: The Liberal State Response.* Cass Series on Political Violence 9. London: Frank Cass.

Winer, Jonathan M. and Roule, Trigin J. 2003. "Follow the Money: The Finance of Illicit Resource Extraction," in Ian Bannon and Paul Collier, eds., *Natural Resources and Violent Conflict: Options and Actions.* Washington DC: The World Bank.

Wright, Quincy. 1942. *A Study of History.* Chicago: University of Chicago Press.

——. 1965. *A Study of War.* Chicago: University of Chicago Press.

Zajtman, Arnaud. 2001. "Ore Fuels West's High-Tech Gear." AP Online, April 9.

Zawahiri, Ayman al-. 2004. "Knights Under the Prophet's Banner," in Walter Laqueur, ed., *Voices of Terror: Manifestos, Writings, and Manuals of Al Qaeda, Hama, and Other Terrorists from Around the World and Throughout the Ages.* New York: Reed Press.

Zinnes, Dina. 1967. "An Analytical Study of the Balance of Power Theories." *Journal of Peace Research* 4: 270–85.

INDEX

CPSIA information can be obtained
at www.ICGtesting.com
Printed in the USA
LVOW04s0111031115

460806LV00020B/227/P